BEYOND LIBERALISM

Economics, Philosophy, Politics

BEYOND LIBERALISM

Economics, Philosophy, Politics

Prabhat Patnaik

Tulika Books

Published in India in 2025 by
Tulika Books
86/1 (ground floor), Shahpur Jat, New Delhi 110 049, India
www.tfortulika.com

ISBN: 978-81-956392-3-6 (hardback)

For sale only in India and South Asia

Printed at Chaman Offset, Delhi 110 002

To the memory of my parents,
Manjari Patnaik and Prananath Patnaik

Contents

Preface

The process of writing this book has been a long and arduous journey for me. During this journey I have had to rethink my own understanding of Marxism and socialism. In making this journey I have been helped by many friends, among whom Akeel Bilgrami has been the most generous and encouraging. He has not only discussed the ideas of this book innumerable times with me, but has read the entire manuscript with care and meticulousness. Rajendra Prasad too has unstintingly spared his time to read and comment on several versions of my chapters.

Others who have helped me greatly in writing this book are Subrata Guha, Malini Bhattacharya, Akbar Noman, Anamitra Roy Choudhury, Margit Koves, Utsa Patnaik, Carol Rovane, Nishad Patnaik, Smita Sirkar, C.P. Chandrasekhar, Indu Chandrasekhar and Jayati Ghosh. Wendy Lochner of Columbia University Press was a great source of help during the final preparation of the manuscript. I wish to extend heartfelt but non-incriminating thanks to all of them.

PRABHAT PATNAIK

CHAPTER ONE

Introduction

About the Book

In his remarkable work, *The General Theory of Employment, Interest and Money*, John Maynard Keynes had said that 'the ideas of economists and political philosophers, both when they are right and when they are wrong, are more powerful than is commonly understood. Indeed the world is ruled by little else.'[1] His putting only these two disciplines, and that too such apparently dissimilar ones, as being so decisive in human affairs seems intriguing at first sight; some may even see in it a defence of his own disciplinary turf. But on a closer look, Keynes' remark has a soundness that is worth exploring, as this book hopes to do.

Political philosophy provides the basis for political praxis, whether such praxis takes the form of preserving *laissez faire*, or of constructing a social democracy, or of working towards mobilizations for yet more radical transformations that transcend capitalism. But this political philosophy is developed on the basis of an understanding of the working of society in which – in the complexity of modern times, at any rate – the economy is an extraordinarily significant component. An understanding of the economy is an indispensable element on the basis of which any political philosophy is built; thus, economics provides an important *intellectual* input for political philosophy, something that is especially true under capitalism. Indeed it is for this reason that economics as a discipline was developed in the first place, and developed originally by philosophers concerned with political praxis. Adam Smith was a philosopher who wrote *The Wealth of Nations* with the purpose of putting across a *political* agenda. This was also central to the thinking of his friend, the philosopher David Hume, who provided an ingenious, though in retrospect not convincing, critique of mercantilism.

So far, I have mentioned three interrelated elements: political philosophy, economics and political praxis. That is to say, two disciplines of theoretical inquiry, and the arena of human engagements which is always integrated with these disciplines of inquiry, serving both as a form of background motivation for the inquiry as well as a foreground field that marks the great relevance of the outcomes of the inquiry. Thus the relationship between the three elements is complex; and part of the complexity is that it has a certain familiar dynamic. The development of each of these two theoretical disciplines of inquiry, with their myriad details, with the nuances and the minutiae of individual arguments, tends to have the effect of giving them quite separate identities to a point where we might lose sight of their essential integrity or unity. However, we find ourselves recovering the unity when, in the realm of praxis, a new political agenda comes to the fore. The proponents of such a new political agenda – which, like all political agendas, is founded on a political philosophy – seek vitally new intellectual inputs from economics, which in turn requires constructing new perspectives in economics and integrating them once again into the political philosophy.

Such was the case with the agenda of socialism as it emerged in the nineteenth century. Karl Marx, again a political philosopher, felt the need to study political economy, to provide a critique of classical political economy, and by doing so constructed and presented an alternative analysis, for working out the agenda of socialism. This makes clear that Marxism is all at once a political philosophy and an analysis of political economy, both geared to and motivated by an agenda of human engagement that we tend to call 'praxis'. But ironically – conforming to the dynamic that I mentioned above – the process of refining and explicating particular arguments within Marxian political economy has given rise to a degree of specialization within it, to such an extent that it has obscured the nature of Marxism's highly elaborate and detailed critique of the *political philosophy* of liberalism which preceded it, and to which it was, to a considerable extent, intended as both a theoretical and practical response.

The present work attempts to elaborate that critique in its detail. So I am, right at the outset, declaring my hand. The book will essentially be a Marxist critique of liberalism. The Marxism that is the source of this critique will be a considerable reconfiguration of some of the orthodoxies that have attached themselves to Marx over the last century and a half of commentary on him, a reconfiguration with two important features. First, it will make central to an understanding of Marxism, the long history of imperialism that has been at the heart of capitalism since its inception. And second, it will see through the relevance of Marxism, so integrated with an analysis of imperialism, to the contemporary period of globalization, in particular financial globalization. What I propose to do in successive chapters, therefore, is to present a quite dramatic contrast between these two alternative doctrinal strands within economics – liberalism and Marxism (as I understand them) – each in sync with a particular political philosophy, and each advocating a particular political praxis.

It will come as no surprise that the dramatic contrast that I describe myself as presenting in the coming pages turns heavily on differential perspectives on the subject of *individual freedom*. Ever since one of the founders of liberal political philosophy and liberal economic theory, John Locke, was declared to have generated a notion of 'possessive individualism' (Macpherson 1962) by critics of liberalism, this perspectival difference has been well known. Yet exactly how an outlook of individualism pervades *in detail* the great range of liberal *economic* arguments and assumptions in the centuries after Locke is not as widely noted as it needs to be, and so will be carefully expounded in these pages.

But this very point about its detailed pervasiveness in the context of the contrast with Marxist arguments and assumptions is prone to a common misconception, which it will be one of my briefs to correct. This is the belief that while liberalism is concerned with individual freedom, Marxism, and the socialist agenda it advances, is unconcerned about it, emphasizing instead a contrasting sphere of the collective. I will argue instead that liberalism and Marxism have very different analyses of the status of the individual within *capitalism,* that the Marxist analysis of capitalism leads to the conclusion that the freedom of the individual itself can be realized only through a transcendence of capitalism through collective action. One can already see, in this brief capsule of what is to come, a point I have been at pains to stress in this introduction – that economic theory, political philosophy and an agenda for action are deeply integrated.

One last but very central point remains in making these introductory remarks to give an advance sense of the overall direction of the book. I will state it briefly here and then elaborate it in the next section. I have declared a dramatic and integrated contrast between liberalism and Marxism as my subject, and it may seem as if I am ignoring a vast and familiar middle ground of social democracy in order to set up the starkness of that contrast. But, as the reader will see in the later reaches of my discussion of Keynesian economic and philosophical ideas, which are the most paradigmatic theoretical basis for the political agenda of social democracy, that middle ground does not do anything to undermine the overarching contrast that I take to be fundamental in the philosophical, political and economic disputes at stake. The Marxist analysis of the status of the individual differs not only from that of the pre-Keynesian strand of liberal economic theory represented by Hayek and other neo-classical economists, a difference that is widely acknowledged, but also from the Keynesian strand adopted by post-war social democracy in its political programme, that sees the individual coming into his or her own, not under conditions of *laissez faire,* but in a capitalism marked by state intervention.

The Marxist critique, in short, covers not just capitalism as it is integrated with liberal democracy and without state intervention in the realm of the economy (what we might call 'classical liberalism'), but also capitalism where social democracy has effected state intervention designed to push the system to full employment. Keynes ([1931] 2010) had coined the term '*new* liberalism' to express his political philosophy, as distinct from the old liberalism championed by pre-Keynesian economists, of both classical and neo-classical persuasions. The Marxist analysis of the status of the individual under capitalism differs from what both classical as well as new liberalism envisage. Let me briefly elaborate these claims.

Classical Liberalism

'Liberalism' as a doctrine gets its most typical exemplification in what have come to be called 'liberal democracies'. Though there is no doubt that liberal democracies have evolved considerably since their early inception in post-Westphalian Europe, throughout this evolution they were shaped by a guiding conceptual framework of ideas and principles (which, no doubt, *themselves* evolved in this process); and it is those ideas and principles that I have in mind in using the term 'liberalism'. Moreover, the evolving liberal democracies were typically accompanied by the evolving economic formation of capitalism; the political ideas and principles that make up the doctrine of liberalism are therefore deeply integrated with economic ideas about the nature of capitalism. My objective is to look at the notion of 'freedom' in the context of this integrated political and economic framework that we have come to call 'liberalism'.

Liberalism is concerned with the freedom of the individual. Within liberalism however, as already mentioned, there are two strands: one is what I call 'old' or 'classical' liberalism, which sees this freedom as being threatened by *specific agents* – either by other individuals, or by the state, or even by such economic aggolmerations as monopolies. It does not, however, see the functioning of the *economic system as a whole*, as distinct from specific agents, as being a constraint on individual freedom. By contrast, the second strand of liberalism, what I call 'new' liberalism, borrowing the term from John Maynard Keynes who had described his own views thus, recognizes that the system itself, and not just some specific agents, can also constrain individual freedom.

Since the state is required for protecting the freedom of the individual from being suppressed by other individuals, classical liberalism defends the role of the state in this regard. It also defends the role of the state as a bulwark against the oppression of the individual by monopolies and oligopolies. In short, it sees the role of the state as being confined to upholding and preserving 'law and order' and the 'rules of the game' of *a competitive economy* (however we define it). But it sees any intervention by the state that exceeds this limit as being inimical to individual freedom, and hence a phenomenon to be opposed.

Classical liberalism's perception of the threat to individual freedom does not *per se* entail the defence of a competitive *capitalist* economy. But the fact that it invariably approves of a competitive *capitalist* economy suggests that it does not see the employer–wage-labourer relationship that is typical of capitalism as being inimical to individual freedom. It follows from this that if the employer–labourer relationship was not always the dominant form but came into prominence only at a certain time, then it must have been a voluntary arrangement that individuals entered into. It must represent then, from the point of view of every individual, an improvement over his or her condition as it would have been in a competitive pre-capitalist economy, if that is supposed to have preceded competitive capitalism.

Every strand of classical liberalism, in short, whether or not it says so explicitly, *must believe* that the emergence of capitalism, that is, of the employer–wage-labour relationship, in so far as it has a history (and has not been a dominant form for ever), was a voluntary process. And since it is a voluntary process based on the freely given consent of all individuals, a competitive capitalist economy represents the *only* economic system under which individual freedom can be fully realized.

Both classical and neo-classical economics can provide, in different ways, the economic theoretical basis for classical liberalism. Though there are major differences between the two, especially with regard to the notion of competition – the former believing in *free* competition (where the wage-rate and the rate of profit are equalized across sectors) while the latter believes in *perfect* competition (where additionally the rate of profit is zero) – they both see the threat to individual freedom as arising, other than from oppression by other individuals (which is a 'law and order' problem and can be ignored here), from the existence of monopolies and from excessive state interference. This belief is sustained by their respective theoretical systems that are very different from one another; but on the basis of either, it can be and has been sustained.

The second strand of liberalism, as we noted earlier, recognizes the possibility of individual freedom being constrained by the operation of the system itself, and on this basis, it does not believe that *laissez faire* capitalism is conducive to individual freedom. This is because *laissez faire* capitalism is associated, as Keynes had argued, with large-scale unemployment, except for occasional 'brief periods of excitement' (when investment rises to sufficiently high levels); and unemployment is destructive of individual freedom. True, the concept of freedom according to this second strand is not the same as according to the first, as we shall see; but it would be a travesty of *any* concept of individual freedom if the workers in a society characterized by large-scale unemployment are claimed to be enjoying individual freedom; or, put differently, the 'negative liberty' of an individual in the sense of absence of interference from others (or other *agents*) that Isaiah Berlin had talked about is simply inadequate as liberty in any meaningful sense.[2] The recognition that the constraints on individual freedom can arise not just from identifiable agents, such as other individuals, the state, or monopolies and oligopolies, but *from the working of the economic system itself*, thus has profound implications.

Overcoming such systemic constraints on individual freedom requires intervention by the state. The state therefore has to take on a far wider role than merely maintaining 'law and order' and the 'rules of the game' of competitive capitalism, even for promoting individual freedom. The interference by the state in economic affairs, far from being a *constraint* on individual freedom, is *essential* for it, which is why Keynes called his position 'new liberalism'.

New Liberalism

But it is not just with regard to unemployment that the state must intervene for promoting individual freedom. The functioning of the system can be associated with poverty, income inequality, hunger, malnutrition and other manifestations which are inimical to individual freedom, understood not just in the sense of the individual being free to enter into what appear to be 'non-oppressive' relationships with others, or the individual making the most of the situation in which he or she happens to be placed, but in the sense of being able to realize his or her *potential.* Modern-day liberalism, or 'new liberalism', sees state intervention to be necessary for overcoming these deprivations that prevent the individual from realizing his or her potential. It thus redefines individual freedom, and considers state intervention as essential for realizing it.

But this redefinition does not amount to an abrogation of the earlier definition; it leads rather to a widening of the earlier definition so that it goes beyond the market outcome of competitive capitalism. 'New' liberalism therefore also sees individual freedom as achievable only under capitalism, but a capitalism that is marked by state intervention.

But if classical liberalism did not recognize the possibility that the functioning of the system could also place a constraint on individual freedom, new liberalism also does not recognize the possibility that the functioning of the system can place a constraint on the capacity of the state to intervene, and hence on the realization of individual freedom in the broader sense that it defines. It sees the state simply as a *deus ex machina* to overcome the limitations of the system, and not as something which too is constrained by the system itself. This trait, which is obvious in Keynes, characterizes more or less all strands of new liberalism.

The ways in which the system constrains the state are multifarious and will be discussed later, but the general point can be made by taking up just one specific instance, namely when the domain of functioning of capital is much larger than the domain over which the state's jurisdiction runs. This is exactly what happens in a regime of economic globalization when globally mobile capital, or what one may call international capital, exists in a world of nation-states.

For overcoming what Keynes had called involuntary unemployment, for instance, the state must expand aggregate demand through larger expenditure of its own; but this requires that such state expenditure must be financed either through a fiscal deficit (which means that larger state spending is not counterbalanced by any reduction in private spending) or by taxing those who save a part of their incomes, typically the rich (so that larger state spending is not counterbalanced by an *equivalent* reduction in private spending). Both these avenues however are closed in a regime of economic globalization: globalization of capital entails above all the globalization of finance, and finance is invariably opposed to larger fiscal deficits (which is why most countries have enacted 'fiscal responsibility' legislation, limiting the size of the fiscal deficit relative to gross domestic product); if the state did not obey the dictates of finance, then finance would flow out of its domain, precipitating a crisis. Likewise, any unilateral increase in taxes upon the rich can also drive away finance from the country, causing a crisis, apart from also driving productive investment away from the country to other shores and thereby lowering the country's growth rate. (This is why nation-states vie with one another in providing tax *concessions* to the capitalists, and the rich in general, within a regime of globalization.)

Put differently, when the state remains a nation-state but capital is globalized, the nation-state willy-nilly must obey the dictates of capital, especially of finance which can move across country-borders at a dizzying pace. This makes fiscal intervention by any particular nation-state to augment employment within its borders almost impossible. As for monetary policy intervention, apart from the well-known infirmity of monetary policy in stimulating the level of economic activity, there is also the fact that in a world with global mobility of capital, there are serious limits to the extent to which the interest rate can be independently fixed by a country.[3]

Thus, in a world of nation-states where there is globalization of capital, including of finance, no individual nation-state can overcome involuntary unemployment even if it wishes to.[4] This is true even of the United States. Since its currency is generally considered 'as good as gold' by wealth-holders across the world, it may be thought that it should be less worried about financial outflows in the event of its state providing a fiscal stimulus; but a good deal of the demand generated by this stimulus would leak out abroad, increasing the US external indebtedness for the sake of creating employment *abroad,* and this consideration provides a deterrent to the expansionary activism even of the US state.

Overcoming involuntary unemployment in a world where globalized capital coexists with nation-states would require, at the very least therefore, a coordinated fiscal stimulus among several leading economies, so that finance is robbed of any incentive to move from one economy to another. This means, however, a confrontation between these coordinated states and globalized finance, which reduces the possibility of such coordination, and also underscores the limitations of a *particular* nation-state in overcoming the constraints imposed by the functioning of the system on getting rid of involuntary unemployment.[5]

Exactly the same conclusion can be drawn regarding the state's ability to bring about an increase in economic equality, or to eliminate poverty, and so on. In short, the new-liberal faith in the ability of the nation-state to achieve individual freedom simply lacks substance. Thus, if classical liberalism does not comprehend the possibility of the functioning of the system, as distinct from particular agents, constraining individual freedom, new liberalism does not comprehend the possibility of the system constraining the ability of the nation-state to overcome the limits on individual freedom.

Marxist Critique of Liberalism: Classical and New

Marxism, while emphasizing along with new liberalism the constraints on individual freedom imposed by the spontaneous functioning of the system, differs from the latter in also recognizing the constraints on the state imposed by the system. It does so by making two points: the system has a logic to its functioning with which state intervention interferes and thereby renders the system dysfunctional. To take an example, the system's functioning close to full employment, which is what Keynes had wanted, makes it prone to uncontrollable inflation and thereby makes it dysfunctional. A pool of unemployed workers, or what Marx had called a 'reserve army of labour', is necessary under capitalism, not just for keeping real wages below labour productivity and hence for making surplus value accrue continuously to the capitalists, but also for keeping money wages in check so that there is no inflationary push from the side of wages.

Hence, a certain level of unemployment (not necessarily the entire unemployment that happens to prevail because of a deficiency of aggregate demand) is essential for the functioning of capitalism; if state intervention eliminates it, then the system becomes dysfunctional. In such a case, the choice before the state is either to push its intervention still further, leading ultimately to the transcendence of the system, or to pull back from whatever intervention it had undertaken. The state too, in short, is objectively constrained by the logic of the system. It is never a mere *deus ex machina*, as new liberalism believes it to be.

The second point that Marxist economics makes against new liberalism is that situations like the one where the nation-state confronts globalized capital do not arise accidentally; they arise because of the immanent tendency of the system towards centralization of capital, that is, the organization of capital in larger and larger blocks. Centralization in Marx is what spurs accumulation: since it arises essentially because larger capital 'eats up' or 'devours' smaller capitals, there is a Darwinian struggle among all capitals to escape being small. This is what drives them to accumulate. Centralization is thus both the driving force and the end-result of the process of accumulation of capital.

Centralization also keeps expanding the boundaries within which capital operates, and the globalization of capital is an end-product of this process of centralization. Thus, escaping control by the nation-state, through the globalization of capital that is the end-product of centralization, is inherent to the logic of capitalism; there can never be a stable system, complete with state intervention, as new liberalism envisages. Individual freedom, it follows, is impossible to achieve under capitalism; it requires a transcendence of capitalism and the ushering in of a new system, socialism, that is not driven by immanent tendencies but is malleable enough to permit state intervention and control.

Indeed, from the fact of the capitalist system being driven by immanent tendencies, Marxism derives an image of the system where individual participants play roles that they are *coerced into playing* by the impersonal logic of the system. Marx for instance called the capitalist 'capital personified'. Competition tends to rob individual agents of their 'agency'; they act not according to their own volition but under coercion exercised impersonally by the system. Escaping this coercion through 'combinations' (trade unions) is what the workers attempt to achieve, and undermining such 'combinations' is what the capitalist system spontaneously seeks to achieve. This dialectic reaches a final *denouement* with the overthrow of the system, and the ushering in of a new system that is not based on competition and hence is not spontaneous.

In the chapters that follow, I develop this argument in detail. I first examine the political economy underlying the classical liberal position, then look at new liberalism's critique of it, and then Marxist economics' critique of both. But before doing so, I must remove certain misconceptions that have characterized the discipline and that stand in the way of a proper understanding. This is done in the next chapter.

Notes

[1] Keynes ([1936] 1949, p. 383). All references to *General Theory* in this book are to the 1949 edition.

[2] Of course the strands of economic theory that sustain classical liberalism simply do not recognize the possibility of unemployment as a persistent phenomenon under capitalism, as we shall see later; but this is their theoretical failure, namely an acceptance of Say's Law that has little validity in a money-using economy. Besides, as I mention below, unemployment is not the only circumstance that robs 'negative liberty' of any meaningfulness; substantial inequalities in income and wealth, the

existence of poverty, and other such phenomena in society that can be associated with the functioning of the system, also have the same effect.

[3] This was first pointed out clearly by Robert Mundell (1963) and Marcus Fleming (1962). If the interest rate in the United States happens to be i, and the relative risk compared to the US associated with putting one's funds in India requires compensation by a risk premium δ, then the interest rate in India cannot be lower than $i+\delta$. Global mobility of finance therefore places a restriction on India's monetary policy.

[4] This is a point that Keynes was aware of, as is clear from his 1933 remark that finance must be national, and also from the fact that the Bretton Woods system he helped to set up provided for controls by the nation-state over cross-border capital flows. This awareness on the part of Keynes may be cited to question our assertion that new liberalism does not take cognizance of the constraints imposed upon the state by the logic of the system. But while Keynes was aware that *if capital got globalized*, it would disempower the nation-state, he thought that such globalization of capital could be *permanently* prevented by the nation-state under capitalism. This turned out to be wrong because the logic of the system, manifested in the tendency towards centralization of capital (the formation of larger and larger agglomerations of capital) overcame the state's capacity to control capital flows; that is, the logic of the system undermined the state's capacity to control this logic. Our criticism of new liberalism for not being cognizant of the constraints imposed by the system upon the state therefore continues to remain valid.

[5] During the Great Depression of the 1930s, a group of German trade unionists and also Keynes had suggested such a coordinated fiscal stimulus. But the idea was not taken seriously at the time; at present, it has not even been mooted with any degree of seriousness. See Kindleberger (1974).

CHAPTER TWO

Some Misconceptions in Economics

Economics as a discipline often proceeds on the assumption that the same terms used in two different theoretical frameworks stand for the same concept or mean the same thing. This is particularly true in the case of theories that are apparently close to one another, or in theories in which one emerges via critical reflection on another. Marx has been especially misunderstood in this respect; since he took classical economics as his starting point, identical terms used by Marxian and classical economics have been presumed to have the same meaning, when they do not. As a result, while some differences between Marx and classical economics – for instance, with regard to the appropriation of surplus value and associated issues that Marx himself had emphasized – have been well recognized, other basic differences have remained unrecognized.

In particular, what has not been recognized is the fact that there are two different, almost diametrically opposite, perceptions of capitalism *in its totality*, not just between classical and Marxian economics, but between Marxian economics on the one hand and *both* classical and neo-classical economics on the other. Each of these perceptions is comprehensive, in the sense of permeating all aspects of the system, and each generates a different political agenda. One is what I have called the agenda of 'classical liberalism' which emanates from the perception of both classical and neo-classical economics (the differences between which are not as serious in *this* respect as usually made out)[1] and the other is the agenda of socialism that emanates from the perception of Marxian economics, whose fundamental differences from classical economics are usually understated because of an inadequate understanding of the difference in their perceptions.

Contrasting Notions of Competition

Let me illustrate this point by taking some particular terms, on the basis of which we shall recreate the contrasting conceptual totalities. The first difference relates to the term 'competition'. There are important differences between the classical and neo-classical conceptions of competition, but these are overshadowed by the difference between both these on the one hand and the Marxist conception on the other, of competition under capitalism. While classical economics talks of *free* competition, which entails an equalization of the wage-rate and the profit-rate across sectors through the free mobility of labour and capital, neo-classical economics visualizes *perfect* competition where additionally there is free entry into the ranks of capitalists (presumably from the ranks of labourers, that is, free *class* mobility), which brings profits down to zero in equilibrium. While this is an important difference, one recognizing barriers to entry into the ranks of capitalists which the other does not, both visualize an equilibrium where there is full employment. In classical economics this happens through the adjustment of labour supply to labour demand, while in neo-classical economics this happens through the choice of techniques (the presumption being that there are lots of techniques along a production function and in equilibrium, given the flexibility of all prices, the economy produces by using the technique at which all 'factors of production' are fully utilized).

The Marxian perception however visualizes the perennial existence of an excess supply of labour (a reserve army of labour). This reserve army plays a number of roles: by keeping real wages tied to some (historically given) subsistence level, it ensures a positive rate of surplus value. Joseph Schumpeter (1952) had believed that since a capitalist economy tended to settle at a full employment equilibrium, surplus value would disappear at this equilibrium through capital accumulation;[2] but the perennial existence of a reserve army of labour prevents this and always ensures a positive rate of surplus value. In addition, a reserve army also keeps the value of money intact (P. Patnaik 2009) by preventing accelerating inflation arising from competing claims over a given output.

But a reserve army also gives a specific character to the nature of competition. The existence of unemployment in the form of the reserve army makes competition among the workers intense. It makes getting a job and holding it down a matter of life and death. This is what introduces, through the coercive threat of unemployment, work discipline and work ethics among the workers. It also means that capitalists too, who get displaced from their position in the system and have to join the ranks of workers, run the risk of remaining unemployed, which also disciplines them into behaving in a manner that does not expose them to such risk. This threat of unemployment thus introduces a Darwinian struggle into the system where individual economic agents act not according to their own volitions, but in a manner dictated by the logic of the system. This is the source of *universal alienation* under capitalism.

Capitalists accumulate not necessarily because they want to, but because not doing so would make them lose their position in the system by weakening their viability vis-à-vis other capitalists who introduce technological progress along with their act of accumulation. In fact Marx had called the capitalist 'capital personified', through whose actions the immanent tendencies of the system work themselves out.

By contrast, the notion of competition in a situation where full employment is reached in equilibrium does not entail any such coercive element. What it does is to ensure that all economic agents get their 'appropriate rewards', that relative wages among workers just compensate for the relative difficulties, skills and lengths of training associated with particular occupations. This was Adam Smith's idea and it holds equally for neo-classical economics as well. Competition of this sort has nothing to do with work discipline (how capitalist economies inculcate work discipline remains unexplained by it, a point discussed later), or with any Darwinian struggle, or with acting as a coercive mechanism to make agents behave in a predetermined manner that has to do with the demands of the system rather than the individual's volition.

While the classical and neo-classical views of competition ensure (in different ways) that all workers get their 'appropriate rewards', competition does not achieve 'justice'. The capitalists' rate of profit according to classical economics has nothing to do with any notion of 'justice', and distribution can be improved in favour of the workers if they change their breeding habits: as workers were believed to multiply in numbers whenever real wages rose above the subsistence level (a phenomenon underscored by the Malthusian theory of population), their wages remained stuck at this level. Even neo-classical economics only asserts that distribution is 'appropriate' *given the initial distribution of endowments among the economic agents,* but not 'just' in any normative sense. *Competition in this sense is no different from cooperation among the producers.* We shall refer to the two different notions of competition we have been contrasting, the Darwinian or coercionist notion and the cooperativist notion respectively.

This contrast in turn fits into another contrast with regard to the very origin of capitalism.

Contrasting Views on the Origin of Capitalism

The classical liberal perception, we have noted in chapter one, sees capitalism as an arrangement that emerges through free individuals, who are under no compulsions of any kind, entering into voluntary contracts with one another. In particular, the employer–labourer relationship that constitutes the core of capitalism is seen as a voluntary relationship that is entered into because it makes both the parties to the contract, the employer and the labourer, better off compared *to their respective positions in the pre-capitalist society*. Capitalism, in short, is the product of a contract between individuals in society which is voluntarily arrived at, and which represents not only an advance in individual well-being compared to earlier, but a quintessential expression of individual freedom. It represents that level of freedom where individuals can enter into contracts voluntarily in order to improve their economic well-being.

This view of capitalism presents the system as if it is based, in effect, on cooperation, except that this cooperation is rooted in *individual self-interest.* Capitalism which originates with individuals coming together, as employers and labourers, to improve their material well-being, is also sustained through such cooperation because each is better off compared to the original situation and does not wish to lose that state of being better off. I shall call this perception 'voluntary cooperation-based' or the 'cooperativist' view of capitalism.

As against this, there is the alternative view of capitalism, expressed by Marx, which sees capitalism as emerging not through a voluntary contract among pre-capitalist producers, with some agreeing to work as labourers for the others because it improves their economic condition compared to what it was when they were petty producers, but through an exercise of *coercion*. Coercion displaces some petty producers from their traditional occupations by separating them from their means of production, and they become 'free' wage-labourers in the double sense: of being unencumbered by any means of production, and having full ownership over their bodies and hence their labour power.

Having been displaced from their traditional occupations, these labourers no doubt enter quite voluntarily into contracts with others willing to employ them, but they do so from a position where *they are already dispossessed and have no other alternative*: they can no longer fall back on the option of being petty producers since they have been forcibly separated from their means of production. I call this perception of the system the coercion-based or 'coercionist' view of capitalism.

Both perceptions, the cooperativist perception and the coercionist one, of course see capitalism *functioning through* voluntary contracts. This is an obvious quotidian fact about capitalism on which there can be no possible disagreement; in the sphere of exchange there is a symmetry between the buyer of labour power and its seller, each of whom enters into a voluntary contract with the other. The difference relates to the question of how this situation of exchange emerged, and hence to what lies underneath this appearance that one encounters in the sphere of exchange. While the cooperativist position projects this voluntary contract back into history, suggesting that this voluntarism characterizes the capitalist system from the very beginning, the coercionist perception sees the appearance of voluntary exchange as being based on a reality which is quite different, a reality marked by coercive dispossession. (One recalls here Marx's well-known remark that if the appearance of things coincided with their reality, then there would be no need for science.)

It is a hallmark of the Marxist perception that not all persons displaced from their traditional occupation through coercion succeed in finding employment as wage-labourers. Many remain unemployed. Thus, both wage employment and the reserve army of labour are *simultaneously* created by an act of coercion.

Contrasting Notions of the Commodity

We now come to the third concept where there is a corresponding difference of perception between the classical and Marxist usages; and that is 'commodity production'. To say, as Marxists do, that capitalism emerges as a result of dispossession of some petty producers still begs the question: why does such dispossession occur? If it is because of sheer greed on the part of some, then the question arises: why does greed suddenly become effective at a certain particular juncture? In fact, however, it is not a sudden emergence of greed that explains such coercive dispossession, or what Marx called 'primitive accumulation of capital'; rather, the forcible eviction of some petty producers is itself the result of a certain coercion exercised on *those who exercise the coercion themselves*. Neither a sudden rush of greed nor a happenstance but the impersonal pressure of competition explains why even the coercive dispossession of some petty producers occurs; and this competition arises because of commodity production. If *one* did not carry out primitive accumulation of capital, then *someone else* would.

The fact that commodity production in the Marxist sense also entails Darwinian competition is often not recognized because of a lack of understanding, even among Marxists, of what such commodity production means. Any production for the market or any production in exchange for cash does not constitute commodity production. Classical political economy defined a commodity as embodying both use-value and exchange-value for both the buyer and the seller, and this understanding is usually also attributed to Marx; but this is not Marx's understanding. For Marx, while a commodity is both a use-value and an exchange-value for the *buyer*, it is only an exchange-value, just a sum of money, for the *seller* (Kautsky 1903). In other words, unlike Alfred Marshall's fishermen who take home the surplus of their catch, over what they can sell, for their own consumption, commodity production implies production *solely* for the market – that is, production for buyers who are not near-and-dear ones. It involves an impersonality between the producers and the buyers; and this comes basically with long-distance trade. Even here, however, long-distance trade is only a necessary and not a sufficient condition for the traded object to become a commodity. *It is this impersonality that introduces competitiveness among the commodity producers.* And competition acts as a coercive force upon all commodity producers, forcing them, whether they wish to or not, to adopt changes in the methods of production as new and cheaper ones become available, and to carry out primitive accumulation of capital whenever the scope for it arises, for if one did not do so, then that scope would be utilized by someone else who would then steal a march over the ones who missed the opportunity.

This sort of impersonal competition that introduces a spontaneity or self-drivenness into the process of social change and makes the individual producer an inauthentic agent rather than an authentic one, is supposed to characterize capitalism, according to the Marxist perception (remember Marx's description of the capitalist as 'capital personified'); but it already makes its appearance in the process of commodity production itself and is carried forward under capitalism.[3]

Of course it is not the old pre-capitalist society that suddenly gets the impulse through such coercive competition to carry out primitive accumulation of capital. That society itself has undergone a prior change, for example, the decline of the old aristocracy and its substitution by a new aristocracy that is much more aligned with what Marx called the 'bankocracy', to make it prepared for primitive accumulation of capital in response to the impersonal coercion exercised by competition. Coercion resulting in primitive accumulation, in short, occurs because of the Darwinian competition entailed in commodity production; but it occurs on the basis of a certain history.

A Neo-Classical Argument on the Origin of Capitalism

Each of these two perceptions of capitalism, the coercionist and the cooperativist, about its origin and about the nature of the competition that characterizes it, has a different implication for individual freedom and hence gives rise to a different political programme.

The essence of individual freedom consists, above all, in the exercise of agency.[4] But if the nature of capitalism is such that individuals, while appearing to exercise agency, are in fact being driven by the logic of the system to act in particular ways which are not of their volition, then there is no genuine exercise of agency. If the capitalist is only 'capital personified', then the capitalist too exercises no agency. A system engendering universal alienation entails a universal denial of individual freedom. For Marx and his followers, therefore, socialism becomes necessary for overcoming this coercion exercised by capitalism. If capitalism is a spontaneous system engendering universal alienation, it follows that going beyond capitalism and ushering in socialism that does not have this spontaneity is the only way to achieve individual freedom.

In contrast, no economist who sees capitalism as being a 'cooperativist' arrangement that is voluntarily entered into by individuals, and that improves the conditions of all those who enter into this arrangement, subscribes to the *necessity* of socialism. Many of them may prefer socialism on *ethical* grounds (as the Ricardian Socialists had done), but the political position that *follows* from their cooperativist perception of capitalism is liberalism, that sees at best the need for reforms in the system but not for transcending it.

It would be argued that neo-classical economics, which says little about the origin of capitalism, cannot be simply clubbed together with those who see capitalism as emerging through a voluntary contract. In fact, few modern economists outside of the Marxist tradition even concern themselves about the origin of capitalism, about whether it arose because of the pooling of resources by petty producers with some becoming labourers to others who became employers, or whether some who became labourers did so because they were forcibly expropriated.

Indeed, neither Walras, nor Menger, nor Jevons, nor Marshall, nor even Keynes (except in passing, on which more later) had much to say directly about how capitalism came into being. And if we define our cooperativist and coercionist traditions exclusively with reference to the origin of capitalism, then we would be at a loss on how to categorize them. We can however safely make an inference about their position on the origins of capitalism from what they *say about capitalism in general,* basing ourselves on the internal consistency of their arguments.

Almost all strands of neo-classical economics believe that, save in certain exceptional cases, such as the existence of externalities, the process of exchange and hence, by extension, production based on the hiring of labour power which itself is an act of exchange and is treated as such, makes all participants in the process better off; 'better off' here is defined in a specific sense, namely that some at least become better off while none becomes worse off.[5]

It follows that petty producers entering into capitalist relations among themselves will become better off in the above sense (i.e. Pareto-wise better off) according to neo-classical economics. Of course, even if some petty producers have been expropriated beforehand as the Marxist tradition postulates, even then their getting into wage employment by exchanging their labour power against money with the capitalists would still be explicable by the fact of Pareto-improvement. In other words, the sheer fact of a voluntary coming together of workers and capitalists is explicable whether there has been a prior act of expropriation or whether no such expropriation has occurred and petty producers have been continuing as before; the wage-contract is thus voluntary, *but a prior act of expropriation is not required by neo-classical economics.*

Hence, if we postulate that there had been a petty production economy prior to capitalism, then the transition to capitalism can be explained by neo-classical economics only by its argument about the sheer 'efficiency' of exchange; and no other explanation will be in keeping with the neo-classical perspective. A voluntary transition to capitalism therefore can be inferred from the neo-classical argument even when there is no explicit discussion about the origin of capitalism.

Putting it differently, since all exchange is supposed to be voluntary and no forced exchange is assumed to be occurring, unlike what had actually happened in the colonies of conquest through the imposition of a rigid taxation system (on which more later), and since all voluntary exchange is supposed to improve (at least in the Pareto-sense) the material conditions of the participants (for otherwise they can just withdraw from the process of exchange), if capitalism is supposed to be a system that carries forward the process of exchange a step beyond petty commodity production, then one can infer from neo-classical economics that it must have been voluntarily arrived at.[6] Because of their belief that exchange improves the condition of the participants, neo-classical economists who say nothing about the origin of capitalism can therefore be considered as belonging to the cooperativist school. Thus, both the classical tradition that does say something even if indirectly about the origin of capitalism (as we discuss later), and the neo-classical tradition that does not do so, can be categorized as belonging to the cooperativist tradition in economics and to the liberal tradition in politics.

But unlike John Locke and Adam Smith who suggested some ways in which pooling of resources improves productivity, neo-classical economics does not explicitly address this question. Technological progress as seen by it cannot explain pooling of resources, for its benefits (at least those of Harrod-neutral or purely 'labour-augmenting' technological progress which it generally assumes)[7] accrue equally to all producers, no matter what the ratio of their endowments. But 'convexity' of the production function which neo-classical economics assumes does provide an explanation. This may be seen as follows.

Suppose land per unit of labour is plotted on the horizontal axis and output per unit of labour on the vertical axis, with land and labour being the only two 'factors of production'. The convexity of the neo-classical production function will then mean that its graph is concave downwards, which means that the weighted average of the outputs of two producers who have the same production function but different 'factor endowments' will be less than the output from the weighted average of the two endowments when they are pooled together.[8] On this argument, if a petty producer with larger labour input per unit of land combined with another with smaller labour input per unit of land, then both of them can be better off. Hence, it is worthwhile for a petty producer with smaller land per head to offer himself as a labourer to one with larger land per head, and to simultaneously lease out his land to the latter. The shift from independent production to capitalist production therefore enhances 'efficiency', which would explain on the basis of neo-classical economics the voluntary emergence of hired labour.

Individual 'Rationality' and the Question of Work Discipline

Both classical and neo-classical economics, however, by presuming full employment as the equilibrium towards which the system tends to gravitate, get into a problem which we must mention in passing here. Capitalism above all is a system of *production* where large numbers are assembled under one roof to undertake productive activity. Any such system of production requires not just a pooling of all factors involved in production, but above all a certain level of coordination and hence discipline that must be followed for realizing this coordination. The conveyor belt depicted in Charlie Chaplin's film *Modern Times* may be a stark presentation of the situation, but the discipline it shows as being required from the workers is no exaggeration and remains quite central to production under capitalism. The most potent means of enforcing this discipline according to Marx was the threat of the 'sack', of being thrown out of work into the ranks of the unemployed; but this threat means little if there are no actual unemployed, no 'reserve army of labour' into whose ranks anyone violating the discipline demanded at the work-place can be consigned. Economic traditions that do not see the coercion exercised by the prospect of unemployment as being necessary for production under capitalism, must *ipso facto* therefore believe either in some other coercive mechanism, or in some non-coercive means of enforcing work discipline. If they do not invoke any other coercive mechanism, as they certainly do not, then they must *ipso facto* believe that voluntary cooperation exists under capitalism between the capitalists and the workers, so that the workers automatically imbibe work discipline. And by this reasoning, Walras, Marshall and Menger must all be categorized as implicit believers in voluntary cooperation as the mainspring of capitalism. Even Keynes, whose notion of 'full employment', that he believed could and should be achieved, did not leave any room for the existence of a reserve army of labour which could be used for enforcing work discipline, must *ipso facto* be categorized as implicitly subscribing to the same position. And so must the classical tradition that too postulates a full employment equilibrium.

But what may underlie such voluntary cooperation is never made clear. And as far as the neo-classical tradition is concerned, since it assumes economic 'rationality' on the part of the individual, the problem gets compounded because *individual 'rationality', that is, the pursuit of a course of action by the individual that is based on a calculation of the gains and losses of that individual alone,* goes against voluntary cooperation.

Such 'rationality' which is necessarily self-centred (an issue discussed in chapter seven) is supposed to be exercised within a bounded area. For instance, taking an apparently extreme and outlandish example, employees are not supposed to pilfer the final product that is produced by a factory. This can be reconciled with individual 'rationality' only under two circumstances: either if individual 'rationality' itself is bounded, that its exercise is self-consciously restricted only to a certain domain, the domain that is considered legally permissible, but not beyond; or if 'rational' behaviour when it transgresses the legal limit is so severely punished that it becomes prohibitively expensive and hence effectively outside the agent's calculation.

Now, there is no justification for the first of these constraints; there is no reason why the exercise of individual 'rationality' should be *self-consciously* bounded. And as for the second circumstance, the idea of pilferage becoming prohibitively expensive *in a neo-classical world* is scarcely convincing. True, if the person pilfering is imprisoned for it, then that may make pilferage prohibitively expensive for many; but imprisonment requires evidence and conviction which are not easy to secure, and are time-consuming and expensive even for the employer.

By contrast, the dismissal of an employee on the suspicion that he was engaged in pilferage is easier for the employer; and it can become prohibitively expensive even for the most self-centred ('rational') employee if he is thereby thrown into the ranks of the unemployed. This presupposes a permanent presence of the unemployed, in the form of a reserve army of the unemployed, which neo-classical economics denies. No doubt neo-classical economics recognizes a certain proportion of the work-force as being unemployed at any point of time, but these only include the voluntarily unemployed and those 'between jobs' (for each of whom in fact a job supposedly is waiting); and those dismissed for alleged pilferage are not a part of this 'frictional unemployment'. And, if we assume for argument's sake that they should also be included in the definition of frictional unemployment, then the term 'full employment' would lose all meaning. The existence of any unemployment could then be passed off as full employment, on the grounds that all those who are supposed to be unemployed are really the transgressors who are receiving punishment for pilferage by the employers.

It follows, therefore, that at full employment, if it is to be defined meaningfully within neo-classical economics, there can be, conceptually, no unemployment of anyone for transgressing injunctions against pilferage, which implies that the exercise of individual 'rationality' through pilferage in a neo-classical universe is perfectly possible.

This vindicates our claim that individual 'rationality' as defined by neo-classical economics is incompatible with persistent cooperative behaviour. Put differently, the existence of a reserve army of labour is essential for work discipline under the system without which there can be no *production.* The cooperativist view of capitalism which assumes full employment is incompatible with individual 'rationality'.

A simple example will clarify the point. A capitalist enterprise produces 100 units of output by employing 20 workers, each paid a wage of 3 units of output. Any of the workers will have an incentive to take away, say, 5 units of output, which is so small that it either goes undetected or its loss cannot be traced. From the point of the worker who takes the 5 units, the cut in the wage-rate on account of the loss will at the most be (5/20), obviously less than 5; 'rationality' then will demand taking the 5 units.

Such taking away no doubt violates the law. But a truly 'rational' individual will not be deterred by the provisions of the law *per se;* only his calculations will become more complex by bringing in the probability of being caught and the severity of punishment. And unless legally caught, the assumption of full employment in the *neo-classical universe* implies that there is no *de facto* punishment for anyone making away with some output from the capitalists' factory.[9] A capitalist unit, in short, cannot function only by relying on the punishment provided by the law of the land; it must have its own punishment system, which the existence of a reserve army of labour allows it to have. Production therefore cannot be seen as a mere extension of exchange, as neo-classical economics does.

The point being made can be put generally as follows. Individual rationality that is assumed by neo-classical economics entails behaviour based on maximizing an objective function subject to certain constraints. But logically, such rationality must mean that even the constraints should be 'rationally' accepted as constraints. Maximizing behaviour must also incorporate behaviour that considers the costs and benefits of violating the constraints themselves. And it must not only make the constraints themselves open to maximizing behaviour in a *particular* context, but also more generally. In other words, the 'consumer's 'rationality' must not only be confined to maximizing a utility function subject to a budget constraint and a set of prices; it must also extend to the possibility of enlarging the budget constraint by 'illegally' snatching from someone else's budget; and so on. The constraints in any constrained maximization exercise must themselves be the outcome of 'rational' calculations, the gains and losses from relaxing them at someone else's expense, and so on *ad infinitum*, which robs meaning from any optimization exercise. Thus, when we talk of 'constrained optimization', we have to recognize that the constraints themselves must be the product of an optimization exercise.

While a simple act of exchange may not offer much scope for going beyond the act itself, more complex processes like production clearly do. Considering production, therefore, as a mere extension of the act of exchange is fraught with serious problems. And the cooperation argument that underlies exchange and is implicitly extended from exchange to production is incompatible with the neo-classical assumption of individual 'rationality'. In fact the view of capitalism as based on voluntary cooperation, supposedly arising from individual rationality, is logically flawed, since individual rationality will militate against such cooperation.[10] But let us move on from this issue to which we shall return later.

Classical economics of course does not postulate individual 'rationality', and hence is free from this criticism; but then it provides no explanation whatsoever for how and why 'work discipline' is maintained by the workers, and indeed for what motivates workers to behave the way they do.

The Ensuing Discussion in the Book

The purpose of this book, as mentioned in chapter one, is to elaborate on these two contrasting perspectives on capitalism and individual freedom. The first part of the book is devoted to an examination of the 'classical' liberal position which itself as we saw is based on two alternative strands of political economy, the 'classical' and the 'neo-classical' strands. Indeed the book begins with the writings of John Locke who was a precursor of classical political economy, and follows the discussion on Locke by one on Adam Smith. The historical validity of the presumptions underlying the positions of Locke and Smith is then examined with reference to data relating to European, especially British, history.

Neo-classical economics of course is essentially ahistorical. It invokes the concept of an optimizing self-absorbed individual who has existed since time immemorial, who sees the benefits of entering into an exchange relationship with others, and whose entering into such exchange relationships with others, whenever the opportunity for it arises, is the foundation of capitalism. Unlike Locke or Smith who saw capitalism as arising because it entailed improved production methods, neo-classical economics sees the virtue of capitalism as lying essentially in an extension of the benefits of exchange, as entailing a market equilibrium that represents a more complex arrangement of exchange.[11]

Central to neo-classical economics, we have seen, is the concept of 'rationality', which believes that all economic agents are always optimizing some objective function subject to the constraints they face; capitalism, according to it, constitutes an arrangement worked out by such 'rational individuals'. The threat to the freedom of the individual arises not from capitalism but from constraints on its full flowering. Such constraints arise from the state meddling in the operation of this system or from monopolies and oligopolies which entail a departure from a state of competitive equilibrium that best captures the benefits of exchange. The state interfering in the operation of the system up to a certain point, which is warranted by 'externalities', may be acceptable to classical liberalism, but certainly not beyond that.

John Maynard Keynes, a liberal who, we have seen, coined the term 'New Liberalism' ([1931] 1963) to describe his own creed, was the spokesperson *par excellence* of heterodox liberalism; his work ([1936] 1949) which emphasizes the need for state intervention to sustain a liberal position, critiques and undermines the basis of neo-classical economics and the strand of liberalism based upon it.

In contrast to all these strands is the Marxist position, which sees capitalism as a 'spontaneous' system driven by its own logic in which individuals are trapped, and in which they are compelled to play out their respective roles; the state presiding over capitalism cannot overcome this 'spontaneity' since the state itself is trapped within it. The last section of this book is devoted to a discussion of the Marxist position.

The Concept of 'Spontaneity'

I have referred several times above to the 'spontaneity' of capitalism and the concept plays a central role in the argument of this book. Even though it is discussed at length in several chapters below, I should still provide a preliminary explanation of what I understand by 'spontaneity'. 'Spontaneity' obviously refers to self-drivenness, but the self-drivenness I am talking about refers not to any individual but *to the capitalist system as a whole.* In fact, this self-drivenness of the system *precludes* any freedom for the individual economic agents: it is based on the individual agents being coerced by a process of Darwinian competition, which characterizes capitalism, to act in *specific ways*, for fear otherwise of losing their position within the system; it is the aggregate of this mass of individual actions which individual agents are obliged to undertake that makes the system self-driven.

This self-drivenness of the system however can be interpreted in two different ways. One way, which is a minimalist interpretation of 'spontaneity', refers to the fact that the aggregate outcome of the actions of individual economic agents, in terms of the behaviour of the system, turns out to be *completely different* from what the agents had envisaged. An obvious example of this is the 'paradox of thrift', where everybody's decision to double his or her savings propensity leads in the aggregate not to a doubling of savings, but to a halving of income.

Before proceeding further I should emphasize that even this minimalist interpretation must be distinguished from another phenomenon, where the aggregate outcome, while not being different from what the agents had envisaged, turns out also to be *something more* than what they had envisaged. The proposition of classical economics that unfettered individual economic agents, while looking after their own interests, also achieve social progress in the aggregate, in the sense of an increase in the wealth of the nation; or the proposition of neo-classical economics that individual economic agents, while exhibiting 'rational' behaviour by maximizing some objective function that relates exclusively to themselves, achieve nonetheless a 'social optimum' in the aggregate, are instances of this *something more*. In these cases, however, quite apart from this 'something more', the agents also succeed in achieving their own interests. But 'spontaneity' in the minimalist or 'weak' sense refers to a situation *where they do not succeed in achieving even their own ends*. Keynesian economics may be said to have highlighted the 'spontaneity' of the capitalist system in this 'weak' sense.

I use the term 'spontaneity' in this book, however, in a different, 'strong', sense, which I believe is the sense in which Marx had used the term. 'Spontaneity' in the strong sense differs from 'spontaneity' in the 'weak' sense in two fundamental ways. First, as already mentioned, competition which characterizes the system coerces individuals to act in *specific ways*, for fear of otherwise losing their place within the system. Second, the aggregate outcome in terms of the behaviour of the system is not just different from, or unrelated to, what the individual agents had envisaged; it also consists of certain immanent tendencies. The system realizes these tendencies by coercing the individual economic agents to act in specific ways, whence it follows that these agents act not out of their own volition: while appearing to be free, they are mere cogs. 'Spontaneity' in the weak sense is subsumed under 'spontaneity' in the strong sense: Keynesian 'involuntary unemployment', for instance, is a feature of capitalism which Marx had recognized even before Keynes.

'Spontaneity' in this strong sense refers of course to the system in its *pure state*. Over time, economic agents engage in praxis to transcend this 'spontaneity': workers enter into 'combinations' to fight for a higher share of wages, and they put political pressure on the state to overcome mass unemployment and to reduce wealth and income inequalities in society. But even when some of their demands are immediately met, and 'spontaneity' appears to have been rolled back by praxis, this victory of praxis *within the confines of the system* is only temporary: the system not only seeks to reassert its 'spontaneity' and roll back the gains achieved through praxis, but actually does so over a period that may be more or less prolonged. This dialectic between 'spontaneity' and praxis, and the manner in which the reassertion of 'spontaneity' is effected, are discussed in several places below, especially in chapters ten and twelve; what this discussion shows is that individual freedom can never be achieved under capitalism.

Spontaneity and Class

The logic of the system, according to this position, manifests itself through the aggregation of actions which individuals undertake, not through an optimization exercise carried out on a clean slate, but because they are compelled by competition to undertake these actions. This conception leads to the conclusion that the individual is not free, and cannot be free, under capitalism since the individual lacks agency. This is palpable in the colonies, semi-colonies and 'outlying regions' that capitalism annexes for itself. But it is also true in the metropolis itself.

Of course, the 'unfreedoms' of different participants of the system, though identical in the sense of robbing each of them of agency, do not place them on a par. The capitalists and the workers, though both are 'alienated' within the capitalist system, are not on an equal footing. And the genesis of this inequality in footing lies in the fact that the employer–labourer relationship, though no doubt voluntarily entered into, presupposes a state of deprivation or destitution of independent producers. This relationship, in other words, is entered into not on a clean slate, but after a process of destitution or deprivation of independent petty producers, which is visited upon them by some other producers themselves or by an overlord, within a Darwinian-competitive setting introduced by commodity production; or by the state acting on their behalf to short-circuit and hasten the process.

Spontaneity of the system, in short, must not be taken to mean symmetry between its different participants or any blurring of class divisions. But different participants in the system, placed differently within it, are nonetheless subjected to this common experience, whereby what each does is because of the coercion exercised by competition rather than because of that individual's voluntary choice. This is what justifies the use of the term 'coercionist'.

Since this 'spontaneity' is immanent to capitalism, going beyond it requires going beyond capitalism; and going beyond capitalism to overcome its 'spontaneity' becomes an essential condition for individual freedom, whence it follows that socialism is the economic system under which *alone* the achievement of *individual freedom* is possible. The central argument of the book is that this conclusion follows from the specific political economy developed by Marx, which is both unique and often unappreciated even amongst his followers.

Freedom of the individual therefore has to be part of a project of human liberation in general; it must entail overcoming the 'spontaneity' that constitutes the essence of capitalism, through a collective effort. Social ownership of the means of production alone therefore cannot define socialism, though it is a necessary condition for overcoming 'spontaneity'; there must be a collective effort to control human economic destiny through the use of political praxis to determine the contours of economics rather than the other way around, as happens under the 'spontaneous' system that is capitalism.

Socialism, it follows, is not about equality *per se*. Liberalism's concern, too, is not so much with equality as with freedom; in fact it sees the two as being in a certain sense contradictory, a point we discuss later. But even socialism is not motivated by the desire to ensure or move towards equality *per se*; it is above all for keeping alive the collective spirit, the sense of belonging together, for which an egalitarian society would be necessary. To talk of equality among individuals *per se* is still to treat them as 'monads', as disparate atomized elements among whom comparisons are being made. The concept of 'equality' does not transcend the atomization of individuals characteristic of capitalism. The concern for equality still remains conceptually trapped within a 'monadic' existence. The essence of socialism is to overcome 'monadic' existence.

But then, why has socialism as it has been practised till now not achieved individual freedom as it is theoretically supposed to do? This is not just the result of socialist practice under the specific historical circumstances in which socialism developed; it is also caused by a flawed understanding of Marxism, for which Marx himself cannot be absolved from blame. The last chapter of the book, which is in the nature of a postscript, discusses the question of individual freedom under 'actually existing socialism' (whose existence, of course, has shrunk greatly). A critique of actually existing socialism is essential for carrying forward the project of human liberation.

Notes

1 As I made clear in chapter one, I use the term 'classical' liberalism throughout this book to distinguish it from 'new liberalism' that comes with Keynes. The economic basis of 'classical' liberalism is provided in *different* ways by *both* classical and neo-classical economics. Classical liberalism should not therefore be taken to mean liberalism based on classical economics alone.

2 Schumpeter's argument, based on the assumption of a constant work-force, was that capital accumulation, resulting in greater and greater 'capital deepening', would eventually reach a 'capital saturation' point where the marginal product of capital (and hence the rate of profit) would be zero.

3 The argument presented in the rest of this section is developed in P. Patnaik (2021a).

4 It may be argued that individual freedom should be defined with reference to the *ability* to exercise agency, in which case a person having the ability to exercise agency but unwilling to do so, would still be considered free. But defining freedom in this way implies that in a situation of lack of exercise of agency we have to find out whether this was because of inability or unwillingness, which may not always be possible. Besides, *in the context of the argument of this book*, whether we define lack of freedom in terms of inability to exercise agency or simply as lack of exercise of agency, makes little difference, since our argument is that the 'spontaneity' of capitalism entails a lack of exercise of *authentic* agency by negating the individual's *ability* to do so.

5 An individual, of course, is presumed to become better off by having *ceteris paribus* a vector-wise larger bundle of goods and services.

6 Even if there had been an exercise of coercion that dispossessed petty producers before the act of exchange that makes some work as labourers for others, then that coercion is an issue separate from the origins of capitalism; for even if it had not occurred, capitalism according to neo-classical economics should still have come into being.

7 Harrod-neutrality means the following: suppose the rate of technical progress is 10 per cent per year, then 100 persons employed in the current year are equivalent to 110 persons employed last year.

8 This can be expressed as follows: $F(\lambda.(N/L)_1 + (1-\lambda).(N/L)_2) > \lambda.F(N/L)_1 + (1-\lambda).F(N/L)_2$ where N and L refer to land and labour endowments with petty producers 1 and 2, F the output and $\lambda = (N/L)_1 / [(N/L)_1+(N/L)_2]$.

9 It may be thought that since the cut in wages will be imposed on *all workers* because of the pilferage by *any one* of them, other workers will have an interest in preventing pilferage by anyone of them. But as long as even a part of the loss on account of pilferage is borne by the capitalist (via a cut in profits), which it must be, all workers, guided by individual 'rationality', will have an incentive to pilfer rather than spy on possible pilferage by their colleagues. The pursuit of individual rationality in such a case may even dictate implicit or explicit collusion between them.

10 Since the argument of this book is that individual freedom is possible only through the individual exercising agency *as part of a collective*, it follows that individual

freedom and individual rationality (as defined by neo-classical economics) are mutually incompatible. A kindred argument is advanced in Bilgrami (2022a).

11 The assumption of constant returns to scale which neo-classical economics makes ensures that the sheer coming together of employers and employees to form a larger-scale production unit compared to the unit under individual petty production, yields no benefits whatsoever, unless, as shown above, the 'factor endowments' were different to start with. Even when there is technological progress, its benefits do not remain confined to any particular firm or firm-size. The arguments for a voluntary employer–employee relationship advanced by Locke and Smith therefore become irrelevant for neo-classical economics.

CHAPTER THREE

John Locke on Hired Labour

We saw in the previous chapter that there are two very different perspectives on the emergence of wage-labour within a world characterized by the pervasive presence of self-employed producers. One perspective sees some producers being forcibly excluded from access to their means of production or to common property resources by some other producers (or, alternatively, the bulk of the self-employed producers being denied such access by some overlord); this then leads to a loss of their incomes, or makes them completely unviable in economic terms, so that they are willing to take up wage employment. Their willingness to be hired as labourers is the result of some specific act or process of absolute *deprivation* inflicted upon them.

The other perspective sees the emergence of wage-labour as being caused by no such act of absolute deprivation, but by the desire on the part of some producers to improve their condition by working for an employer who offers them an even higher standard of living than they were earning through their own independent effort. This normally presupposes (outside, that is, of the assumption of concavity downwards of the production function that neo-classical economists make) that the employer uses some method of production that is superior to what the now-turned labourer used in his capacity as a self-employed producer.

Both these perspectives see the labour-contract between the employer and the labourer as being *voluntary*; but while the contract itself is entered into voluntarily, which is what distinguishes wage employment from slavery or serfdom, what led up to this voluntary arrangement is the point of difference. In one case, it is a process of deprivation that more or less coerces the labourer into entering into this voluntary contract; in the other, there is no such deprivation or coercion, only a desire to do even better than one was doing before. Put differently, the coercionist perception of capitalism visualizes what we shall call 'wage-labour by deprivation', while the voluntarist or cooperativist perception visualizes 'wage-labour by assimilation'. These two perspectives belong, respectively, to the Marxist and the Classical Liberal traditions.

John Locke was among the pioneers of the second tradition, i.e. was among the first to visualize 'wage-labour through assimilation' that is central to the voluntarist perception, an idea that was then taken over by Adam Smith in his *opus* a century later. Locke, the Social Contract theorist, who saw the emergence of organized society and the state as the result of a contract voluntarily entered into by its individual members, also saw the emergence of the employer–labourer relationship as the result of a voluntary contract with no history of deprivation or coercion preceding it. It arises, according to him, even in what he had called 'the state of nature', where there is plenty of land for everyone to cultivate.

Locke on Property

Locke, as is well known, sought to reconcile his defence of private property with his view that God 'hath given the world to men in common', by locating the origin of property in human labour. Since human beings undoubtedly had property over their own bodies and hence over their own labour, the application of labour to nature in order to obtain things for oneself established a natural right to property over what was so obtained. What was thus 'appropriated' with the application of labour belonged to one. As he put it:

> … everyman has a property in his own Person. This nobody has any right to but himself. The labour of his body, and the work of his hands, we may say, are properly his. Whatsoever then he removes out of the state that nature hath provided, and left it in, he hath mixed his labour with, and joyned to it something that is his own, and thereby makes it his property. It being by him removed from the common state nature placed it in, it hath by this labour something annexed to it, that excludes the common right of other men. (Locke 1689, Book II, para 27)

Locke recognized two limits to such a natural right to property: one, what was appropriated must not exclude other people's right to similar appropriation; and two, what was appropriated must not be such as cannot be used by the one appropriating, and hence will perish.

In the state of nature when there is plenty of land available for all, these limits do not become constraining. My enclosing a plot of land to satisfy my wants does not preclude anyone else's enclosing a similar plot of land to satisfy his wants; and in a world where goods are perishable, there would be a natural limit to what I can enclose, for anything in excess of what would meet my wants would only lead to waste, and hence be violative of my natural right to property.

This natural limit to what I can enclose disappears, however, when money comes into existence. With money making its appearance, in the form initially of precious metals, a form of holding wealth comes into existence that did not exist before. I can then enclose a much larger plot of land, far in excess of what is required for satisfying my wants, because whatever produce from this land I do not consume myself, I can exchange with others to obtain precious metals which I can store *ad infinitum*; there is no question of its being wasted or perishing.

This has two implications. First, my natural right to property is not confined any longer to only what I can consume, for holding my excess produce (over what I can consume) in the form of money, obtained through exchange with others, does not entail a waste, and hence does not violate Locke's second criterion for defining a natural right to property. Secondly, people will *actually* begin to hold wealth when a form in which wealth can be held becomes available; and when this happens, the amount of land that a person will find worth enclosing will greatly increase. This leads to the total using up of the land area (or more generally natural resources), greater conflicts over property and hence the need to provide protection for property, for which people enter into a social contract to form a civil society, complete with a state.

But before we enter into a discussion of this transition from the state of nature to civil society, an important point is worth noting. What is striking about Locke's view is that, in the state of nature, cultivation is carried out by *individuals*, meaning not isolated *persons* but *households*. The individual is the 'subject' in the state of nature and retains his 'subject'-hood throughout, carrying it into civil society itself.

It has been argued by Macpherson (1962) that the social contract which brings civil society into existence is one between individual *property-owners* and not between all individuals, and that Locke's civil society therefore involved strict gradations within it; but let us leave this issue aside for the moment. We note only the fact that since the employer–labourer relationship improves, according to Locke, the conditions of both the employer and the labourer (compared to the time when the latter was an individual producer), the strife within the state of nature before the social contract was entered into can also be taken to be damaging to both; the entry to civil society by the former will therefore be supported by the latter – that is, the social contract according to this perception can be deemed to enjoy general support.

What is of note is that the individual entering into civil society as a subject derives his subjecthood and also his property from being the subject of the *production process.* This, of course, is historically inaccurate. Men lived collectively and produced – in Locke's sense (i.e. hunted) – collectively, long before individual cultivation of land came into being. Any recognition of collective production would also entail collective property by Locke's definition: since the labour applied to nature is not that of an individual but of a group (say, a hunting group), the product of the application of that labour would belong to the group as a whole.

This would have two implications. First, there has to be now a separate set of rules about how this product which becomes the property of the collective as a whole should be distributed among the individuals constituting the collective. Second, a civil society of a sort would have already existed quite before any social contract entered into by individuals could create one.

True, Locke's theory asserting the rights of the individual against an absolutist state, for example an absolute monarchy, is in a sense meta-historical; it has a philosophical-axiomatic significance that is not derived from a literal reading of history. But the problem is that a liberal defence of individual freedom (not, of course, to withdraw from civil society but to change the government that violates the basic terms of the social contract), such as what Locke is providing, is also closely enmeshed with the liberal perception of the origin of private property, and hence of capitalist property (as we discuss below). Since the benign-ness of capitalist property is by no means unquestionable, unlike the benign-ness of freedom from an absolute monarchy, Locke's defence of individual property and hence of capitalist property cannot be accepted only on philosophical-axiomatic grounds; its verisimilitude has to be interrogated by referring to real history. Anyway, the point to note here is that individual subjecthood is an *axiom* in Locke's theory.

Insufficiency of Locke's Explanation of Transition

Locke's explanation of the transition from the state of nature to civil society raises a number of questions. On the one hand, there is in Locke a view, reminiscent of Hobbes, of the state of nature itself being unsustainable and necessitating such a transition anyway. This is because the state of nature cannot preclude an individual being in a 'state of war' against others. As he put it,

> To avoid this *state of war* (wherein there is no appeal but to heaven, and wherein every the least difference is apt to end, where there is no authority to decide between the contenders) is one great reason of men's putting themselves into society, and quitting the state of nature: for where there is an authority, a power on earth, from which relief can be had by *appeal,* there the continuance of the *state of war* is excluded, and the controversy is decided by that power. (Locke 1689, Book II, para 21)

But of course, the need to enter into society from the state of nature arises overwhelmingly for a somewhat different reason, viz. the protection of private property, which in turn is crucially linked to the emergence of money. With the introduction of money, the protection of property becomes necessary for two reasons. First, the precious metals that now also constitute property in the possession of the individuals need to be protected; and second, with the limit on the land that can be enclosed being lifted the pressure on land increases, which gives rise to conflicts over property in the form of land. The resolution of such conflicts among people and the protection of property now requires the institution of a state. The state, in short, becomes essential for defending property, and the need for such a state arises as a consequence of the fact that money has come into being.

The above is a fairly standard view of Locke's theory of the transition from a state of nature to organized society and the institution of a state. In this account, however, there is an obvious lacuna. Even in a world into which money has entered – in which, in other words, there is a convenient form of wealth-holding – an individual, even a hypothetical one who has no qualms about simply piling up wealth in the form of money, would not enclose land beyond what he can *cultivate*. There is a constraint on the amount of land that an individual can *cultivate*, in addition to the constraint arising from what he can *use for satisfying his wants*. Even if the latter constraint ceases to be effective because money has come into existence and can now provide a means of storing wealth so that production need not be limited by a person's wants, the former constraint does not disappear.

True, the amount of land that a person can cultivate is not some fixed magnitude: it depends on the crops he grows, the equipment he uses and so on. But taking all that into account, there is still a limit to the amount of land that a single person can cultivate. And even the amount of equipment that can be used is constrained by the fact that a single person (or household) has to use it. Even in the state of nature, therefore, the mere appearance of money should not make individuals enclose inordinately large amounts of land.

Hence, when Locke says that with the introduction of money the tendency would be to increase greatly the amount of land that an individual would enclose for himself, he does not appear to be taking this constraint into account. In fact there is a mention of it in one place in Locke's writing, but it soon drops out.

> The *measure of property* nature has well set by the extent of men's *labour and the conveniencies of life:* no man's labour could subdue, or appropriate all; nor could his enjoyment consume more than a small part; so that it was impossible for any man, this way, to intrench upon the right of another, or acquire to himself a property, to the prejudice of his neighbour, who would still have room for as good, and as large a possession (after the other had taken out his) as before it was appropriated. (Ibid., para 36)

Locke's remark that 'no man's labour could subdue or appropriate all' recognizes the labour constraint on enclosing land, which money as such cannot overcome. But soon this constraint drops out of consideration, and the view that money encourages the unlimited enclosure of land by providing a durable form in which wealth can be held, takes over.

Even though Locke visualized the employment of wage-labour in the state of nature, on which more later, unless there is an *unlimited supply of wage-labour*, the labour constraint on the amount of land that can be enclosed for cultivation still remains. If, for instance, we assume a fixed population, which automatically puts a limit on the number of wage-labourers that can be employed, the amount of land that can be enclosed for cultivation also becomes bounded. True, the accumulation of 'stock', if it can be 'labour-saving', that is, reduce the number of workers per unit area for raising any particular crop-mix, can raise the limit on the amount of land that can be enclosed for cultivation; and if accumulation of this sort is continuous, then the limit keeps rising steadily. And Locke did visualize accumulation of 'stock'; he did not visualize wealth only in the form of money. Besides, he also referred to population growth, which would keep raising the limit on the amount of land that can be enclosed.

For instance, he mentions in passing:

> Men at first, for the most part, contented themselves with what unassisted nature offered to their necessities; and though afterwards, in some parts of the world (where the increase of people and stock, with the *use of money,* had made

> land scarce, and so of some value) the several *communities* settled the bounds of their distinct territories. (Ibid., para 45)

Here he rightly refers to the 'increase of people and stock' *and* the use of money *together* making land scarce; but in much of his writings there is only an emphasis on the use of money to the exclusion of everything else, which would suggest as if the labour constraint simply dropped out of reckoning.

There is, however, an alternative possibility suggested by this paragraph. Since Locke refers here to land itself having 'some value', it may be presumed that enclosing land was not necessarily only for cultivation (where the labour constraint would count); it could be because land itself begins to acquire value and is expected to do so. The pursuit of land enclosures then would proceed independently and parallelly with enclosures for *cultivation.* But Locke does not make this point anywhere else; and even here it is alluded to only fleetingly.

To sum up, the primary reason that Locke adduced for the using up of the entire land in the state of nature, viz. the introduction of money, was insufficient as an explanation. He did mention other factors which, together with the introduction of money, could explain this phenomenon, but he mentioned them only in passing, though they too are essential.

Wage-Labour in the State of Nature

Let us now come to what is for us the crucial aspect of Locke's discussion of the state of nature; and that is his recognition of the existence of wage-labour in that state. This is suggested, for instance, in the chapter on property in the *Second Treatise* (chapter 5), when he is connecting labour with property rights. He writes: 'Thus the grass my horse has bit; the turfs my servant has cut; and the ore I have digged in any place where I have a right to them in common with others, become my property' (ibid., para 28).

This remark is puzzling for two reasons. First, in the state of nature where *ex hypothesi* there is plenty of land for everyone, why should there be any farm servants at all? And secondly, why should the labour of my farm servant provide *me* with a natural right to property over what *he* has produced, even if one accepts Locke's principle that labour is the basis of property?

The answer to the second question is given by Locke as follows:

> … for a Free-man makes himself a servant to another, by selling him for a certain time, the service he undertakes to do, in exchange for wages he is to receive: and though this commonly puts him into the family of his Master, and

> under the ordinary discipline thereof; yet it gives the master but a temporary power over him, and no greater, than what is contained in the contract between them. (Ibid., para 85)

In other words, the labourer has property rights over his own body and the labour it performs, and hence upon the products of his labour which he can hand over to the employer in exchange for a wage. By virtue of paying him the wage the employer acquires property rights over what the labourer produces, exactly as he would over the products of his own labour. (Incidentally, it is only a short step from here to Marx's theory of surplus value.)

The first question however remains, namely, why should there be farm servants at all in the state of nature where there is plenty of land available for all? An obvious answer to it could be found in the exercise of coercion, but Locke, in keeping with his classical liberal perspective, does not see any coercion underlying wage-labour. Such coercion, incidentally, was employed in India in earlier times through the caste system, whereby the Dalits, those at the bottom of the caste hierarchy, were not *allowed* to own land, so that they could provide an army of labourers to work on the land of others. And if any of them left the village to occupy virgin land that lay outside the village boundaries, then troops were sent to bring them back forcibly (Habib 1995). But there is no scope for such coercion in Locke's state of nature (and, of course, there is no state as yet). Why, then, should there be a class of labourers in Locke's state of nature, where there is plenty of land available for anybody to enclose as part of his natural right?

Oddly, Locke does not provide any specific answers to this fundamental question. To quote a Locke scholar,

> Locke does not give a specific reason why a freeman would want to sell his labour to someone else when he could work for himself and acquire his own property. Presumably he believed a man would sell his labour only if it were to his advantage. Locke believed that not all men are equally capable, so he might have believed also that a less capable man would prefer working for another rather than taking the risk of having to live on what he could make for himself. (Karen Vaughn 1980)

There are two obvious problems with this explanation attributed to Locke. First, Locke himself wrote extensively elsewhere, not in *The Two Treatises,* about the subsistence level at which the wages of labourers were stuck. To believe that a person could not, with his own labour, work land which was available without limit to earn even a subsistence for himself, appears far-fetched. This is especially so when there are no reasons for any difference in terms of land productivity between the method of production used on the employer's plot and that which the labourer would have used on his plot if he had decided not to seek wage employment. Besides, even if there was a difference to start with, since the employer enjoys no monopoly over the method of production he uses, the labourer could easily have copied it on his own farm to earn an amount no less than the wage he would earn from the employer. There is no reason, therefore, why there should be any inducement for anyone to become a labourer in the state of nature when there is plenty of land for everyone to cultivate.

Secondly, it is methodologically unsound to base an explanation for an observed phenomenon on a proposition for which there is no independent evidence and which can only be inferred from the observed phenomenon itself. Since there is no independent evidence for the lesser capability of the labourers compared to the employers of labour, other than the fact that the former are labourers and the latter are employers, 'lesser capability' simply would not do as an explanation for the fact of some becoming labourers.

Since Locke in his economic writings had anticipated Adam Smith, and talked of employers having accumulated some stock which they would advance to the labourers before they could employ them, that is, of a degree of thriftiness on the part of the employers, it may appear that this thriftiness constitutes a difference between them; that the employers have the virtue of being more thrifty than the labourers.

But this thriftiness is a completely separate issue, which does not explain why some would become labourers rather than cultivating on their own when there is no land constraint. And if it is argued that in periods of natural calamity the less thrifty become indebted to the more thrifty and thereby lose their freedom to cultivate on their own, becoming labourers instead in the employment of the latter to pay off their debt, then we are talking of a form of *coercion*, through debt-bondage, as the origin of wage-labour. We are no longer, in other words, in a world of 'wage-labour through assimilation', which underlay classical liberalism, as distinct from 'wage-labour through deprivation'. We are then talking about a class-divided society, where one class exercises coercion upon another.

This is in fact what Macpherson had read into Locke's state of nature. Not only was it a class-divided society according to him, but one already characterized by 'possessive individualism' reminiscent of a bourgeois society: why else should the introduction of money make individuals wish to enclose more and more land in order to convert the growing surplus of what is produced on such land over what is needed to satisfy their own wants (including of labourers employed by them and being paid a subsistence wage) into a growing stock of money being accumulated?

But whether or not we can infer from Locke's account an immanent bourgeois individualism in the state of nature itself, it is certainly true that such an individualism emerges clearly with the introduction of money, and hence of production for exchange (against money), as distinct from production for use that characterizes the state of nature. Enclosures of larger and larger amounts of land, or 'land-grab', follow in the wake of this transition from production for use to production for exchange, or from the 'natural economy' to a 'commodity economy' as later economists were to put it. Since this transition, and the associated process of 'land-grab' (or what Marx was to call 'primitive accumulation of capital', though Locke would have *rejected* the Marxian perception), has a central place in Locke's analysis, he would appear to Marxist eyes as a philosopher of the process of primitive accumulation of capital, though advancing a different, liberal, narrative on this process (a narrative whereby wage-labour is *not* generated as a *consequence*).[1]

The purpose behind Locke's invoking a 'social contract' as a meta-historical narrative then becomes clear. It is to obtain a general social acceptance of, and commitment to, the defence of capitalist property that was emerging through this process of primitive accumulation of capital. The social contract is not exclusively a contract among property-owners but supposedly encompasses the entire population including the wage-labourers, who also stand to gain from it as the defence of private property is in their interests as well (since they have become 'wage-labourers through assimilation'). The social contract therefore enjoins upon everybody in society to live up to their contractual obligation by standing for the defence of capitalist property, and to demand of the state that it must also fulfil its contractual obligation for doing so.

Let us, however, move on. What is relevant for the argument of this book is the basic fact that while Locke believes in 'wage-labour by assimilation', he does not provide any satisfactory explanation, except only by allusion referred to above, of why there should be 'wage-labour by assimilation' in his state of nature.

Complexities Associated with the Introduction of Money

There is one aspect of Locke's theory which deserves notice, if only in passing. Since wealth-holding in his account begins essentially with the introduction of money, one may conclude that money is the main form in which wealth is held; for had this not been the case, then wealth would have been held even before the arrival of money, and hence the transition from the state of nature would not have awaited the arrival of money. But if money is the main form in which wealth can be held, then the bulk of the product from whatever land an individual has enclosed, in excess of his own wants, must be exchanged against money; and this must be true for all individuals who have such surplus product. Hence the bulk of the excess output from land over the producers' own requirement must be sold to those individuals who are engaged in producing money.

This already suggests a division of labour in the state of nature, between those engaged in producing money and those engaged in producing agricultural and related goods, which develops alongside the introduction of money. The transition from the state of nature to civil society, in short, is accompanied by a growing division of labour. Locke thus envisions a division of labour long before Adam Smith; but of course, unlike Smith, he does not attribute any 'efficiency gains' or productivity benefits to it.

Once money is introduced, a number of other thorny questions also arise. Money production must be occurring within the state of nature itself. This production must therefore adjust to the total surplus of all individual producers of non-money goods over their own requirements. How does this adjustment take place? In the absence of such adjustment, there would be un-saleability of either the non-money goods or of the money-commodity at the going relative price. In other words, the introduction of money even in the state of nature would bring to the fore all the complex problems of a monetary economy, of imbalances between supply and demand of non-money goods (and hence *ipso facto* of money) – which Locke, of course, does not go into.

The general idea of selling non-money goods to import gold, which is the primary form of holding wealth, is a desideratum of late mercantilism, under which the balance of trade (in non-money goods) is sought to be kept favourable to a country in order to have the balance settled by the import of gold and silver which then get accumulated in the country (Dobb 1946). Since gold and silver were considered the primary form of wealth, this was supposed to enrich a nation.

This idea was strongly criticized later by David Hume and Adam Smith. Hume argued on the basis of the Quantity Theory of Money, of which he was an early proponent, that if a country had more gold than was required to circulate its non-money goods at their going prices, then these prices would rise, making that country uncompetitive in international trade. Its balance of trade would then become unfavourable, leading to an exodus of gold to settle its payments, which would reduce the stock of gold in the economy. Eventually, therefore, the distribution of gold across countries will be in the same proportion as the distribution of the value of the goods and services produced across countries at their respective 'equilibrium' prices.[2] Smith argued on this basis that it is the amount of goods and services that a country can produce, which depended upon its capital stock, that really mattered, and not the amount of money stock it held; hence the true index of the wealth of a nation was its capital stock, with the help of which its inhabitants produced its volume of goods.

Hume's criticism however does not affect Locke's argument (or even the argument of the late mercantilists). Locke (like the late mercantilists) was talking of precious metals *as a form of holding wealth* and *not just as a medium of circulation*, while Hume and Adam Smith (and David Ricardo later) were talking of money *exclusively* as a medium of circulation. A rise in the stock of precious metals therefore need not raise prices as Hume visualized, as it would be simply stored and not increase the demand for non-money goods and services. Besides, Locke was talking not about a real-life *nation* but about the state of nature.

However, even though Locke was not talking about a nation but about the state of nature, with the introduction of money into this state the behaviour of all individuals in this imaginary state was visualized in effect to resemble, in the aggregate, what a nation pursuing a mercantilist trajectory would pursue. Locke's state of nature after the introduction of money represents in some ways, therefore, a *projection backwards* of the mercantilist economy of his time which was amassing gold and silver, and which, far from seeing anything wrong in it, revelled in such amassing.[3] His entire account of the transition from a state of nature to a civil society, however, is fraught with a lack of coherence arising *inter alia* from his insistence on the emergence of 'wage-labour through assimilation'.

Notes

[1] It is often not appreciated that the process of primitive accumulation of capital in Marx, including even the 'enclosures' in Britain, were associated with the emergence of the commodity economy (P. Patnaik 2021a). The emergence of 'possessive individualism', in short, is associated with the emergence of commodity production stimulated by overseas trade (see chapter two), in the manner suggested by Locke though he had a different narrative, even within the Marxist perception.

[2] David Ricardo was to provide a precise definition later to these equilibrium prices or 'natural prices'.

[3] Unlike Spain, which obtained gold directly from the New World, England had to obtain its gold from Continental Europe by having a positive trade balance (in non-gold commodities) vis-à-vis the continent which had to be settled through gold inflows, exactly the way that Locke depicts the situation in the state of nature.

CHAPTER FOUR

Adam Smith and the Division of Labour

Individual Agency

Adam Smith did not invoke Robinson Crusoe as the starting point of his analysis, as was to become common in economics later; but he did invoke something not dissimilar, namely a 'rude state of society, in which there is no division of labour, in which exchanges are seldom made, and in which every man provides everything for himself' (Smith 1981, p. 276). The example he gave of such a society was the set of scattered residents of the Highlands of Scotland. Such a resident could not indulge what, according to Smith, was his 'propensity to truck, barter and exchange', and lived perforce a life where there was scarcely any room for exchange and division of labour. As he put it:

> In the lone houses and very small villages which are scattered about in so desert a country as the Highlands of Scotland, every farmer must be butcher, baker and brewer for his own family. In such situations we can scarce expect to find even a smith, a carpenter, or a mason, within less than twenty miles of another of the same trade. The scattered families that live at eight or ten miles distance from the nearest of them, must learn to perform themselves a great number of little pieces of work, for which in more populous countries, they would call in the assistance of those workmen. (Ibid., p. 31)

While arguing famously that division of labour was limited by the extent of the market, Smith suggested that an increase in the size of the market could come about either through an increase in the density of settlement (the contrast he drew between towns which had greater division of labour and the countryside where one perforce had to be a 'jack-of-all-trades'); or through the development of transport facilities linking one's habitat with more distant lands (he underscored the role of the Mediterranean Sea in promoting trade). In either case, as the size of the market increased, people could engage more fully in exchange and division of labour.

But while the increase in the size of the market made greater division of labour possible, the *motive* for division of labour, according to him, lay elsewhere: in the *propensity to truck barter and exchange one thing for another.* This assertion by Smith had two implications. First, it made exchange, and hence division of labour, the outcome of individual *agency.* People made a conscious decision to enter into an exchange relationship with others voluntarily, without being coerced into it in any way. Secondly, in locating the motive for exchange in a *propensity*, i.e. a psychological trait, Smith did not bring in the question of expected *gain* from exchange. Exchange, resulting in division of labour, no doubt brought gains to the individuals engaging in them, but these were not why they engaged in exchange. Smith indeed is quite clear on this:

> The division of labour from which so many advantages are derived, is not originally the effect of any human wisdom which foresees and intends that general opulence to which it gives occasion. It is the necessary, though very slow and gradual consequence of a certain propensity in human nature which has in view no such extensive utility; the propensity to truck barter and exchange one thing for another. (Ibid., p. 25)

Though the motive for division of labour does not lie in any calculation of gain, when division of labour does get established the interdependence among people is such that each person supplies goods to others in order to obtain goods for oneself in return. Self-interest, in other words, while not being the motivating factor behind exchange, comes to determine individual behaviour in a world characterized by exchange.

Smith had famously remarked that

> it is not from the benevolence of the butcher, the brewer, or the baker that we expect our dinner but from their regard to their own interests. We address ourselves not to their humanity but to their self-love, and never talk to them of our necessities but of their advantages.

This remark, referring to the role of self-interest (self-love), is not in contradiction with his perception of division of labour being caused not by calculations of gain but because of a propensity. This particular remark refers to a world where division of labour has got established and made people interdependent, while the 'propensity to truck barter and exchange' explains why such a world at all comes to get established.

Smith did not, in other words, accept the concept of the so-called innate 'rationality' of the individual that is so common in modern neo-classical economics. This postulates that the individual is *by nature* self-interest-maximizing and that the individual enters into exchange because of this trait. Smith's conception, rather, was that behaviour promoting individual self-interest is not the cause but the consequence of entering into exchange relations. The cause is an innate propensity to enter into exchange relations; but once the individual has entered into exchange relations, he or she becomes concerned with self-interest promotion (or with 'self-love', to borrow Smith's term).

Likewise, Smith was of the view that the difference in talents visible among men is not the cause but the consequence of division of labour (which may also be taken as being in implicit opposition to the argument attributed to Locke about wage-labour arising in the state of nature because of differences in natural abilities). Given the great significance of this view, it is worth quoting Smith in full here:

> The difference between the most dissimilar characters, between a philosopher and a common street porter for example, seems to arise not so much from nature as from habit, custom, and education. When they came into this world, and for the first six or eight years of their existence, they were perhaps very much alike, and neither their parents, nor playfellows, could perceive any remarkable difference. About that age, or soon after, they come to be employed in very different occupations. The difference in talents comes then to be taken notice of, and widens by degrees, till at last the vanity of the philosopher is willing to acknowledge scarce any resemblance. (Ibid., pp. 28–29)

The Accumulation of Capital

While the cause for entering into exchange and division of labour lies, according to Smith, in a human propensity, and while the ability to do so depends upon the extent of the market, the actual doing so requires an accumulation of 'stock'. Consider a person who starts out perforce as a 'jack-of-all-trades', a counterpart of the Scottish Highlander, and at a certain point finds that conditions have become propitious for exchange and division of labour. In the very first period when that person devotes himself exclusively to producing, say, corn, and therefore produces a larger amount of corn than his own requirement, so that he can exchange his surplus with the butcher and the brewer while he himself ceases to act also as a butcher and a brewer, that is, when he diverts his resources from producing meat and drink to producing only corn, he would be short of meat and drink.[1]

His extra corn will become available only at the end of the period, which he can then exchange with the butcher and the brewer to obtain his meat and drink for the *next* period; but in the current period, his decision to specialize in corn production will cause a deficiency in his meat and drink supply, *unless he has already accumulated a stock of it beforehand* which he can consume in the current period. Division of labour therefore requires some previous accumulation of stock; and individual producers obtain this stock either through themselves exercising frugality, by refraining from consumption earlier, or by borrowing from others who in turn have exercised this frugality earlier. As Smith put it:

> But when the division of labour has once been thoroughly introduced, the produce of a man's labour can supply but a very small part of his occasional wants. The far greater part of them are supplied with the produce of other men's labour, which he purchases with the produce of his own. But this purchase cannot be made till such time as the produce of his own labour has not only been completed but sold. A stock of goods of different kinds therefore must be stored up somewhere sufficient to maintain him and to supply him with the materials and tools of his work. (Ibid., p. 276)

Smith's concept of 'previous' accumulation, which is in sharp contrast to Marx's notion of a 'primitive' or 'primary' accumulation of capital, is of great significance for understanding his *weltanschauung*. But it raises an immediate question: while Marx's concept of 'primitive' accumulation of capital explained simultaneously the emergence of a class of displaced petty producers who were to constitute the ranks of the proletariat, wherefrom do labourers come in Smith's conception? The obvious answer is that the division of labour which the previous accumulation of stock gives rise to raises labour productivity immensely, because of which it now becomes profitable to employ workers even by offering them a higher wage than what they were earning earlier as independent producers in the 'rude state of society'.

Put differently, in the 'rude state of society', as the possibility of exchange and division of labour arises – through, for instance, the opening up of a sea route – some producers restrict consumption and accumulate stock in order to be able to indulge their propensity to truck barter and exchange. This raises labour productivity so much that others who have not exercised such frugality nonetheless find it more beneficial to work as labourers for those who have accumulated stock than to continue as producers in the way they were doing in the 'early and rude state'.

The 'early and rude state of society', in other words, gets bifurcated into two groups: those who have accumulated stock and are willing to employ others, and those who have not accumulated stock and are willing to work for others. There is no question of any dispossession of earlier producers, or any coercion being employed against them: *both the accumulators of stock (or capitalists) and the workers employed by them gain, compared to what they were earning in the 'early and rude state of society'.* And the fact that the transition from the early and rude state of society to capitalism characterized by wage-labour and stock accumulation benefits *everyone* is made possible by the advantages that accrue from the division of labour. Thus Smith provides an explanation for 'wage-labour through assimilation' that was elusive in Locke.[2]

This explanation however may appear at first sight to be contradictory to what some, including Marx (1969), have seen as Smith's *deduction theory of profits* which hints at a theory of exploitation. Smith's words are worth quoting here:

> In that early and rude state of society which precedes both the accumulation of stock and the appropriation of land, the proportion between the quantities of labour necessary for acquiring different objects seems to be the only circumstance which can afford any rule for exchanging them for one another. ... In this state of things the whole produce of labour belongs to the labourer ... as soon as stock has accumulated in the hands of particular persons, some of them will naturally employ it in setting to work industrious people whom they will supply with materials and subsistence, in order to make a profit by the sale of their work. ... The value which the workmen add to the materials therefore, resolves itself in this case into two parts, of which one pays their wages and the other the profits of their employer. (Marx 1969, pp. 65–66)

He then goes on to add: 'As soon as the land of any country has all become private property, the landlords, like all other men, love to reap where they never sowed, and demand a rent even for its natural produce' (ibid., p. 67). This so-called 'deduction theory' of profits and rent, which, in Smith's work, is immediately followed and apparently contradicted by an 'adding-up' theory of price, that sees the natural price of a commodity as consisting of the amounts of different factors that go into the production of a unit of that commodity multiplied by their respective 'natural' rates of reward, has been held to hint at an exploitation theory of the sort that Marx was to advance later.

This, however, is not an issue that need detain us here. Reconciling such a 'deduction theory' with the claim that everybody benefits from the transition from the early and rude state of society to capitalism, poses no great difficulty. Such 'deductions' would cause a reduction in the level of wages of the workmen compared to what they were earning in the early and rude state of society, *only if the methods of production remained unchanged between the two states*. But since the methods of production do change, with the capitalist economy being characterized by pervasive division of labour and hence much higher levels of labour productivity compared to the early and rude state of society, it becomes possible for everyone to benefit, including the workers compared to their earlier state.

But while the transition to capitalism *permits* wages to rise above what they were earlier, why should wages be *actually* any higher than before?

Wages and a 'Progressive' Society

To answer this question, we have to go to Smith's theory of wage determination. Smith's theory is based on the distinction between the market price of labour and the natural price of labour; the market price will be above the natural price if the demand for labour exceeds supply at the natural price, while the opposite will be true if the demand for labour falls short of supply at the natural price. And labour demand in turn depends upon the magnitude of capital stock.

Smith argues that wages would be higher in a more 'thriving' country, one 'advancing with much greater rapidity to the further acquisition of riches', than in a stagnant country. This is because the demand for labour in the former keeps outstripping supply, necessitating perpetually higher wages compared to the initial state. Smith implicitly assumes that the initial state, before the drive towards the 'further acquisition of riches' began, was characterized by a level of the wage-rate that kept the population, and hence the work-force, constant; this rise in wages above the initial level serves to raise the population growth. And as accumulation keeps occurring, wages remain above the initial level, so that labour supply keeps getting adjusted to the growing demand.

In Smith's words,

> it is in the progressive state, while the society is advancing to the further acquisition, rather than when it has acquired its full complement of riches, that the condition of the labouring poor, of the great body of the people, seems

> to be the happiest and the most comfortable. It is hard in the stationary, and miserable in the declining state. The progressive state is in reality the cheerful and the hearty state to all the different orders of the society. The stationary is dull; the declining, melancholy. (Smith 1981, p. 99)

Since the transition from the early and rude state of society to capitalism is marked by continuous accumulation, and hence by a continuous rise in the demand for labour which keeps outstripping the rising supply of labour, the wages under capitalism, to say the least, must be higher than under the early and rude state of society.[3] The transition from the early and rude state of society to capitalism, in other words, not only makes higher wages *possible* because of the rise in labour productivity, but also brings about an actual increase in real wages because of the rise in the demand for labour compared to the initial state.

But, what of the stagnant and declining states of society? As an example of a declining society Smith chooses Bengal, where even the existing capital stock is not maintained. America, by contrast, constitutes a 'progressive' society where there is rapid accumulation of stock, a rapid increase in labour demand outstripping labour supply and hence a high level of real wages. Smith attributes this difference to the fact that America was governed directly by the British crown while Bengal was ruled by a merchant company, namely the East India Company.

There can be no two opinions about the fact that the East India Company's rule over Bengal was marked by extraordinary rapacity. Indeed, so sharp was the increase in land revenue after the Company had obtained the revenue-collecting rights for Bengal from the Mughal emperor in 1765, that as much as one-third of the population of the province, or about 10 million people, died from a famine in 1770 that was a consequence of this increased burden of land revenue (Dutt 1900). But to say that rule by the British crown would have alleviated the people's distress is just a fanciful notion on Smith's part. Direct crown rule was introduced in India in the aftermath of the Revolt of 1857; but it did not bring any relief to the people from such exactions. On the contrary, the period of direct rule also saw a series of terrible famines in Bengal, including one in 1896–97 and culminating in the Great Bengal Famine of 1943 which killed 3 million people (Sen 1981; U. Patnaik 2018).

The real difference between Smith's two examples, Bengal and America, actually lay elsewhere; it lay in the fact that one was a *colony of settlement* to which there was an inflow of capital from the metropolis, while the other was a *colony of conquest* from which there was an outflow of resources without any *quid pro quo* to the metropolis (called the 'drain' of surplus by Indian nationalist writers). Even if Bengal had been ruled by the British crown from the outset, given the overall scheme of things under the British imperial arrangement, no difference would have been made to the fact of its decline.

The 'declining' state, therefore, is not a 'normal' phenomenon in any capitalist economy which is a part of the metropolis; it characterizes the situation of a colony of conquest. The only case where, even within the metropolis, a declining state could possibly arise, is if there is shift of capital from one country to another. But even here there is no reason to expect that capital stock in the original country would actually *shrink.* The more likely scenario is where accumulation of stock in the original country gets located not in that country itself but in another country; and in such a case, there would at best be a stagnation in the level of capital stock in the original country.

Historically, there was such a shift of capital to the American colonies primarily from England, which was a shift *within* the metropolis itself. This did not cause a 'declining' state within the metropolis as a whole, or even within England; but it explains several of Smith's observations about wages in England and America.

Thus, leaving aside the colonies of conquest, the only two cases that remain relevant are: one, where the capital stock is growing, and the other where the capital stock is stagnant. Smith takes labour demand to be moving in the same direction as the capital stock, so that labour demand would be rising in the first case and stagnant in the second.

If the 'natural rate of wages' is defined as that wage-rate at which the work-force simply reproduces itself, neither increasing nor diminishing in size (Dobb 1973), then it follows that we can distinguish between two cases: one, where the capital stock is growing and hence labour demand outstrips labour supply, keeping the level of real wage above its 'natural rate'; and two, where the capital stock is stagnant and hence labour demand is not increasing – labour supply has adjusted to it and the wage-rate is at its 'natural' level.

The argument that the real wages will be higher in a capitalist society than in the early and rude state of society follows directly from the fact that in the former, characterized by rapid accumulation of stock, there will be a rise in labour demand which will continuously exceed supply. True, Smith himself never compared incomes of workers in the early and rude state of society with those of workers under capitalism to which it had transformed itself; but it is clear from his remarks that the workers were better off under the latter.

In fact, one can go a little further in analysing Smith's theory of wages. He compares wages in England with those in Scotland, and finds them to be higher in the former. Likewise, he compares wages in urban areas with those in rural areas, and finds urban wages to be higher. The inference is that where stock accumulation (and hence the division of labour) is proceeding more rapidly, the wages are higher than where it is slower. One facet of this cross-sectional picture, we have seen, is a comparison between a growing capitalist society, and the early and rude state of society; the former would clearly have higher wages than the latter.

But does this proposition continue to hold when the capital stock begins to stagnate in the capitalist country? Does a *stagnant* capitalist society still have a higher wage-rate than the income per worker in the early and rude state of society? Smith does not say anything directly on this, but can something be inferred from his other remarks on this issue?

The Natural Rate of Wages

The very fact of sustained high wages in the transition from the early and rude state of society to capitalism must affect the 'natural rate of wages'. Smith does not say so, but it is consistent with his other ideas. The natural rate of wages, we have seen, can be defined as that rate which leaves the population and hence the size of the work-force unchanged. But this rate cannot be taken to be a fixed magnitude: it should certainly depend, among other things, on the actual time-profile of wages that the workers may have been experiencing.

Smith himself talks of higher income lowering the mortality rate among working class children, and thereby increasing the population size, which is how it adjusts the supply of labour to increased demand. But he also talks of the number of children born to families being larger for poorer families than for better-off families. As he put it: 'Poverty, though it discourages, does not always prevent marriage. It seems even to be favourable to generation. A half-starved Highland woman frequently bears more than twenty children, while a pampered fine lady is often incapable of bearing any, and is generally exhausted by two or three' (Smith 1981, pp. 96–97).

While Smith talks of 'capability' for child-bearing and of 'exhaustion', one need not take these literally; cultural factors, including a desire for a life of some comfort which gets strengthened with a better standard of living, are likely to play an important role in limiting the number of births in better-off families. The basic point, however, is his observation that the number of children born in poor families is higher than in better-off families.

But if so, then the rate of wages at which the population remains constant need not be one unique number; on the contrary, if wages remain high for long, then both the death rate and the birth rate can come down, so that the natural rate of wages itself can move up.

The fact that the wage-rate in England remained higher than in Scotland was not just on account of the higher rate of capital stock accumulation in the former than in the latter; even after, according to Smith, the rate of accumulation in England had come down, even as it was going up in America, the wage difference between England and Scotland had continued. The rise in the natural rate of wages in England, so that even if England had been a stagnant society, the wage-rate would still have been higher than in Scotland, could be adduced as a possible Smithian explanation.

Smith says:

> In England, the improvements in agriculture, manufactures and commerce began much earlier than in Scotland. The demand for labour, and consequently its price, must necessarily have increased with those improvements. In the last century accordingly, as well as in the present, the wages of labour were higher in England than in Scotland. They have risen too considerably since that time, though on account of the greater variety of wage paid there in different places, it is more difficult to ascertain how much. (Ibid., p. 94)

When a wage difference persists over such a long time, the explanation for it must lie not just in the market wage-rate being higher than the natural wage-rate in one place compared to another; within the parameters of Smithian theory, one must also bring in differences in the natural wage between the two regions and the *rise* in the natural wage in England as compared to Scotland.

It follows, then, that the wage-rate under capitalism would be higher than in the early and rude state of society, not just during the period when rapid accumulation occurs within the former but even when the former settles down to a stagnant state. Because of this, any possible conflict between capitalism and individual *agency* disappears. Being a member of a capitalist society is not forced upon the individual but is an expression of his agency, a part of a transition which leaves *everyone* better off, not just temporarily during the period of transition itself when the pace of stock accumulation is high, but permanently.

The Smithian position can be reconstructed as follows. While the introduction of exchange *per se* (for instance, by simply exchanging the surplus produced by each person over his or her own requirements) constitutes an expression of a human propensity, its further development through stock accumulation into division of labour and specialization also has the effect of making everyone better off perennially. Capitalism, in short, is a voluntarily entered-into arrangement which has the effect of making everyone better off compared to what he or she had been earlier. This is because the appearance of capitalism is invariably associated with an increase in labour productivity caused by technological progress, which in Smith is associated with division of labour.

Technological Progress

What, it may be asked, are these benefits of division of labour? Smith, as is well known, mentioned three main benefits. The first is the increase in dexterity that comes about when a total manufacturing process is broken up into a set of simple activities and each worker specializes in one of these. The repeated action of doing a simple thing increases the worker's speed; and when this happens to all the workers, the total time taken for completing the manufacturing activity as a whole gets greatly abridged. The second advantage is that the time taken in changing from one task to another when the same person is doing all the different tasks gets eliminated when the tasks are divided among different workers, each doing only one task. True, some time would still be required for transferring material from one group of workers to another. But the total time taken for it would be greatly reduced compared to when the same person does all the tasks. The third advantage is that when the complex manufacturing job is broken up into a set of simple activities, it becomes easier to mechanize each of these activities.

Smith, in discussing the advantages of division of labour, talks only of the division of labour within an enterprise through the splitting up of a manufacturing process into its simple component activities; in fact, he takes pin-making as his classic example. He does not distinguish between division of labour within an enterprise and division of labour in society as a whole. Now, taking Smith's argument itself, the advantages arising from the first two of the factors mentioned by him will get exhausted soon. Beyond a point, any further subdivision of a production process will not increase dexterity much. Likewise, the time saved in switching from one activity to another also has its limits.

As for the third advantage, while the introduction of machinery, or more generally of changes in the process of production, is a continuous phenomenon, the contribution of division of labour *per se* to this phenomenon also has its limits. Process innovations are introduced steadily, but this is because new inventions arising from fresh scientific advances keep occurring, which have nothing to do with the extent of division of labour *per se*. There is, in other words, no discernible advantages beyond a point from the sheer fact of division of labour. And the same holds true for division of labour in society at large.

The breaking of an integrated manufacturing activity that has been occurring of late and the location of its different components in different countries in a global value chain, is caused by the low wages in the third world rather than any greater prospects of technological progress.

But while Smith's emphasis on division of labour *per se*, though perhaps apposite for its time, may have been overstated as a general theoretical proposition, his view of capitalism being marked by what subsequent authors like Nicholas Kaldor (1978) have called 'increasing returns', is of great significance. In fact, without going specifically into Smith's discussion of division of labour, we can state his general position as follows: if the output–capital ratio (or capital productivity) is denoted by α, the output–labour ratio (or labour productivity) by β, and the rate of capital accumulation $(dK/dt)/K$ by g (with $g \geq 0$), then

$$(d\alpha/dt)/\alpha = f(g), \text{ with } f(0) = 0 \text{ and } f'(.) > 0$$

$$(d\beta/dt)/\beta = F(g), \text{ with } F(0) = 0 \text{ and } 0 < F'(.) < 1$$

$$g + (d\alpha/dt)/\alpha - (d\beta/dt)/\beta = h(g) \geq 0, \text{ and } h'(.)>0.$$

This means that the rate of growth of capital productivity is positively related to the rate of capital accumulation, as is the rate of growth of labour productivity, and that the rate of growth of labour demand (assumed to be always satisfied) is always positive when the rate of accumulation is positive and is also positively related to it.

When technological progress has this character, the wage-rate will be above the natural rate, and hence above what it was in the early and rude state of society. And even when the rate of accumulation is zero, i.e. in Smith's 'stagnant society' when the wage-rate will be equal to the natural wage-rate, this natural wage-rate itself will be above what it was in the early and rude state of society, for reasons discussed in the last section. Hence, the transition to capitalism will invariably entail an improvement in the condition of life for all; and continuous capital accumulation will entail a continuous increase in labour demand, for which the wages will be maintained higher than the natural rate, to enable an increase in the population and hence in the work-force.

Concluding Observations

The claim that capitalism represents the realization of individual freedom, which informs classical liberalism, can be sustained only by a certain perception of capitalism. Classical liberalism as a political position presumes at the same time a certain view of the economics of capitalism.

This view sees capitalism as the outcome of a self-transformation of society which leaves everyone better off than before and which therefore enjoys the support of everyone. And it leaves everyone better off than before because this self-transformation is associated with technological progress as a more or less continuous process. Adam Smith was among the early proponents of this view, as this chapter has shown. Even though Locke too had talked of the introduction of employer–labourer relationship in the state of nature, he had provided no satisfactory explanation for it, a lacuna which Smith overcame.

It is implicit in both Smith and Locke, however, that the emergence of the employer–labourer relationship in a world where agriculture is the main activity should be accompanied by an improvement in production, in particular an improvement in land productivity. Even though the genesis of this relationship in both authors belongs more to a meta-historical narrative than a historical one, it is nonetheless worth examining whether there were any such improvements in land productivity around or preceding the time that they wrote. This is what we do in the next chapter, keeping a theoretical critique of the Smithian conception of the origin of the employer–wage-labour relationship for a later chapter (chapter eight).

Notes

1 There is an implicit assumption in Smith's account of the transition from the 'rude state of society' to one where division of labour is introduced. This assumption is that the average time-lag between the application of labour and the acquisition of necessaries increases in the latter compared to the former. This would happen, for instance, if a certain minimum amount has to be produced before it can be sold.

2 Such an explanation becomes particularly necessary for Smith since he has rejected the argument, used by Locke in passing, about differences in natural ability leading to some persons' labour being more productive than that of others in the state of nature.

3 With demand outstripping supply the real wages should be *rising* over time. But Smith does not assert this. All that his theory states is that real wages are higher than what prevailed initially and what would be compatible with a stagnant population. In any case, the exact dynamics of wage adjustment was not worked out by Smith. We shall therefore stick to this 'minimalist' assertion, of wages being *higher* than initially, in what follows.

CHAPTER FIVE

Historical Evidence on Land Productivity

Classical liberalism, we have seen, locates the genesis of wage-labour in a voluntary coming together of an independent petty producer-turned-employer and an independent petty producer-turned-labourer, each of whom becomes better off through such coming together. While this coming together itself may be 'voluntary', the real question is what led up to it; and classical liberalism answers it by saying that even the lead up to it was voluntary.

Such a voluntary coming together between employers and labourers is possible only if the pooled resources of the two produce an output greater than the sum of the outputs being produced on their individual units in the initial situation. With agriculture as the main activity, this presupposes an increase in output per acre on the pooled land compared to what obtained earlier on individual plots.

If it was only the increase in scale, i.e. the mere fact of pooling, that was responsible for such an increase in output per acre, then there would be a symmetry between the two producers, the would-be employer and the would-be labourer, which might make them cooperate by pooling their lands; but it would not make one of the producers become a landless labourer working for the other producer and therefore coming under the employer's *direction*. It is not, therefore, a question of the larger scale of operations being responsible for the increase in land productivity.

Neo-classical economics, while it does not believe in scale effects, assumes that the production function is concave downwards, which would make pooling of resources increase land productivity. And the question why some should become labourers subject to direction by others if two petty producers simply pool their resources does not concern neo-classical economics because it does not discuss the specificity of *production*, seeing it as no different from exchange; different 'factors of production', according to it, simply come together to produce the output without any direction or supervision of the labour process involved.

Of course, the concept of a production function of the neo-classical kind, which we discuss in a later chapter, has little basis either in logic or reality, and was not in any case invoked by either Locke or Smith. The increase in land productivity must come about, plausibly, according to the 'cooperativist' conception of capitalism, through some *new* method or manner of production. And the access to this new method or manner must lie exclusively with the person who becomes the employer and not the one who becomes the labourer, for otherwise each would have introduced the new method without one becoming a labourer for the other.

The same is true if it was a mere case of a change in the cropping pattern, for such a change could have been introduced on both farms, benefiting both producers, instead of making one into a labourer for the other.

The Relevance of Land Productivity

For the classical liberal story to be true, therefore, there must have been the introduction of some land productivity-raising innovations, the knowledge of which lay only with some producers and not all. Locke no doubt talks of some being simply better at cultivating than others, but there is no reason for believing this to be the case; a more plausible argument in defence of Locke's view would be if those supposed to be better at cultivating have access to, or manage to develop, some method of production that others do not have, which raises land productivity.

The question is: is there any evidence of such an increase in land productivity having occurred in Europe, especially in the medieval period, on the basis of which the story of the origin of wage-labour that Locke for instance, or even Smith, had developed, can be defended?

It may be thought that the absence of any such innovation, while being unfavourable to Locke's theory, cannot be held against the theory presented by Adam Smith about the origin of wage-labour. Smith's theory was that some independent producers, each of whom in the 'early and rude state of society' had perforce been a 'jack-of-all-trades', started accumulating 'stock'; on the basis of such accumulation they employed other producers, who agreed to become labourers because they were tempted by the higher incomes that would come to them owing to the benefits of the division of labour which became possible by the increase in the scale of production.

While the benefits of division of labour could in principle accrue to any increase in the scale of operation, i.e. while these benefits themselves did not discriminate between producers, the distinction between those who became employers and those who became labourers lay in the greater thriftiness of the former. It is this which resulted in their accumulating stock and hence being in a position to offer employment to others.

In Adam Smith's account, however, land productivity scarcely enters the picture. Division of labour increases labour productivity; in fact, all the three ways in which division of labour enhances output, according to Smith, relate to an increase in the output *per worker.* The three ways, it may be recalled, are: greater dexterity of the worker; less time spent in passing from one 'species of work' to another; and the greater amenability of production processes to the use of machines once they have been separated out by the division of labour. In all this, Smith is making no claims about any increase in *land* productivity. Why then should we drag *land* productivity into his argument?

The reason is as follows. If land productivity does not increase and hence food output does not increase through the division of labour or any other means, then there would scarcely be much temptation to work for someone else on the presumption that one becomes better off thereby. Since the income elasticity of demand for food is positive and quite high at the level of income we are talking about, a person would not be tempted to move out of independent production in the 'early and rude state of society' to become a wage-labourer in a capitalist setting, unless there is a distinct increase in the amount of *all the major goods including foodgrains* that the person can command compared to what the person was having as an independent producer in the 'early and rude state'. A person could scarcely be tempted by the prospect of having more pins (as Smith's pin factory example would suggest) unless there is also more food. And since food output will not increase an iota unless land productivity increases, Smith's account too requires a concurrent increase in land productivity as a precondition for the introduction of 'wage-labour through assimilation', and hence for carrying forward division of labour.

It may, of course, be argued that with more pins being produced, pins can be exchanged for food through foreign trade, so that even if more food is not domestically produced, division of labour nonetheless enhances food availability and hence makes every one better off compared to the 'early and rude' state of society. But this only shifts the argument to a different geographical terrain. It presumes that the amount of food that can be imported into the economy where pin output has increased through division of labour can be raised. Such a rise can occur, however, only if either the area under food or land productivity can increase *in the food-exporting country*; otherwise food price in terms of pins will increase, which will lower employment in pin production (and hence the average real income) via 'deindustrialization' in the food-exporting country, making that country unwilling to engage in free trade and eager to put tariffs on pin imports (*unless it happens to be a colonial adjunct to the metropolitan economy where division of labour is proceeding apace*).

It follows, therefore, that if colonialism is ruled out (as no matter how important in practice, it did not enter Smith's argument) and since unused land is not necessarily available, there must be an increase in land productivity, if not in the pin-making country, then in the food-exporting country. An increase in real wages, in short, such as what division of labour is supposed to make possible, cannot occur unless there is an increase in land productivity.

Thus, any story about a voluntary transition from a pre-wage-labour to a wage-labour-based society, or for the emergence of 'wage-labour through assimilation', requires for its validity an increase in land productivity. This entire line of argumentation we have been pursuing may appear to be unnecessary nit-picking with regard to what were perhaps no more than casual, impressionistic statements about the origin of wage-labour. But given the philosophical importance of the account of the origin of wage-labour, namely that it was a voluntary coming together of employers and workers to reap the benefits of the greater abundance made possible by such coming together, these impressionistic statements must be closely examined. The question that arises is: what historical evidence has there been of an increase in land productivity?

Indirect Test for Wage-Labour through Assimilation

No doubt, confronting a philosophical argument with historical data may appear inapposite and unfair; but we are talking here of philosophical arguments which not only have profound practical implications for individual freedom, but also stand in contrast with other philosophical arguments, such as those of Marx and his followers. Hence, some confrontation of such arguments with historical data becomes necessary.

There is, however, a further problem. The phenomenon of wage-labour of some kind had existed long before capitalism made its appearance (we discuss this in a later chapter); we are not talking therefore, strictly speaking, of *the* origin of wage-labour, such as what Locke or Adam Smith were talking about. The confrontation of their theories with historical data is not a simple matter for this reason. We can, however, leave aside issues of *the* origin of wage-labour and still ask the question: is there any historical evidence that exists to support the view that innovations in production practices in agriculture were responsible for a *voluntary* transition on the part of *many independent producers* to becoming wage-labourers? This question, being of importance in its own right even if it did not have any philosophical significance, deserves careful attention.

We answer this question in two ways: in an indirect manner (since direct evidence is hard to come by), and in a direct manner wherever possible. The indirect manner consists in this: had wage employment increased because independent petty producers preferred to become wage-labourers despite not undergoing any process of destitution and only because of the attractive wages they expected to get as labourers, then we would have found wage employment to have increased alongside the real wage-rate. When the real wage-rate increased, then, according to this hypothesis, it would have been more attractive for petty producers to become wage-labourers than otherwise; and in such a case, there would have been an increase in wage employment. Likewise, when the real wage-rate went down, it would have been less attractive for independent producers to take up wage employment than otherwise, in which case wage employment would have shrunk – if not absolutely, then at least relatively.

Put differently, if the taking up of wage employment is a voluntary decision with no coercive antecedents, then the magnitude of such employment would be expected to vary directly with the level of the real wage-rate. What we do for testing this theory, therefore, is to examine whether the real wage-rate and the magnitude of wage employment moved up together. This is the indirect way of testing. The direct way of testing is by looking at whatever evidence we can find on land productivity. Our focus in what follows will be on Britain, though developments on the continent were generally in sync with what was happening in Britain.

What we find from the history of Britain, and of Western Europe in general, however, is *just the opposite of this*; that is, we find that periods when the real wage-rate went up were periods when there was a (relative) contraction in wage employment, while periods when the real wage-rate went down were periods when there was an expansion (in relative terms) in wage employment. This is not very surprising, for it amounts to saying that in very long booms (we are talking here of booms and slumps that are far longer than even the Kondratieffs) the real wage-rate goes down, while in very long slumps the real wage-rate goes up.

The twelfth and thirteenth centuries, especially the period between 1150 and 1300, constituted a period of boom in Western European agriculture, when not only was there a rapid rate of population growth but also a rapid expansion in the supply of money. Whether the boom was stimulated by these factors, as some historians have suggested, or by something else, is not a matter for discussion here; but the boom was widespread across Western Europe. Cereal prices rose rapidly, much more rapidly than money wages. The rise in population led to an expansion in arable area, a shift of the margin of cultivation to less and less fertile land, and also a subdivision of holdings resulting in a fall in average farm size. In fact it was not possible to support a family on the small farms, which meant that many small farmers supplemented their incomes by working as agricultural labourers as well. There was thus a rise in output and employment over this period, with wage employment increasing relative to total, which simultaneously however witnessed a reduction in the real wages (say, money wages divided by wheat prices). Hence, the extent of wage employment was negatively correlated with the level of real wages.[1]

By contrast, the fourteenth and fifteenth centuries, especially the years between 1300 and 1450, were a period of prolonged slump. The Black Death in the mid-fourteenth century was by no means the cause of this contraction, which had begun even earlier. There was an absolute decline in the population of Europe, from 73 million in 1300 to 60 million in 1450, according to one estimate. But this hides a sharp fall because of the Black Death till the middle of the fourteenth century, followed by some recovery, especially in the fifteenth century. At the same time, there was a reduction in the net availability of precious metals in Europe which characterized this long depression.

We obviously do not have country-wide data for the movement of real wages, but there are records of individual farms from which we can get a picture of what was happening to real wages. The wheat wages (i.e. the money wage divided by the wheat price) on the estate of the Bishop of Winchester for the years 1320 to 1479, taking two-decade averages, were as follows:

1320–39: 100
1340–59: 107
1360–79: 106
1380–99: 169

1400–19: 153
1420–39: 148
1440–59: 171
1460–89: 158
Source: van Bath (1963, p. 138).

We have taken 1320 as our starting point rather than 1300, because the early years of the century were marked by famines in 1315 and 1316 when wheat prices were exceptionally high; this would overstate the subsequent decline in wheat prices and hence the rise in real wages, giving exaggerated support to our argument. Starting with 1320 avoids this exaggeration. The real wage trends elsewhere in Europe, especially in Germany, were similar. The real wages, in short, rose notably when there was a long recession, just as they had gone down quite sharply when there had been a prolonged period of boom.

The rise in real wages was not confined only to the agricultural sector. Industrial prices relative to agricultural prices were higher almost throughout this period compared to 1300, reaching the ratio of 1300 only towards the middle of the sixteenth century in England. Since industrial wages more or less moved in tandem with industrial prices, these wages too, deflated by agricultural prices which figured prominently in the cost of living, went up during the fourteenth and fifteenth centuries. It follows that real wages in the industrial sector too must have gone up noticeably over this period of long recession.

The rise in real wages was accompanied by a decline in the total cultivated area, with many farms remaining fallow because of the fall in farm prices.

> Reclamation and polder-making had come to a stop. ... The cultivated area shrank in almost all the countries of Europe; in many parts, farms, and even whole villages, were abandoned. In England these are known as 'lost villages', in Germany as Wustungen. The same phenomenon was seen in France, Norway, Sweden, Denmark, the Alpine Regions and Hungary. (van Bath 1963, p. 142)

This in turn must have meant an increase in the extent of unemployment, especially a decline in wage employment. The period of rise in real wages, in other words, could hardly have been one when peasants abandoned their own lands to work for an employer, since the prospects of finding employment as a wage-labourer would have been particularly bleak.

At the most they could have supplemented their incomes from cultivation with income from supplementary work, but that is a reflection of the distress to which the peasantry had been reduced, not of 'wage employment through assimilation'. In fact there would be a reversion from such supplementary work to greater engagement with agricultural work by cultivators when agricultural prices started rising again.

The period after the middle of the fifteenth century marked a revival from the depression. Silver mining was revived in Central Europe in 1460; and the population too started increasing. This revival was sustained by the inflow of gold from the New World conquered by Spain, which caused the sixteenth-century price inflation that lasted into the seventeenth century. Once again we find a fall in real wages during the boom. The price indices for food and industrial products along with the index of money wages of builders (which more or less reflected the movement of money wages in general) for three European countries for the period 1475–1620 were as follows (1451–1475 = 100):

	England	France	Germany
Food	555	729	517
Industrial goods	265	335	294
Builders' wages	200	268	150

Source: Phelps-Browne and Hopkins (1957, p. 298), cited in van Bath (1963, p. 197).

The point to note here is again the coexistence of lower real wages along with boom conditions entailing an increase in output and employment, especially wage employment. This runs completely contrary to the view that the boom, associated with technical progress, induces an increase in wage employment at the expense of independent petty production through a rise in real wages.

From around 1650, however, European agriculture once again moved into a slump that was to last a whole century. Slicher van Bath sums the general picture as follows:

> The depression was of a far milder sort than the serious economic decline of the late middle ages, but its chief symptoms were the same: falling cereal prices, relatively high real wages, little reclamation activity, conversion of arable to pasture, expansion of animal husbandry, cultivation of fodder crops and various industrial crops, in some parts a transition from agriculture to rural industry, few innovations in farming technique and little interest in questions of an agrarian nature. Even those most characteristic and distressing features of the late medieval depression, the lost villages, the empty farms and neglected fields, were not absent. (van Bath 1963, p. 206)

From the reference above to the growth of industry at the expense of agriculture, one may get the impression that higher industrial wages during the agricultural depression, while it reduced wage employment in agriculture, actually enlarged wage employment outside agriculture in industry, thereby, in a sense different from the way we have understood till now, validating the classical liberal view of 'wage employment through assimilation'. But this impression is erroneous. First, the decline of agricultural population was accompanied by either a decline in overall population (Germany and Spain) or an absolute stagnation in it (Western Europe as a whole), so that wage employment even outside agriculture would have increased little if at all. Second, even the diversification towards industry was a forced diversification that occurred because of agrarian distress; when the depression came to an end around the middle of the eighteenth century, a good deal of such rural industry did not survive.

Direct Evidence on Land Productivity

Let us now move to whatever direct evidence exists. In fact, the increase in land productivity in Europe over the entire period of the middle ages appears to have been quite insubstantial. Sporadic data, again from individual farm level, exist which suggest that while there was a certain change in the pattern of crops cultivated, with barley and pulses, for instance, being produced to a greater extent in England than before, there was little evidence of any significant increase in productivity per acre either of particular crops or of foodgrains as a whole.

Increase in manure use was one reason for whatever increase occurred in land productivity in particular crops. This was also the main reason why productivity increase was more pronounced in the depression period than in the boom years. During the depression period, since cereal prices were low, there was a tendency to move towards growing livestock by shifting land use from cereals towards pastures. This had the effect of raising the input of manure on the residual land that still remained devoted to cereals, and hence the cereal output per hectare on that land. But aside from such fluctuations and the incidental consequences of changes in cropping pattern, there does not seem to have been any noticeable changes in the technology of production.

For instance, on the land belonging to the Bishop of Winchester, the average amount of wheat given by a hectare of land over the period 1200–1499 was 815 litres. The maximum and minimum yields were 849 litres and

733 litres respectively, which are not too far apart. For individual periods the average figures are:

1200–49: 733
1250–99: 819
1300–49: 849
1350–99: 840
1400–49: 833

The average productivity for England as a whole for modern times (1895–1914) was 2,817 litres, which is more than three times what it was in the medieval period on this particular farm. But for an entire period spanning three centuries between 1200–1499, the increase in yield, even if we take the ratio between the maximum and the minimum as an approximation to it, was a mere 15.8 per cent. The idea of yield-raising technological progress in medieval European agriculture therefore seems to be quite far-fetched. This direct evidence throws doubt on the view that the transition from independent petty production to wage employment could have occurred because of the increase in productivity per hectare, which supposedly made higher output and hence higher wages on such advanced farms possible; there was in fact very little increase in output per hectare.

This conclusion remains unaffected even when we look at the sixteenth and the seventeenth centuries. The period until the middle of the seventeenth century had witnessed, as we have seen, a significant 'profit inflation' during which real wages had fallen; even though the agricultural depression after 1650, marked by falling cereal prices, started raising real wages, the level of real wages in 1700 according to Keynes, citing expert opinion, was still about 50 per cent lower than in 1500 (Keynes 1979, p. 141). Innovations in farming techniques during the depression were insignificant, which means that land productivity increases because of technological innovations were also insignificant; the *observed* land productivity increases which were associated with slumps occurred because, apart from greater manure use on the remaining farms, less fertile farms abandoned cultivation owing to the falling prices that eroded their viability.

In booms, the opposite happened, with cultivation being extended to newer and less fertile areas which could become viable because of the high agricultural prices. At any rate, there could hardly have been much prospects of attracting independent petty producers to become wage-labourers through the lure of real wages being higher on wage-labour-based farms: the increase in land productivity being limited, the wage-labour-based farms could hardly have provided a higher wage-rate than the incomes of independent petty producers. Thus, land productivity increases were hardly a significant factor till the end of the seventeenth century.

Evidence for the Eighteenth Century

What is more surprising however is that even for the eighteenth century, for which we have proper country-wide data for Britain, there is little evidence of any significant increase in land productivity. This is surprising because there is supposed to have been an 'agricultural revolution' in Britain preceding the industrial revolution, which, if it were true, could have provided *prima facie* support to the idea of a voluntary transition to wage-labour at least for that period, though not for the earlier one. But the data from the period 1700 to 1800 provide little support to any such idea of an agricultural revolution (U. Patnaik and P. Patnaik 2021).

Between 1701 and 1801, the total cereal output in volume terms in Britain increased by only 43 per cent, according to Chambers and Mingay (1966). Since the population over the same period increased by 73 per cent, according to the estimates of Lee and Schofield (1981), the per capita cereal output declined over the century as a whole. The per capita decline, which was almost 20 per cent between 1701 and 1801, caused rapid food price inflation towards the end of the eighteenth century and imposed a drastic squeeze on the living standards of the working class. This created a strong and persistent demand for the repeal of the Corn Laws which had stood in the way of cheap imports of corn from abroad. This became the most prominent political issue for almost half a century between the 1790s and the actual repeal of the Corn Laws, in the teeth of bitter opposition of the landlords, in 1846.

Even the value of agricultural output as a whole at constant prices in Britain, according to W.A. Cole (1981), went up by about 80 per cent over the entire century, which meant, in view of the 73 per cent increase in population, a very marginal increase – indeed virtual stagnation – in per capita terms.

But of course, our concern has been with productivity per acre and not with per capita output. Even productivity per acre, however, hardly increased over the century as a whole. Over the entire eighteenth century (1700 to 1800 to be precise) we find, according to estimates by Turner, Beckett and Afton (2001), that area under wheat in England and Wales together went up by about 25 per cent, while *gross* output per acre went up only by about 11 per cent. The overall increase in *net* output over the century as a whole was

37 per cent, which means again an increase in net output *per acre* of a little over 10 per cent over the entire century.

Obviously, if over the entire century there was just a little over 10 per cent increase in output per acre of wheat, which was the most important food crop, then the question of there being any radical introduction of land productivity-raising agricultural technology simply does not arise. And much the same can be said of non-foodgrain crops as well, namely that while the yield per acre of some of them may have been higher than of foodgrains, this yield did not go up much over the eighteenth century.

It can of course be argued that 10 per cent represents the increase in land productivity *over time*; but it does not represent the cross-sectional difference in land productivity *across farms*, which could have been larger and hence provided an incentive to independent farmers to seek employment as labourers in high land productivity farms. But, if at all these cross-sectional differences were because of differences in technology (and not just land quality differences), then the period we are talking about is long enough for this technology to have got diffused across the entire land area, and hence the average land productivity to have asymptotically approached the highest level prevailing among farms at the beginning of the period. An observed 10 per cent increase in land productivity over the century therefore does not suggest significant technological differences across farms at the beginning of the century. Of course, if technological change occurred towards the end of the period, then the cross-sectional difference in land productivity towards the end of the period could still be quite high without being reflected in the rise of land productivity. But that would still not negate the proposition that for *much* of the eighteenth century there was little innovation raising land productivity in Britain.

Even the marginal absolute increase in constant price value of agricultural output in the eighteenth century that we mentioned earlier was because of a shift to higher-value crops on larger, capitalist, farms which had already come into being through processes other than the voluntary transformation mentioned above, i.e. through processes other than those which entailed that some petty producers voluntarily became agricultural labourers while others became their employers.

We come back to these processes in a later chapter, but the point to note is that we have to be careful not to take the observed tendency towards capitalist farming as vindication *ipso facto* of the *liberal perception* of the process of shift to capitalist farming.

We have seen that by the end of the nineteenth and the beginning of the twentieth centuries, notable land productivity increase had occurred in Britain compared to medieval times. The question would then arise: how do we square this with our argument about the stagnation in land productivity until the eighteenth century and even over much of the eighteenth century? This could partly of course be the result of the introduction of modern scientific agricultural methods during the nineteenth century; but this could also be because the British economy had by this time diversified substantially from its dependence on agriculture that had characterized the medieval period. And this must have entailed moving cultivation away from less fertile marginal lands and concentrating it only on more fertile lands, a tendency that is likely to have got strengthened to a great extent after the repeal of the Corn Laws.

Britain's sluggish agriculture during the eighteenth century, which necessitated the repeal of the Corn Laws, also resulted in substantial dependence upon the colonies of conquest for meeting its foodgrain requirement. This had an added advantage for Britain, since the imports from the colonies of conquest were in effect not paid for (U. Patnaik and P. Patnaik 2021); they were financed from the appropriation of economic surplus through the taxation mechanism, constituting the commodity form of the 'drain' of surplus that has been much discussed. So, Britain could avoid not just any serious inflation in food prices in the latter half of the nineteenth century, but also any serious strains on its balance of payments.

Note

[1] Much of the data for the assertions in this chapter are taken from Slicher van Bath (1963).

CHAPTER SIX

Neo-Classical Economics and 'Rationality'

By neo-classical economics I mean the various strands of theory that emerged in the early 1870s with the work of Stanley Jevons (1871), Carl Menger (1871) and Leon Walras (1874), and were carried forward separately in Cambridge, England by Alfred Marshall (1890), and which in one form or another continue to occupy centre-stage in mainstream economics to this day. Within these strands there are, of course, important differences. Nonetheless there is a certain commonality, which is what I will be highlighting and discussing in the present chapter.

The main element of commonality is the view that the capitalist arrangement is formed and sustained by 'rational' individuals who are 'rational' in a very specific sense. These are individuals whose behaviour is determined by their optimizing some objective function subject to constraints, and who enter into a relationship of exchange with one another in order to derive its benefits. These benefits accrue not just to individuals separately by improving their condition compared to before exchange; they give rise to a situation of equilibrium under competitive conditions, which is also socially 'rational' (leaving aside 'externalities') in the sense of being a Pareto-optimum, a state from which nobody can be made better off without someone else becoming worse off.

The competitive equilibrium, it would be argued, is just a logical construct, a starting point for analysing a real world that is significantly different from the assumed competitive universe; and economists *have been examining* this world by making departures from this assumed universe. On what basis, then, can we call any of them neo-classical? The hallmark of neo-classical economics is not the belief that the world is characterized by a competitive economy, but the core analytical proposition that in a capitalist economy with flexible prices and price-takers, there would be a tendency for all markets to clear, including the labour market, as happens in a competitive economy. This means that a capitalist economy would tend to reach full employment if all prices including the money wage-rate are flexible, that its spontaneous tendency is to reach full employment in the absence of price rigidity.[1] This proposition, accepted by neo-classical economics in general, is elucidated by the benchmark competitive equilibrium model, which is why we focus below on the competitive economy while discussing neo-classical economics.

The idea of individual self-seeking behaviour leading to a socially desirable outcome pre-dates neo-classical economics; it characterizes classical economics as well (and can even be traced back to Bernard Mandeville's 'private vices public virtues' in *The Fable of the Bees*). But the positions of classical and neo-classical economics on this issue differ significantly in at least three respects.

First, classical political economy had not talked of 'rationality' and maximizing behaviour, which came to characterize post-Jevonian theory. Second, it had not visualized a kind of symmetry of social positioning between the different individual agents, as post-Jevonian theory did. Individuals differed with respect to the endowments in their possession and also in their tastes and preferences, but there were no 'workers' and 'capitalists' as in classical political economy. In the latter both workers and capitalists followed rules of behaviour dictated by material interests, such as workers moving to jobs that were *ceteris paribus* better paid or capitalists moving to spheres of production that fetched higher rates of profit; but there was no suggestion of any maximizing behaviour, and that too among symmetrically placed individuals. Third, the 'social good' that such pursuit of individual interest was supposed to achieve consisted, according to the classical economists, in more rapid capital accumulation or more rapid growth of the 'wealth of the nation', rather than in the optimization of any particular social objective or even in any improvement in the condition of the people at large. (Such improvement, according to the classical economists, would demand their curbing the propensity to procreate, which was a separate issue.) It was, in short, a more general desideratum than some specific social objective.

We have seen earlier the problem that arises when production is treated as a mere extension of exchange, namely, that the question of work discipline and work motivation remains unaddressed. In the present chapter, we mainly discuss the problems associated with the neo-classical concept of 'rationality'. Some problems with 'rationality' have been mentioned in chapter two; in this chapter we go beyond what was briefly discussed there. We also highlight some other logical problems that beset neo-classical economics.

The Self-Centred Individual

The individual in the neo-classical view is supposed to be entirely self-absorbed and self-centred: the producer, for instance, maximizes profits accruing exclusively to him, and the consumer maximizes the utility that he alone derives from the goods and services in his possession. There is no scope for any situation where *my* utility depends on the goods in *your* possession. True, much effort has been made towards introducing 'externalities' into neo-classical analysis. But the introduction of 'externalities' typically takes the form *not of moving away from the self-centredness of the individual's decision-making*, but of moving away in two other quite different ways: first, in analysing the effects of others' decisions on the data on the basis of which such self-centred optimizing is carried out by an individual; second, in getting the state to push the economy towards a different equilibrium from the one that comes about through the aggregation of individual optimization exercises.

Such a self-centred individual, maximizing, subject to constraints, an objective function that pertains entirely to his or her own state, is what is defined as being 'rational'. 'Rationality', in other words, gets associated exclusively with a self-centred possessiveness. All individuals in the economic universe are supposed *ideally* to be endowed with this quality; anyone free of such self-centred possessiveness is supposed to be 'irrational', a deviant constituting an exception. Moreover, by ignoring history and assuming that economic life as depicted by it has always existed, it makes such meticulously planned self-centred behaviour a permanent attribute of human nature rather than an attribute that gets inculcated under capitalism. Looking at it differently, *neo-classical economics sees individual behaviour supposedly characteristic of capitalism not as a phenomenon that arises in society at a certain point of time, but as one embedded in human nature.* It sees capitalism, therefore, not just as conforming to human nature, but as its highest expression.

The question may be asked: how essential is the presumption of *self-centred* individual optimizing behaviour for neo-classical economics? True, this is always the way that the story of capitalism is told within this tradition; but is it conceivable that this tradition can visualize a capitalism based on individual optimizing behaviour but without *self-centredness* – where people, for instance, are optimizing agents, but also act 'morally' for the social good in some sense?

The plain answer to this question is, 'no': moral behaviour and optimizing behaviour are mutually incompatible. To see this, let us assume that the individual hands over a part or the whole of the goods in his possession to others who are in need. Now, the 'cost' to an individual who puts in labour for acquiring goods, no matter how these goods are used, is the disutility of his work. If the individual is to look at the benefit side, then this disutility must be offset by the utility he obtains from the goods that this labour entitles him to possess. In fact the commensurability of the 'cost' and the 'benefit' is ensured by taking disutility on the 'cost' side and utility on the 'benefit' side.

The typical presumption in neo-classical economics is that this utility arises from the individual's (and his family members') direct *enjoyment* of these goods, but this presumption can be abandoned. As long as the disutility of work is compared with the utility obtained from the goods acquired through such work, the individual can carry out his optimization exercise: whether the utility of the goods to him is because of his own enjoyment or because of the satisfaction he obtains from giving them to others, makes not an iota of difference to the optimization exercise. But an optimization exercise where one's utility is derived from giving goods to others is no less self-centred than an exercise where one's utility is derived from one's own enjoyment.

The very act of optimization, in other words, entails the presence in the optimand of one's utility derived from the possession of goods, no matter what destination one has in mind for these goods – whether one's own stomach or that of someone else towards whom one is being 'generous'. *And it is this presence of one's own utility in the optimand of one's optimization exercise that amounts to self-centredness.* Behaviour based on optimization therefore is necessarily self-centred even when the person doing the optimization exercise is proposing to hand over the whole or a part of his goods to others.

Moral behaviour, by contrast, is not based on any optimization – that is, any *calculation* of costs and benefits. It is based on a transcendence of individual's interest altogether, which giving away goods to others does not entail *per se*. The mindset underlying moral behaviour therefore is basically different from the mindset underlying optimizing behaviour.

This has an important implication. In a socialist society where people own the means of production collectively, it is the commitment to the collective that is visualized as inducing people to work, without any optimization calculations. In a capitalist society, according to the Marxist perception, it is the fear of being unemployed and hence the fear of destitution that induces people to work, and that too in a disciplined manner; and for this mechanism to be effective there must always be an actual pool of the unemployed, a reserve army of labour. But neo-classical economics neither claims that some collectivist spirit motivates people to work under capitalism (for then, there would be no scope for any optimization and hence for the exercise of what it considers 'rationality', which it believes is universal), nor recognizes the existence of any unemployment or reserve army in its concept of the equilibrium state. For it, therefore, work discipline under capitalism remains inexplicable;[2] and a dissociation of incomes from the amount of work that is put in is inconceivable.

All this, however, is on the assumption that the individual optimizes while obediently accepting the constraints imposed upon him. But we have already seen in chapter two that optimization behaviour must also mean that the constraints themselves are arrived at as a result of such behaviour, that the individual must calculate the costs and benefits of violating the constraints. But let us leave aside this aspect here and discuss the implications of optimization behaviour as discussed conventionally in the neo-classical literature.

Optimization by economic agents in this perception is necessarily self-centred optimization. Central to the perception of neo-classical economics, therefore, is a society fragmented into individual economic agents, each concerned with his or her own utility which depends on the goods and services that he or she possesses.

A Basic Problem with the Assumption of 'Rationality'

In such a society, we have seen, the emergence of the employer–labourer relationship from within a universe of petty production can be explained on the basis of the convexity of the production possibility set, or, put differently, the concavity downwards of the graph of the production function when capital (land)/labour ratio is plotted on the horizontal axis and labour productivity on the vertical. Petty producers with different endowments of 'factors of production', if they got together, would be better off in the sense of getting a larger output for the same amount of total factor endowments. This getting together can take the form of some offering their labour services to others together with their (relatively) meagre land (or 'capital') endowments.

The concept of the production function however raises a problem. A complete production function is not visible at any point of time; only one point on it, which is the actual point where production is occurring, is visible. All other points are invisible; they exist only hypothetically, as points that *would be* visible if there were a change in the ratio in which factors are used. Then, how do those who get together as employers and labourers come to know of the benefits of their getting together? How, in other words, do they know that the total output will be larger than what they jointly have before getting together if they pooled their resources, since no other point on the production function other than where they are currently producing is visible to them and hence known to them?

This problem may not be a serious one when we are discussing the transition from petty production to capitalism, for among the numerous petty producers, since the factor endowments would be different, numerous points of actual production would be visible, each corresponding to a different 'factor endowment'. In other words, the myriads of hypothetical points on the production function must be actually getting realized before pooling has occurred; the benefits of pooling 'factor endowments', and hence of evolving the employer–labourer relationship, can in principle therefore be recognized. Let us assume in what follows that there are in fact actual points of production in real life corresponding to the different points on the production function, so that different economic agents come to realize the benefits of pooling their resources by observing those points.

This however remains a basic problem with the production function approach for analysing capitalism (though not necessarily the transition *to* it); and we shall come back to it later. But let us first discuss a second basic problem, which has to do with the concept of 'rationality'. A decision taken on the basis of 'rational' calculations must get more or less realized in practice if this 'rationality' is to have retrospective justification and hence meaningfulness. Put differently, the outcome of one's action must more or less coincide with the intention with which one had undertaken that action if one is to keep one's faith in 'rational' calculations. If there is a persistent and inexplicable deviation between the two, then one's doing 'rational' calculations and acting upon them would lose all relevance; indeed one would not even make any 'rational' calculations in the event of such persistent divergence, and there would be nothing 'rational' about 'rational' calculations in such a case.

The problem which the breakdown of this assumption of the broad coincidence between the intention behind an action and its outcome causes can be illustrated with reference to the 'paradox of thrift'. According to this paradox, if I decide to double my savings and so does everyone else, the outcome of this action on my part and that of everyone else is not a doubling of savings but a halving of income. If my decision to double my savings was based on 'rational calculations', i.e. an optimization exercise, then this exercise has landed me in a situation I had not bargained for and for which I have no explanation. If this keeps happening, then how do I do any optimization?[3]

The problem here arises *not* because of the simple fact of interdependence, i.e. the fact that *your* decisions affect *my* outcome (in addition to my decisions). Optimization can be done while taking into account such interdependence, and while nobody can be sure about how others may be behaving, some extrapolations can be made from the past, on the basis of which the optimization exercise that is carried out can be expected to give an outcome that is not way off the mark. But the *problem that arises here* is not because of the sheer fact of interdependence; it is because of the perversity of the theoretical model that underlies such optimization exercises. This model does not recognize the possibility of a deficiency of aggregate demand.

If the problem of deficiency of aggregate demand did not exist, if the output of the economy was always at full employment, then the divergence between intentions and outcome would not be a serious problem. In the above example, if suddenly everybody put a lower weight on current consumption compared to the future and hence saved more, they will all end up with larger savings and a lowering of the interest rate (according to neo-classical economics) until everybody is satisfied with his or her division of income between consumption and savings. But when output can fall below its full employment level because of a deficiency of aggregate demand, 'rational' behaviour becomes a problematical concept.

Neo-classical economics assumed that Say's Law, which states that supply creates its own demand, was always satisfied, and there could never be a deficiency of aggregate demand. But once we recognize the possibility of such a deficiency, the aggregate of individual decisions can lead to an outcome that is very different from what each decision-making agent had planned. The idea of optimization in such a case ceases to be meaningful.

If the aggregate outcome of the decisions of all economic agents taken together is different from what anybody singly had anticipated, then it follows that *even the outcome for the individual agent itself will be different from what that individual had anticipated.* To put the matter differently, the exercise of individual 'rationality' produces neither socially 'rational' outcomes (of which the mass unemployment generated in the aggregate through each individual agent acting 'rationally' is an obvious example), nor even the fulfilment of individual 'rationality'.

The lack of recognition in neo-classical economics of the possibility of deficiency of aggregate demand in turn arises from the fact that it does not recognize money as a form in which wealth can be held in a capitalist society.[4] This is not only factually wrong, for money which has played the role of being a store of value since time immemorial (which Locke recognized even in his 'state of nature') continues to play that role under capitalism too; but it is also logically erroneous. After all, capitalism is a pre-eminently money-using economy, where the role of money as a medium of circulation is quite central. Neo-classical economics believes that money plays *only* the role of a medium of circulation but not that of a form of wealth.[5] But in playing the medium of circulation role, money is in fact also acting as a store of value for a brief period. In the C–M–C circuit, money which interposes itself between the sale and purchase of commodities acts *ipso facto* as a form of wealth in the period between the sale and the purchase. To ignore the form of wealth role of money nonetheless, while recognizing its medium of circulation role, is tantamount to believing that money is reconverted to commodities in the C–M–C circuit *after a fixed definite interval*, which means that the 'rational' individual does not act 'rationally' when it comes to deciding the length of time for which money is held.

Looking at the matter differently, this fixity of the length of the period between sale and purchase is what is entailed by the assumption of a constant velocity of circulation of money. But the moment the possibility of money being held for a longer (or shorter) period is recognized, the form of wealth role of money must intrude into the analysis. To believe that money can play the medium of circulation role but is never a form of wealth is therefore logically untenable; it amounts to believing that people like automatons convert money into commodities after a fixed definite period under *all* circumstances, never a longer or a shorter period. Such a belief has no basis. In fact it amounts, ironically, to denying the very 'rationality' in the realm of asset choice that the theory emphasizes as central to human behaviour; and even more ironic is the fact that without *this* denial of 'rationality', its assertion of rationality in other spheres becomes a *logical* non-starter.

The concept of 'rationality' that underlies neo-classical economics is thus not just unhistorical, but also logically untenable. People simply cannot be 'rational' in the sense claimed by neo-classical theory in a money-using world where the possibility of a deficiency of aggregate demand is ever-present; such a possibility negates any pursuit of individual rationality.

Say's Law and 'Rationality'

Almost every strand of established neo-classical economics sees money only as a medium of circulation and not as a form of holding wealth. Accordingly, it sees the demand for money as being a stable function, usually a constant ratio, of money income; and more recent attempts to introduce the idea of holding money as wealth into neo-classical economics have turned out to be largely unsuccessful in the sense of requiring all kinds of special assumptions, for which there is no justification, to create a coherent theory (P. Patnaik 2009). Put differently, since money being used only as a medium of circulation is a *sufficient* condition but not a *necessary* one, for Say's Law to hold, as standard neo-classical economics believes it does, it is *possible* to think of cases where money can be a form of wealth and yet to tell a neo-classical story; but these would require special assumptions of all kinds which have no justification.[6]

The reason why ruling out money as a form of wealth validates Say's Law is quite simple: Say's Law would not hold and there would be an excess supply of goods at full employment output only if there is some other non-goods commodity for which there is an excess demand. In other words, a deficiency of aggregate demand for goods is possible only if it is matched by an excess of demand over supply in some other non-goods market (since the sum of all excess demands must be zero). This, typically, is the money market; and for such excess demand for money to be possible, the demand for money must not be strictly tied to the value of the output of goods (at given prices); it should be able to move around independently. Recognizing only the role of money as a medium of circulation strictly ties the demand for money to the value of the output of goods (at given prices). It thereby precludes any possibility of an excess demand for money and a corresponding excess supply of goods at full employment, if at the money wages and prices that prevail at full employment, the amount of money required for circulating the goods equals the supply of money. In fact, wage and price flexibility is supposed to ensure that exactly this level of money wages and prices actually prevail at full employment. With money not being held as a form of wealth, there is no question of this not happening.

Neo-classical theories can be divided into two broad strands, to start with. One is the Walrasian strand which basically looks at a short-period general equilibrium involving several markets, but where the concept of a rate of profit being equalized across sectors, or even the very concept of a rate of profit, does not play any role. The second strand is where the distribution of income between the various 'factors of production' is determined in accordance with their full employment 'marginal productivities', that is, the reward of each factor is determined by what a unit of it would contribute at the margin to total output (with the use of other factors remaining the same) at that point of production where all factors are being fully employed. The Austrian and the Cambridge theories before Keynes are examples of this second strand.

The ruling out of the role of money as a form of wealth is done differently in the different strands. In the second strand, this is done through the so-called Cambridge quantity equation, according to which $M_s = k.P.Q$ where M_s denotes money supply, P the price level, Q the output (which is taken to be at full employment level), and k, the reciprocal of the income velocity of circulation of money, is a constant; the r.h.s. denotes the demand for money which is supposed to depend exclusively upon the level of money income.

The same thing, of ruling out the role of money as a form of wealth-holding, is sought to be achieved in a different way in the Walrasian system. The stability of the system, which is essential for a meaningful full employment general equilibrium, requires the assumption of 'gross substitutability' (again a sufficient condition). This requires that a reduction in the price of all other goods in terms of any one good must lead to a reduction in the excess demand for (i.e. an increase in the excess supply of) the latter (Mukherji 1990). A reduction in money prices of every other good must lead accordingly to a reduction in the demand for money, which will happen only if money is required exclusively for transaction purposes, i.e. if money has only a medium of circulation role.

It follows that since, for the concept of 'rationality' underlying neo-classical economics to be meaningful, Say's Law must hold, for which again the role of money as a form of wealth-holding must be ignored, the neo-classical perception typically assumes away this role of money. But since to imagine that money is a medium of circulation but not a form of wealth-holding is both in principle and in practical terms quite untenable, the concept of 'rationality' underlying neo-classical economics is also untenable.

The Problem of 'Externalities'

The fact that the aggregate outcome of decisions taken on the basis of individual 'rationality' may turn out to be socially 'irrational' has for long been noted. It was the crux of the earlier critique of the market equilibrium by the Cambridge School, notably by A.C. Pigou, prior to Keynes' *General Theory*. That critique highlighted *inter alia* the existence of 'externalities', which the markets as they exist are incapable of taking fully into account. The market equilibrium therefore is not socially optimal. For instance, if a factory produces pollution for which there is no price to be paid by the polluter, then the market equilibrium will entail substantial pollution and hence be socially inoptimal.

There is a view that such externalities can be handled by having appropriate additional markets. For instance, if a polluting factory can be set up in a neighbourhood, and if there is a market where the producers of pollution can buy the consent of those exposed to pollution by paying an agreed price, then the problem of externality would have been taken care of. The problem of externality, in other words, arises because of the absence of appropriate markets.

There are, however, two obvious problems with this argument. The first is ethical. If those exposed to pollution are poor people, then the producers of pollution will be able to get away with paying a lower price for polluting than if those exposed to pollution are rich people. The mere introduction of markets to resolve the problem of pollution, therefore, is ethically objectionable, since it violates the principle that all human lives are of equal value. This is exactly the kind of objection one has to the suggestion that polluting industries from the advanced capitalist world should be shifted to the third world (even when such relocation is accompanied by a compensation payment to the latter), namely the objection that such a course does not treat all human lives as of equal value.

This of course is a general problem with the market, namely that since purchasing power is unequally distributed among people, the weights they command on the market are necessarily unequal, unlike in the political arena where every vote in a democratic election has equal weight. Since democracy entails equal weight for everyone, it follows that the market in a fundamental sense is anti-democratic; and if democracy is in conformity with our ethical demands, then the market solution must be unethical. The question however may be raised: why do we find a market solution to pollution ethically objectionable if we do not find the market solution to other aspects of economic life ethically objectionable?

Equality, in other words, has never been a primary concern of liberalism, which has been much more focused on individual freedom. The attitude towards equality has varied across the different strands of neo-classical economics and hence also across the different strands of liberalism. Keynes argued for a reduction in the prevailing levels of inequality on the grounds that it would prop up aggregate demand. But within neo-classical economics, the main concern has been that if redistribution is to be effected, then it must be effected in a manner that does not disturb the efficiency properties of the market equilibrium, whence emphasis has been placed on 'lump-sum' transfers which are supposedly non-price-distorting. Since such 'lump-sum' transfers which do not impinge on relative prices are difficult to bring about in practice (even an income tax can be seen as altering the relative price of work vis-à-vis leisure), it is reasonable to say that equality has not been a priority for neo-classical economics and the strand of liberalism based on it.

But while equality has never been a primary concern of liberalism, it is not as if extreme inequality has been approved by the liberal tradition; in particular, more recent liberal writers have emphasized the need to curb extreme inequality on a variety of grounds ranging from ensuring 'justice' (Rawls 1971) to preserving 'democracy' (Piketty 2014). Even these strands would not shun the liberal suspicion of extreme equality on the grounds of its being destructive, if not of efficiency then at least of effort; but they would certainly find a market solution to the problem of pollution, by filling the gap of a missing market, ethically objectionable.

The second objection to the argument of having a market where the compensation for pollution should be decided is that people are not the best judges of their own welfare in this sphere. This is generally true in most spheres, alcoholism and drug addiction being obvious examples of lack of knowledge about one's own welfare; but it is even more true in the case of pollution, where understanding the damage done to people by pollutants requires a certain level of scientific knowledge which people in general may not have.

To decide on the penalty to be paid by the polluting firm, as well as to ensure that people are not sold a 'lemon' in the name of being compensated for pollution, it is necessary that the state should intervene in the case of pollution. In general, for all cases of externalities, state intervention in the form of taxes and subsidies, or even in the form of direct bans, is the way towards resolution. And the Cambridge tradition before Keynes wanted the state to intervene in the form of taxes and subsidies in the functioning of the market to ensure that the market equilibrium was nudged towards a socially optimal state (Pigou [1920] 2013).

But while the discussion of the disjunction between individual and social 'rationality' in the period before the Keynesian revolution was more or less confined to the case of externalities (and of course income distribution which we shall not consider here), Keynes' highlighting of the problem of effective demand made it clear that the problem went far deeper. The aggregation of individual decisions taken on the basis of individual 'rationality' produced not only a socially 'irrational' outcome in the form of mass unemployment; it also produced an outcome that was 'irrational' from the point of the very individual who had taken a supposedly 'rational' decision. With the Keynesian revolution, therefore, the very idea of the exercise of individual 'rationality' producing in the aggregate an outcome that, barring externalities, was 'rational' both from the individual and from the social point of view, got discredited. It is not surprising that Keynesian ideas were fought so bitterly by neo-classical economics.

While 'rational' individuals coming together to pool resources to increase output is to be welcomed according to neo-classical economics, *the exercise of 'rationality' must be within a bounded domain.* Any exercise of 'rationality' whereby individuals come together to obtain a gain *that is at the expense of some other individuals* must be prevented. In other words, the individuals, while coming together to form coalitions, must not be allowed to exercise any monopoly power, i.e. must not cause any deviation of the market equilibrium from the competitive equilibrium. Such a deviation must be prevented by the state for it hurts other individuals. The classic case is when workers come together through trade unions to enforce a real wage higher than the market clearing wage, which, according to neo-classical economics, is the cause of non-frictional unemployment. Neo-classical economics would recommend state intervention to enforce 'labour market flexibility', to prevent the forming of such coalitions that end up hurting others. Preventing *such* coalitions must then be one of the constraints upon the exercise of individual 'rationality'.

The state on the neo-classical conception must be an entity which ensures that markets work freely. For the state to be able to do this, however, it must not be influenced by those who gain from the deviation of the market equilibrium from competitive equilibrium. It must not be swayed by money power. It must not be influenced by the trade unions enforcing wage rigidity into not acting on behalf of the unemployed; and so on. Put differently, the coming into being of coalitions through an exercise of individual 'rationality' must leave the state unaffected; or, the domain of politics must be kept outside the exercise of individual 'rationality'. Within its own logic, therefore, the neo-classical concept of individual 'rationality' cannot be a *comprehensively* applicable one; how these *different* applications are ensured across different domains is never explained by neo-classical economics.

A Critique of the Marginal Productivity Theory

The strand of neo-classical economics that bases itself on the marginal productivity theory, that talks of 'factors of production' and takes 'capital' as a factor of production on a par with labour, has been very effectively criticized by the work of Piero Sraffa (1960). There are two different parts of this critique. In a fundamental sense, as already mentioned, there is only one point on the production function that is visible at any time, which is the point of actual production. All other points are supposed to come into effect in the event of a hypothetical change. Their material reality therefore is suspect. This problem was assumed away earlier by us because in a world of petty production, one can imagine the simultaneous existence of several points at the same instant of time (though even here one has to answer how they coexist without some being competed out). But when we are talking about a competitive equilibrium, explaining such an equilibrium in terms of a non-observed hypothetical change is problematical.

The second critique relates to the concept of capital. Since capital can only be a value sum, with individual elements of fixed and circulating capital being evaluated at their equilibrium prices – that is, at prices that would prevail when the wage-rate and the rate of profit are equalized across sectors in a world where commodities are produced with the application of labour to produced means of production – this sum can be known only when the rate of profit (or the wage-rate) is specified. Instead of the rate of profit being determined by the ratio in which 'capital' is applied to labour in the economy as a whole, as the marginal productivity theory of distribution would suggest, the ratio of 'capital' (as a value sum) to labour can be known only when the rate of profit is independently given, thus undermining this theory.

Even the residual value that the marginal productivity theory could have, simply as a *description* of phenomena, if there was a monotonic inverse relationship between the value of capital per unit of labour and the rate of profit, as it predicts, is also negated; it turns out that there is no such monotonic relationship. In fact, as the phenomenon of 're-switching' of techniques shows, techniques cannot be ordered monotonically as being more or less capital-intensive; as the rate of profit is lowered, a technique of production that was more profitable than another at a higher rate of profit, and became less profitable than the other at a lower rate of profit, could become once again more profitable than the other at a still lower rate of profit. Correspondingly, as the rate of profit is lowered the value of capital per unit of labour may rise, but as the rate of profit is lowered still further the value of capital per unit of labour may be lower again. The lack of monotonicity between the value of capital stock and the rate of profit makes the marginal productivity theory logically erroneous even as a means of stylized description (Pasinetti 1977; Bharadwaj 1989).

Neo-classical writers have tended to withdraw to a Walrasian position as a consequence. But as argued above, this presupposes no demand deficiency, for which it needs to assume that money does not have the role of a form of wealth-holding, which is both unrealistic and illogical.[7] In fact the very concept of 'rationality' which is supposed to underlie the behaviour of economic agents ceases to be meaningful.

The liberal argument which bases itself on neo-classical economics is founded essentially on the benefits of exchange, including benefits that arise from exchanging 'factors of production'. Production, in short, is seen essentially as an extension of exchange. Exchange occurs between economic agents, each of whom is 'rational' in the sense of maximizing, subject to constraints, an objective function that is centred upon oneself; such exchange is something which is supposed to have characterized mankind since time immemorial (only its scope may have increased over time), since such 'rational' behaviour is supposed to be part of human nature. The freedom of the individual consists in enjoying this freedom to exchange; the threat to this freedom arises from state intervention other than that required to achieve a *social* optimum in the presence of externalities, and from monopolies and other such institutions which undermine a competitive economy.

The market, however, can do nothing even according to this theory to change income distribution, neither to change the distribution of endowments before exchange nor to change the distribution of gains of exchange. The state must intervene to effect a better distribution of income, the need for which, within limits, cannot be denied even by this strand of liberal thought. And above all, state intervention becomes crucial for overcoming deficiency of aggregate demand which this strand does not recognize. The necessity of pervasive state intervention for preserving individual freedom was emphasized by Keynes and what he called 'New Liberalism'. Let us turn to this now.

Notes

[1] Questions may be raised about whether this or that individual economist can be categorized as neo-classical on our criterion. This question however is not relevant for us; our emphasis is on categorizing not individual economists but the neo-classical *tradition*.

[2] It may be thought that even at full employment, since there is some frictional unemployment, and since being even 'frictionally unemployed' entails a cost (say α) in the sense that the income of the frictionally unemployed is ($w-\alpha$) where w is the real wage of the employed, then this fact itself should induce work discipline even without unemployment proper. But in such a case the wage per period of the employed would also be driven down to ($w-\alpha$). But if a wage less than w which must be the market-clearing wage, prevails in every enterprise, then there will be an excess demand for labour, which can only be met through a disappearance of frictional unemployment. Thus, the existence of frictional unemployment cannot

be a disciplining device; what is more, the very concept of frictional unemployment is an empirical add-on to a consistent theoretical system, even though this add-on itself is not theoretically compatible with this system. This is an instance of inconsistent theorizing, which neo-classical economics is afflicted with, because of such empirical add-ons.

[3] The question will be raised: if meaningful rational calculation becomes impossible, then how do people act? Obviously, they would then be acting on the basis of certain *rules of action*. Some, of course, may still prefer to act 'rationally', i.e. on the basis of calculations of optimality, even when outcomes differ from intentions. But if they do so, then optimizing behaviour itself becomes a mere rule of action devoid of any meaningfulness.

[4] The argument which follows is based on P. Patnaik (2009).

[5] It is not a refutation of our argument to identify individual economists who have produced neo-classical models but who also believe *in their other writings* that money is held as wealth. Our argument is not *ad hominem*; it is concerned with the internal logic of the neo-classical *position*.

[6] One very obvious special assumption that would be required if a neo-classical story is told, with money being a form of wealth-holding, is that no matter what the current value of money may be (vis-à-vis commodities), *it must always be expected to have a positive value in future*, that is, there must be inelastic price expectations for money (at least over a certain range). But in a world of flexible money wages and prices such as what neo-classical economics assumes, there is absolutely no reason why this assumption should hold at all.

[7] Strictly speaking, in a Walrasian system with an auctioneer who announces equilibrium prices, there is no role for money even as a medium of circulation. All transactions can occur in one instant without any actual use of money which can play the role only of a unit of account. But if we do reformulate the system giving money a role as a medium of circulation, as economists like Clower (1967) have attempted to do, then it would be illogical not to give it a role also as a form of wealth-holding (P. Patnaik 2009).

CHAPTER SEVEN

Keynes and the Socialization of Investment

Keynes does not seem to have been particularly concerned with the origin of capitalism. In his *General Theory* there is little on this issue; but in the second volume of *A Treatise of Money* there is a passing discussion on the origin of capitalism, where he sees the birth of this system as being the outcome of the massive and prolonged profit inflation caused by the inflow of Spanish gold into Europe from the 'New World', initially as sheer transfer and subsequently through working the gold mines at Potosi.

The *Treatise*, it may be recalled, was written in an intellectual milieu where the accepted view was that in a capitalist economy all 'factors of production' would be fully utilized in equilibrium; output would be at that level which the full utilization of all factors of production would produce; the real wages would equal the marginal productivity of labour at full employment; the money wages and prices at this output would be determined by the quantity of money; and the level of investment would be equated to the level of savings out of this output through changes in the interest rate.

As against this, Keynes argued in the *Treatise* that the interest rate equalized not investment with savings but the demand for money with its supply; at any given money wage-rate and output, the saving–investment equality was brought about (assuming a closed economy for simplicity) by changes in the price-level relative to this money wage-rate. Hence, if there was an excess of investment over voluntary savings at the given output and money wage-rate, and at the base price-level (equalling the marginal cost of producing this output at the given money wage-rate), then the price-level would rise relative to its base level, pushing up the profit-margin and the profit-share *at the expense of the workers* (whence the term 'profit inflation').

Keynes and the 'Birth' of Capitalism

Keynes in the *Treatise* broke new ground by suggesting that booms under capitalism were financed not by any 'sacrifice' of consumption on the part of the capitalists as preceding 'mainstream' theory had believed, but rather by forcing the workers to consume less per head, i.e. by forcing 'savings' out of them, *for which however they got no credit.* All such 'forced savings' generated by squeezing workers landed on the lap of the capitalists who are the ones that got credit for it. Profit inflation therefore led to 'forced savings' and such 'forced savings', rather than any consumption sacrifices by the capitalists, financed the booms.

Since an excess of investment over voluntary savings is the same as an excess of expenditure over the given output at base prices, profit inflation can be said to have been caused by such an excess of expenditure. The inflow of gold into Europe gave rise to such an excess of expenditure over output at base prices, during the sixteenth and seventeenth centuries, which raised the profit-share and hence made a whole range of investment projects more profitable than before, and thereby caused a massive boom that gave rise to the capitalist system.

To the question why the rise of capitalism was more pronounced in England and elsewhere in Europe than in Spain itself, if the inflow of Spanish gold was the cause of its birth, Keynes' answer was that the gold which came into Spain went more or less straight into the hands of the aristocracy; its domestic use by them was mainly for employing a larger retinue of domestic servants, i.e. for purchasing personal services, which raised money wages and hence prices. Its domestic use, in short, mainly caused an 'income inflation' (where money wages and prices both went up in tandem) rather than a profit inflation (where prices went up relative to money wages). In fact, after a brief period of profit inflation when prices rose faster than money wages in Spain, there was an income inflation when both increased in tandem and even a profit deflation when money wages rose faster than prices. In England, by contrast, gold entered through private commerce and was used to buy goods, which raised prices relative to money wages and hence caused a far more prolonged 'profit inflation', which raised the profit-share and hence the profitability of investment projects.

As Keynes put it:

> It is not safe to believe more – and this is quite sufficient to illustrate our argument – than that the greater part of the fruits of the economic progress

> and capital accumulation of the Elizabethan and Jacobean age accrued to the profiteer rather than to the wage earner. Putting it shortly, we may say that profit inflation in Spain lasted from 1520 to 1590, in England from 1550 to 1650, and in France from 1530 to 1700 (with a serious depression intervening from 1600 to 1625). In England real wages were rising rapidly from 1680 to 1700, while there is no evidence of a similar improvement in France. Never in the annals of the modern world has there existed so prolonged and so rich an opportunity for the businessman, the speculator and the profiteer. In these golden years modern capitalism was born. (Keynes 1979, p. 141)

The reference to the birth of capitalism here is a little misleading. It is not birth in the sense of a transition from a completely different society, a pre-capitalist one with no wage-labour, to a capitalist society that Keynes is talking about.[1] Rather, his analysis refers to the massive boom that occurred in the sixteenth and seventeenth centuries, which resulted in a *strengthening* of capitalism; a 'profit inflation' presupposes 'profits' as a social category and hence some rudimentary capitalism to start with. The transition from this rudimentary capitalism to a consolidated capitalism is really what Keynes is talking about, which is not exactly the same as the birth of capitalism in the sense of classical writers. In Smith's case, for instance, there was a clear transition from an 'early and rude state of society' to one where there was pervasive use of wage-labour. In Keynes there is no such transition; the origin of free wage-labour from the ranks of pre-capitalist petty producers does not figure at all in his analysis.

Within its own context, however, what Keynes had to say about the transition he was discussing is interesting. While Keynes is not exactly discussing the transition that Locke or Smith had been concerned with, what he does say marks a break from the Lockean or the Smithian tradition. An implication of Locke's writing was that those who became wage-labourers in the transition from the state of nature not only became better off because of this transition, but remained permanently better off compared to their condition in the state of nature. Likewise in Smith, as we saw in chapter four, the transition from the early and rude state of society entails a permanent improvement in the condition of the workers compared to what it had originally been. For Locke and Smith, while there may not be a steady improvement in the condition of the workers, there is no slide-back to their condition in the original pre-capitalist state; but Keynes' theory of profit inflation questions this.

Profit inflation arises because of a fall in real wages when money wages do not keep pace with prices; when this happens, there is no reason whatsoever why such a fall cannot carry real wages below what the workers' real incomes had been in the original pre-capitalist state. In fact Keynes quotes the figures of Wiebe, accepted by Hamilton, which show that the 'violence and the duration of the profit inflations in France and England were so great that real wages in 1600 were only half what they had been in 1500', but rejects them as being scarcely 'credible' (though he adds in a footnote that real wages in 1700 might have been 50 per cent lower than in 1500). Even this, however, is a drastic decline. Keynes' perception that capitalism could be associated with such drastic declines in real wages in certain periods suggests a rejection on his part of the 'cooperativist' view of the emergence and functioning of capitalism that underlay classical liberalism. Though he does not directly write about it, he is implicitly rejecting the idea of a voluntary transition to capitalism on the basis of a universal agreement.

In doing so, Keynes too is subscribing to the idea of a 'spontaneity' of capitalism as distinct from an exercise of individual agency, but a 'spontaneity' different from what Marx had visualized. It is not a 'spontaneity' where the overall functioning of the economy arises out of the fact that every economic agent is *coerced by competition* into acting in particular ways irrespective of individual volition, or a 'spontaneity' *in the strong sense* if you like; but it is 'spontaneity' nonetheless, a 'spontaneity' *in the weak sense*, where the system moves in a way that is not willed by anyone or foreseen by anyone. This idea of 'spontaneity' in the weak sense, of which the anarchy of the system is a part, runs through Keynes' writing, starting from his view on the 'birth' of capitalism as discussed in the *Treatise*.

Invalidity of a 'Prisoner's Dilemma' Interpretation of Keynes

'Mainstream' economics before Keynes had seen individual agency in pursuit of individual self-interest achieve in its totality a result for society as a whole that was beneficial for society. Neo-classical economics in particular had seen it in a stark manner, as the pursuit of 'individual rationality' leading in the aggregate to the achievement of 'social rationality' defined in a particular manner (except to the extent that 'externalities' muddied the picture); but even classical political economy had argued a kindred proposition.

Keynes broke with this entire idea of 'pursuit of private interest resulting in social good'. This idea presupposed individual economic agents reacting to market signals without there being any choice regarding the form in which wealth could be held, i.e. no stock choice and hence no stock equilibrium. Money was never considered a form in which wealth could be held, which is why Say's Law was supposed to hold, ruling out any problem of deficiency of aggregate demand. But once money is also considered a form in which wealth can be held, which it must be, since in any case wealth is held even if fleetingly in the form of money when it is being used for transaction purposes in the C–M–C circuit, then the choice of holding wealth either in the form of money or in the form of capital goods or claims on capital goods becomes important. Any such stock choice must be based on expectations about the future, expectations that must incorporate the anticipated actions of others both now and also in the future. And once such expectations are introduced, the simple notion of the pursuit of private interest leading to public good can no longer be entertained.[2]

For deciding on investment, for instance, an entrepreneur must have some idea about what others are deciding. The aggregate result of each economic agent acting 'rationally' on the basis of some assumption about what others are doing can not only be socially undesirable, such as for instance the creation of mass unemployment,[3] but also, for that very reason, be different even from the intentions of the individual. The pursuit of individual rationality then, even if it is assumed that individuals are engaged in such a pursuit, achieves a result that can be considered neither socially rational, nor even rational *ex post* for the individual, a point noted in the last chapter.

The problem that Keynes was opening up, however, was not the same as the 'prisoner's dilemma' in Game Theory, as many have believed. True, both Keynes and the Game theorists discussing the 'prisoner's dilemma' highlight the fact that the pursuit of individual 'rationality' leads to a solution different from what would obtain if they colluded. But the Keynesian argument goes further in several ways. To see just *one of these ways*, let us assume that each entrepreneur believes that others would be acting exactly as he does, so that the 'prisoner's dilemma' solution that arises because of not knowing how others would be acting is actually ruled out. We are, in short, no longer in a 'prisoner's dilemma' situation.

Investment orders in this case will get pushed up to the maximum level possible, since entrepreneurs would believe that they would collectively provide markets to one another no matter what the level of investment. But the *actual* investment will be constrained in such a case by the production capacity of the investment goods sector (as in Goodwin 1951). This actual level of investment will determine via the multiplier, the demand for consumption goods. This demand would not, except by sheer accident, equal the production capacity of the consumption goods sector; if it falls short, then we would have insufficient capacity in the investment goods sector combined with excess capacity in the consumption goods sector. When this happens, the response of the consumption goods sector would be to stop adding to its capacity, or to reduce such addition drastically, *which would also reduce demand for investment goods, create excess capacity in the investment goods sector and hence reduce additions to the capacity of the investment goods sector*, causing a downturn in both sectors.

Keynes, in other words, was not talking only about inadequate investment; *he was talking about inadequate investment causing an overall recession in the economy via the multiplier*. And the latter happens because in a capitalist economy prices cannot fall below the marginal cost without reducing output, so that imbalances are not rectified through price variations alone but give rise to recessions or, in the opposite case, profit inflations (which would happen if the demand for consumer goods exceeds the full capacity output of this sector).

In a socialist economy with state ownership of enterprises this multiplier relationship ceases to hold, since prices of consumer goods can be allowed to fall, to even below the marginal cost without any reduction in output; they can therefore be allowed to fall relative to the money wage-rate, to clear the market, as the planning authority decrees a non-reduction in any enterprise's output. All enterprises being state-owned, their individual profits and losses do not matter. Even without a 'prisoner's dilemma', it follows, there can be mass unemployment in a capitalist economy.

Putting it differently, the problem highlighted by Keynes was not the smallness of investment *per se*, as the analogy with the 'prisoner's dilemma' would suggest, but the fact that there is no mechanism within the system to equate full employment savings with investment, whatever its size. A fall in prices relative to the money wage-rate at full employment output, which can be effected in a socialist economy, is impossible under capitalism; and the interest rate does not equate savings with investment, as pre-Keynesian theory that did not see money as a form of wealth-holding had believed.

Likewise, the Keynesian problem, it can be shown, arises not because of the absence of 'rational expectations' (which amounts to *de facto* perfect foresight). 'Rational expectations' of course are ruled out by the very concept of the speculative demand for money advanced by Keynes, since it presupposes divergent expectations among wealth-holders, and divergence would be ruled out if everybody had rational expectations. But let us reconstruct Keynes' theory without the speculative demand for money, along the lines of Kalecki who postulated only a transactions demand for money but made the size of this demand relative to the value of transactions a function of the short-term interest rate; the expected average of short term rates plus a risk premium then determined the long-term rate.

Even if we reconstruct Keynes in this manner to give 'rational expectations' meaningfulness even in a Keynesian universe, the assumption of rational expectations will still make no difference to the conclusion about the persistence of involuntary unemployment. Keynes' conclusion, in other words, arises for an entirely different reason and not because of the absence of 'rational expectations'. Let us see how with a simple example.

Keynes and 'Rational Expectations'

Consider an economy where each firm has an investment function of the following kind:

$$(I/K)_{t+1} = (I/K)_t + b.(u_t - u^*).(I/K)_t \ \ldots\ldots\ (A)$$

Here, I denotes net investment (net addition to capital stock), and u denotes the degree of capacity utilization which is a pure number that is equal to O/K.β, with β being the technological output–capital ratio, O the output and K the capital stock; the time subscripts refer to periods, and u* is the desired level of capacity utilization by the firm. The investment function states that if the degree of capacity utilization in the current period is greater than the desired level, then the rate of growth of capital stock is stepped up in the next period compared to the present period.

Suppose to start with $u_t < u^*$; then the amount of investment relative to capital stock which the firm will make in the next period will be less than in the current period. Assuming all firms use exactly the same rule for making investment decisions, this will reduce u still further in the next period, i.e. $u_{t+1} < u_t$. This, of course, is the famous 'knife-edge' problem highlighted by Harrod (1939). Now, *suppose every firm correctly foresees this happening*; what can they do? If they curtail investment still further because of this anticipation, that is, if they do not stick strictly to the investment behaviour as shown in (A), then that ironically will only make matters even worse in the next period; u_{t+1} will fall still further.

The only case where 'perfect foresight' *both* informs action by firms *and* also obtains in practice, is where every firm undertakes just as much investment as is required to place the economy on the 'warranted growth path', i.e. where $(I/K)_{t+1} = s.\beta.u^*$, where s is the savings ratio of the economy.

Or, if we make the assumption that all wages are consumed and all profits are saved, then the warranted growth path will be given by $\pi.\beta.u^*$, where π is the share of profits in output.

But given the instability of the 'warranted growth path', a chance deviation from this path, even if the economy happens to be on it to start with, will lead to a cumulative deviation *even if there are 'rational expectations'*, for reasons we have just discussed. While it is certainly true that if capitalists *colluded* in investment decision-making they would put the economy back on the 'warranted growth path', in the absence of any actual collusion, simply being aware of what the future holds in store does not help one iota.

If everybody pursues the same investment function, despite being aware of its implications for the economy as a whole, then that will simply reproduce the knife-edge property. On the other hand, in the event of growth slowing down, if everybody in isolation cuts investment even further than what equation (A) above would have warranted, then the slowing down will be even greater. Nobody however, despite knowing all this, will *increase* investment compared to what would have been undertaken in accordance with (A) in the midst of a slowdown, because then others would not follow him and he would be even worse off than if he had only followed investment behaviour as in (A) above.[4] The 'rational expectation equilibrium', even if the economy started from one, would be impossible to get back to.

There is, in short, a distinction between 'rational expectations' and 'collusion'. There is invariably a belief in 'mainstream' theory that 'rational expectations' ensure a collusive solution, which is not at all the case (P. Patnaik 2009). The two are completely separate entities, and a collusive solution cannot be achieved in the absence of some institutional arrangement that ensures it.

The problem highlighted by Keynes thus inhered in the fact of *individual* as distinct from collusive or cooperative decision-making,[5] and required for its resolution the institution of such collusion which could take the form, in Keynes' words, of the 'socialization of investment'.

Keynes however did not even set much store by the idea of individuals pursuing their self-interest 'rationally'. Even on investment decisions where his depiction of the intersection between marginal efficiency of capital and the interest rate as the point of investment might suggest that entrepreneurs were acting 'rationally', it is clear that his idea was only to show the factors influencing investment rather than to put his faith in some unchanging curve of marginal efficiency of capital. In fact he was quite explicit on the question of individuals not being capable of pursuing self-interest.

> Let us clear from the ground the metaphysical or general principles upon which, from time to time, *laissez-faire* has been founded. It is *not* true that individuals possess a prescriptive 'natural liberty' in their economic activities. There is no 'compact' conferring perpetual rights on those who Have or those who Acquire. The world is not so governed from above that private and social interest *always coincide*. It is not so managed here below that in practice they coincide. It is not a correct deduction from the Principles of Economics that enlightened self-interest always operates in the public interest. Nor is it true that self-interest generally *is* enlightened; more often individuals acting separately to promote their own ends are too ignorant or too weak to attain even these. Experience does *not* show that individuals, when they make up a social unit, are always less clear-sighted than when they act separately. (Keynes 1963, p. 312)

This outright rejection of the premises of classical liberalism was accompanied by Keynes' embrace of a heterodox liberalism that he himself called New Liberalism, whose point of departure lay, in the economic realm, in the 'spontaneity' of the capitalist system in the weak sense defined above.

Keynes and Individualism

The most significant manifestation of this 'spontaneity' is the production of mass unemployment. Keynes wrote:

> The authoritarian state systems of today seem to solve the problem of unemployment at the expense of efficiency and of freedom. It is certain that the world will not much longer tolerate the unemployment, which, apart from brief periods of excitement, is associated – and in my opinion inevitably associated – with present-day capitalistic individualism. (Keynes 1949, p. 381)

Keynes thus saw unemployment as the inevitable outcome of the existing capitalist system, whose spontaneous functioning, far from achieving individual self-interest as well as social good, as earlier theory had believed, actually achieved neither. And this was not just an aberration but its normal state of affairs, 'apart from brief periods of excitement'.

The reason why this happened was clear, namely that, unlike what earlier theory had erroneously believed, money could also be a form in which wealth could be held. For there to be enough investment therefore, so that at the prevailing income distribution the level of consumption is large enough to generate a level of aggregate demand that would produce a situation of (or close to) full employment, holding wealth in the form of capital goods must be sufficiently attractive compared to holding it in the form of money. The schedule of marginal efficiency of capital, in short, which denotes the prospective yield on different levels of investment, must be sufficiently high relative to the interest rate, which indicates the preference for money, or liquidity preference, among wealth-holders. There is absolutely no reason why the marginal efficiency of capital should be high enough to counter the extent of liquidity preference among wealth-holders to produce enough investment for creating a situation close to full employment, except in certain periods of euphoria, or, as Keynes put it, 'brief periods of excitement' (when the marginal efficiency of capital appears high).

Keynes appears to have believed that as capital accumulation proceeded, there would be an inward shift in the schedule of marginal efficiency of capital, so that the maintenance of any particular level of employment will *ceteris paribus* become more and more difficult, i.e. the capacity of the system to remain at any given level of employment, including at full employment if at all it is achieved, will become more and more attenuated. But there is no valid reason for believing this; and this is a feature of Keynes' overall thought not germane to our present argument.

While seeing mass unemployment as a more or less perennial feature of capitalistic individualism, Keynes continued to remain attached to capitalistic individualism for its other advantages. In his words:

> Let us stop for a moment to remind ourselves what these advantages are. They are partly the advantages of efficiency – the advantages of decentralization and of the play of self-interest. The advantage to efficiency of the decentralization of decisions and of individual responsibility is even greater perhaps than the nineteenth century supposed; and the reaction against the appeal to self-interest may have gone too far. But, above all, individualism, if it can be purged of its defects and its abuses, is the best safeguard of personal liberty in the sense that, compared to any other system, it greatly widens the field for the exercise of personal choice. It is also the best safeguard of the variety of life, which emerges precisely from this extended field of personal choice, and the loss of which is the greatest of all the losses of the homogeneous or totalitarian state. (Ibid., p. 380)

If these advantages of capitalistic individualism had to be preserved, then 'its defects and its abuses' had to be purged through state intervention which should ensure that the economy functions as close to full employment as possible by adjusting the level of investment and the marginal propensity to consume through a mixture of monetary and fiscal policy. Otherwise, Keynes feared that the appeal of 'state socialism' would overtake the capitalist system.

Keynes placed himself within the ranks of liberals because of his support for individualism, but for an individualism that thrived by ridding itself of the 'spontaneity' of capitalistic individualism and was enriched by state intervention to bring the economy close to full employment. The apparent paradox of this position, of wanting larger state intervention as a condition for the flourishing of individualism, was expressed by him in the following words:

> While therefore the enlargement of the functions of government, involved in the task of adjusting to one another the propensity to consume and the inducement to invest, would seem to a nineteenth century publicist or to a contemporary American financier to be a terrific encroachment on individualism, I defend it on the contrary, both as the only practicable means of avoiding the destruction of existing economic forms in their entirety, and as the condition of the successful functioning of individual initiative. (Ibid., p. 380)

Keynes' Conception of the State

What was striking about Keynes' theory was the implicit assumption he made not just about the system which he assumed to be 'malleable' (an assumption we discuss in detail in a later chapter) but about the state: namely that the state was not part of the 'spontaneity' of the system, but was both willing to intervene in economic life in the interest of society as a whole and was capable of doing so. The state, in short, was an embodiment of social rationality, which could be influenced by wrong theories but scarcely by vested interests. Keynes even refers to the 'common will embodied in the policies of the state', which places the state outside of the spontaneity of the system. Using the language of mainstream economics we can say that state intervention constitutes the intrusion of social rationality into the domain of the economy, which in its absence is governed by the play of private rationality; and it becomes necessary because the play of private rationality does not ensure a socially rational outcome (or an outcome even conforming to private rationality).

This view of a state unfettered by private interests and embodying the common will is explicitly articulated by Keynes when he says, 'the ideas of economists and political philosophers, both when they are right and when they are wrong, are more powerful than is commonly understood. Indeed the world is ruled by little else' (ibid., p. 383). It follows from this that 'if the ideas are correct ... it would be a mistake to dispute their potency over a period of time'.

If the state is more or less unfettered by vested interests but is driven by ideas, then it places an enormous responsibility for social progress on those 'economists and political philosophers' who deal with ideas. In class terms, Keynes sees them as the 'educated bourgeoisie', but he also believes that they are not to be seen merely in class terms, as just narrowly advocating the interests of a particular class. Unfettered by the interests of the class they belong to, they are engaged in the task of developing ideas that would diagnose the problems of society and suggest the correct way forward along which the state can lead society.

There is a similarity here between Keynes' remarks about the 'educated bourgeoisie' and the Marxist idea of bourgeois intellectuals who rise above their narrow class interests and 'see the historical process as a whole', and hence side with the proletariat in its revolutionary effort to emancipate itself and all other oppressed classes. The difference lies in the fact that the Marxist view sees 'correct' ideas being acted upon through the social activity of a class that sets up a specific state for this purpose which is free of the influence of the previously dominant class, while Keynes sees 'correct' ideas being implemented by a state that is *inherently free of all influence* and capable of espousing reason. His two perceptions – of capitalism being 'spontaneous' in the weak sense, and of the state being an autonomous entity that can stabilize it – thus hang together.

This state representing an embodiment of common will and driven by reason, is expected to carry out an ambitious programme, namely the 'socialization of investment' which, Keynes believes, is quite adequate for overcoming the ills of the capitalist system without requiring any further socialization of economic life, including any social ownership of the means of production. Monetary policy or mere fiscal tinkering may not be sufficient to bring the economy to full employment and keep it there: 'central controls to bring about an adjustment between the propensity to consume and the inducement to invest', and that too on a permanent basis, would be required. The level of investment at all times must therefore be such as to bring about full employment which is the social desideratum. This is the essence of 'socialization of investment', and it becomes the responsibility of the state.

There are two assumptions underlying Keynes' theory of the state. One, which we have been discussing, is that the state, when informed by 'correct ideas', is an embodiment of reason and pursues what it believes would achieve social good without being influenced by any narrow class or vested interests. Two, that the government that is actually elected in a capitalist society would be in sync with such a state, i.e. that the people would not get swayed by racist, xenophobic and divisive agendas to elect political parties that would prevent the state from becoming such an embodiment of reason. The appeal of reason, in short, extends to the electorate; it covers the electorate as much as it covers the state functionaries. Or, looking at it differently, 'extreme' political formations remain always on the fringes, and never succeed in displacing those political formations which are more or less amenable to reason from the centre of power.

In the specific context that he was writing, there may have been some basis for believing that the state could carry through the changes he was advocating without much opposition; but the view that the state would always succeed in pushing through an agenda of reasonable change lacks credibility. In a situation of depression and mass unemployment, getting the economy out of such a situation and pushing it towards full employment *makes everyone better off* (until proximity to full employment increases the bargaining strength of workers to a point where capitalists feel threatened). The workers get larger employment and incomes and the capitalists get larger profits; hence there is a Pareto-improvement in society. This may make all classes agree to an agenda of state intervention for improving the level of activity in the economy. Likewise, in a situation of mass unemployment it is likely to be true that an agenda of improving employment will be attractive to the electorate which will elect a political formation committed to such an agenda. Both the assumptions underlying Keynes' theoretical belief, therefore, are likely to have been fulfilled in that specific context of depression and mass unemployment; but generalizing from that context is problematical.

The Cambridge Tradition

Mass unemployment was only one of the problems that Keynes had highlighted as afflicting capitalism. The other was the 'arbitrary and inequitable distribution of wealth and incomes'. Here Keynes suggested that the basic argument till then used for justifying large inequalities lacked any substance, and this was so for two reasons. First, the argument that capital formation required savings and hence a voluntary sacrifice of consumption on the part of those able to do so, which suggested that a more egalitarian distribution of income would lower the rate of savings, ceased to be valid in a world where the economy was demand-constrained. In such a world, excessive *ex ante* savings was the problem, and more *consumption*, such as would arise from a more egalitarian income distribution, would raise the level of activity, and hence the inducement to *invest* and the drive to wealth creation.

Secondly, Keynes believed that the maintenance of full employment in the future would require much lower levels of interest rate, especially in view of the inward movement of the marginal efficiency of capital schedule. This would entail a 'euthanasia of the rentier' and hence a disappearance of the rentier aspect of capitalism, which would also mean that there would be a general lowering of the non-wage share in income.

A rectification of extreme income and wealth inequalities that typically characterized capitalism, however, was not a non-zero-sum game, unlike the overcoming of depression and mass unemployment. There may be no opposition within society to state action for overcoming mass unemployment, for such action would benefit everyone; but there would certainly be opposition to taking away wealth and income from some in order to give them to others, for, no matter how justifiable it may be on theoretical grounds, it would hurt some who would lose by it. A theoretical argument in the first case, that of depression, is backed by the practical support of almost everybody; but a theoretical argument in the second case, while it would command the practical support of many, would be opposed by others. The two cases therefore are vastly different, and a theory of the state which may appear to get validated by the first case cannot be assumed to hold in the second case.

Such a theory of the state however was not exclusive to Keynes. He may have propounded it most emphatically because his programme of state intervention was more far-reaching than that of any of his non-socialist predecessors, but the entire Cambridge School was more or less committed to such a theory of the state. Keynes has to be seen as the legatee of the Cambridge School with Marshall and Pigou as his illustrious predecessors, though he broke with them on theoretical grounds. Pigou, notwithstanding his softness towards socialism, had advocated on welfare theoretic grounds a set of taxes and subsidies which he expected the state within a capitalist system to implement for achieving the social good.

Keynes was a more forthright advocate of state intervention within the same Cambridge tradition. Unlike his predecessors, who had pointed out certain well-known blemishes in the functioning of capitalism, arising for instance from the existence of 'externalities' which the market was intrinsically incapable of taking cognizance of, Keynes saw the capitalist system as being fundamentally flawed. His version of liberalism, which he called 'New Liberalism', advocated that this flaw should be overcome through state intervention.

The 'newness' of this liberalism consisted in the fact that it saw individual freedom not as being encroached upon by such state intervention to overcome the deficiencies of the economic system, but, on the contrary, as being placed on a sounder footing. But an integral part of this 'New Liberalism' was a theory of the state which saw the state as acting in a manner untrammelled by class or vested interests. Such a theory of the state, which his predecessors in the Cambridge tradition had held in a somewhat rudimentary form, reached its apogee in Keynes. Modern 'liberalism' which stands, for instance, for social justice within a capitalist order, must believe in a theory of the state such as what Keynes had enunciated and which therefore suffers from the same lacunae.

Notes

[1] True, even in pre-capitalist societies there is some wage-labour in the form of farm servants employed in agriculture, as we discuss in chapter eight. But forced savings at the expense of a relatively small number of farm servants would hardly give rise to the birth of capitalism.

[2] Keynes did not just recognize money as a form of wealth-holding, but also adduced a powerful and novel reason why wealth is held in the form of money, namely speculation in the market for claims on capital stock. When these claims become marketable, people do not just buy such claims for 'keeps' (and hence with an interest in the enterprise) but largely for speculation, with a view to what their value would be tomorrow, which in turn entails expectations about what the speculators will do tomorrow. Those who believe that the value of the claims on capital stock will fall at a rate greater than the rate of return on such claims will hold money instead of such claims. Liquidity preference therefore depends *inter alia* on speculators' behaviour, which has significant effects on investment, output and employment.

[3] There is a view, quite prevalent these days, that Keynes' conclusion about mass unemployment resulting from the functioning of the market arose because he assumed a fixed money wage; that if money wages are flexible, then the economy will automatically achieve full employment. This is wholly untenable: firms typically have inherited debt commitments in money terms and if there is a fall in money wages and prices in response to the existence of unemployment, then many firms with such inherited debt commitments will go bankrupt, as their cash flows for meeting their debt obligations would have reduced. This will lead to a collapse of employment rather than an increase in employment. See P. Patnaik (2009) for a more detailed discussion.

[4] It may be thought that even when the economy slips below the 'warranted growth path' everybody would continue to invest in every period at the rate of $\pi.\beta.u_0$ which they know will get them to the 'warranted growth path'. But then a firm which invests less, i.e. 'breaks ranks' with others on the question of following this rule, would be better off, since it would then earn profits larger than its investment while others would earn profits less than their investment. Suppose there are two identical

firms and each has to invest 100 for the economy to stay on the warranted growth path. If one firm invests only 90, i.e. breaks ranks, while the other invests 100, then each will earn 95 as profits. In this case the first firm would be better off than it would have been if it had invested 100, since its investment has fallen by 10 compared to if it had invested 100, while its profits have fallen only by 5 (from 100 to 95). It becomes therefore a 'surplus firm' lending to the other which becomes a 'deficit firm'. In a situation where slipping below the 'warranted growth path' strains finances for all by making all into 'deficit firms' in the period of slip (i.e. if the slip is caused by an unexpected shortfall in consumption), the temptation to break ranks and hope to recover the deficit, at least partially, will be strong. And if this thought strikes everyone, then there is no question of investment continuing in every period at $\pi.\beta.u_0$.

[5] As Michal Kalecki, the co-discoverer with Keynes of the 'General Theory', put it: 'Now, capitalists do many things as a class but they certainly do not invest as a class' (Kalecki 1971, p. 152).

CHAPTER EIGHT

Capitalism: Its Specificity and Origins

Let us summarize the argument so far. Capitalism has been seen in two sharply contrasting ways. One sees it as a voluntary coming together of economic agents in an environment of cooperative competition, in which every agent retains agency and therefore enjoys individual freedom. The other sees it as a system of coercion, whose origins lie in petty producers being coerced into becoming wage-labourers in search of employment (which is not available to all), and where each agent is engaged in a process of Darwinian competition that compels him to act in particular ways, and hence robs individuals of agency and causes *universal alienation*. The former perception of capitalism underlies classical liberalism, while the latter informs the Marxian perspective and points to the necessity of socialism for the achievement of individual freedom.

The claim of classical liberalism was that the emergence of wage-labour out of petty production was because both the employer and the labourer thereby became better off compared to earlier; and that this was because they could get a larger output than before on the same plot of land using better technology which could be employed through such an arrangement. We contested this claim in earlier chapters on two grounds. First, if this perception was correct, then we should find an increase in the extent of wage employment being associated with an increase in the level of real wages, but historical evidence for Western Europe shows just the opposite: periods of increase in the extent of wage employment, such as during prolonged booms, were marked by a decline in the real wage-rate. And secondly, no such technological advances raising land productivity to any notable extent, let alone advances not having the property of 'scale-neutrality', actually occurred, at least in Britain, in the period before the mid-nineteenth century.

Neo-classical economics, the other leg for classical liberalism, implicitly adduces not technological improvement but the convexity of the production possibility set as underlying the voluntary evolution of wage-labour. Economic agents coming together in this manner retain, according to this view, their agency and hence individual freedom.

The neo-classical view has serious problems, of which one was exposed by none other than Keynes, who showed that mass unemployment generally characterized the capitalist system and entailed a lack of agency for the individual. Keynes himself saw the state as an embodiment of 'social rationality' whose intervention could achieve full employment, because of which individual agency could actually come to be realized under capitalism. The problem with Keynes' analysis is that, first, the state itself is generally hamstrung in its intervention; and second, genuine full employment can never be achieved under capitalism as it undermines the functioning of the system by making money wages and prices explode, and also by subverting work discipline (a point that holds with regard to every economic theory underlying classical liberalism). Thus, every theoretical system adduced to support the perception of capitalism as a voluntary coming together of individuals, and the corollary that such individuals retain agency and individual freedom, is deeply flawed.

A *Differentia Specifica* of Capitalist Wage-Labour

We shall further continue that discussion in the present chapter. A point about the origin of the employer–labourer relationship however needs clarification here. The binary between two distinct phases, pre-wage-labour and post-wage-labour, is not synonymous with pre-capitalist and capitalist. Even in pre-capitalist societies, for example under feudalism, agricultural workers working for a wage, whether in cash or in kind, had been a common phenomenon. And Keynes' whole argument about sixteenth-century profit inflation engendering capitalism is based on the assumption that there was already a class of workers who were paid money wages that were not price-indexed. The existence of workers, especially farm labourers, therefore, is not necessarily an exclusively capitalist phenomenon, and can be said to pre-date capitalist wage employment.

This is true of India as well. In Mughal India, as mentioned earlier, there was plenty of land available, yet there were farm labourers who worked for a wage. This was made possible by the caste system where the most oppressed castes, the Dalits, were not allowed to till any land over which they could claim exclusive control; they perforce had to work on the land of others within the village for a living. There were cases where they left the village to set themselves up elsewhere as independent cultivators; but then the Mughal troops were despatched to bring them back to the villages which they had left (Habib 2013). The existence of pre-capitalist wage-labour in India, therefore, was sustained by coercion. This coercion was not always explicit; it often took the form of 'custom' and 'tradition'. Underlying such custom and tradition however, and coming into the open only occasionally as the last resort, was violence.

When we discuss the emergence of capitalist wage-labour, therefore, we are talking not just of this pre-existing wage-labour; we are talking, above all, of the emergence of the employer–employee relationship *from within that sector which had earlier seen only self-cultivation*. When the classical liberals talked of the wage-labour arrangement arising from within a system that was earlier characterized by independent production, they were in effect talking of this phenomenon. The point of debate, therefore, is whether there is any tendency for a system of wage-labour to arise from within the womb of independent petty production, *over and above whatever wage-labour may have already existed in the earlier society*, owing to the emergence of a scope for economic gain for both employers and employees.

In the present chapter, we make a critique from a different angle of the classical liberal narrative about the emergence of capitalist wage-labour out of petty production. This critique states, first, that the emergence of capitalist wage-labour is invariably accompanied by the simultaneous emergence of *unemployment*, and that this constitutes the *differentia specifica* of capitalist wage-labour; second, that the creation of unemployment clearly refutes the classical liberal view that capitalist wage-labour, with which such unemployment is necessarily associated, arose out of a voluntary arrangement; third, that any independent petty producer will be most reluctant to voluntarily abandon his land to join the work-force if there is a chance of his becoming unemployed, i.e. if capitalist wage-labour emerges in this full form; and fourth, that this simultaneous emergence of wage employment together with unemployment from out of petty production is what really occurred in history.

The essence of capitalist wage-labour is that it is characterized by competition among the labourers, which entails above all competition between the employed and the unemployed, and hence the existence of a category called the unemployed. Capitalist wage-labour, in other words, necessarily exists alongside a reserve army of labour, which was not the case with pre-capitalist wage-labour.

Capitalism is impossible to visualize without a reserve army of labour; this is because such a reserve army plays a number of crucial roles under capitalism. First, because of the competition it introduces between unemployed and employed workers, it keeps down the real wages so that the rate of profit is not driven down to zero, as Schumpeter (1952) for instance had believed it would. Second, it restricts the growth of money wages and hence contributes to the relative stability of the value of money, without which capitalism, being above all a money-using economy, would be inconceivable (P. Patnaik 2009). Third, it is essential for work discipline under capitalism. No production system is possible without some method of inculcating work discipline among workers. Under feudalism, work discipline is maintained through coercion, through the use of the *monseigneur*'s whip. Under capitalism, where the use of explicit coercion in the process of quotidian production is ruled out, and where the employer and the employee come into a voluntary contract on the market, work discipline is maintained by 'threat of the sack' (Kalecki [1943] 1971), and this threat can have any meaning only if there is an actual army of unemployed workers. (This, incidentally, is why the picture of capitalism in neo-classical economics, which extrapolates from an exchange economy to cover an economy with production, is so inapposite for capturing production under this system: its conclusion that the economy is always at full employment is not only factually, but also theoretically wrong, for if the capitalist economy always functioned at full employment, there would be no work discipline under it and production would be impossible.) Fourth, the existence of the reserve army also provides the cushion with which the economy can start new projects and throw in large numbers of workers without having to divert them from existing employment, thereby causing large-scale disruptions. Capitalism is thus inconceivable without a reserve army of labour.

Indeed the emergence of capitalist wage-labour from the system of independent petty production has always been associated, as we shall see, with the emergence simultaneously of a reserve army of labour, in the sense of unemployed or underemployed workers, or of workers who would be willing to move into employment if jobs were available. This simultaneous creation of both wage employment and unemployment out of petty production, which invariably marks historically the emergence of capitalist wage-labour, is a direct refutation of the classical liberal narrative of this emergence. This is because the emergence of unemployment clearly entails a worsening of the conditions of the earlier producers now rendered unemployed, which no independent producers would voluntarily embrace, even if it is assumed along with classical liberalism that those who are newly employed as wage-labourers are better off compared to their condition earlier.

The simultaneous emergence of unemployment alongside wage-labour, in short, is a clear refutation of the hypothesis that the emergence of capitalist wage-labour was the outcome of a mutually beneficial arrangement. In fact, the creation of wage-labourers out of independent producers, alongside unemployed workers, *cannot be explained by any process other than coercion.* The origin of capitalism necessarily lies in the exercise of coercion. Without this coercive start, capitalist wage-labour specifically could not have arisen with its immanent feature of competition between workers, which, even if suppressed for employed workers through the formation of trade unions, continues to remain in the form of competition between the employed and the unemployed.

Problem with the Voluntary Transition View

This dual formation of wage-labour and unemployment simultaneously, which together constitute the comprehensive category of capitalist wage-labour, explains another phenomenon which has been noted widely and which has puzzled observers for long. This is the fact that independent producers prefer to remain independent rather than work as hired labourers even when their income as labourers would be higher than as independent producers. This has been observed in many parts of the world and was noted by Otto Bauer, the Austro-Marxist.[1]

This phenomenon, as we noted earlier, refutes the classical liberal view of the origin of capitalism that sees its roots in a mutual agreement whereby the independent producer voluntarily becomes a worker because of the higher income being earned as a worker. The commonly observed phenomenon is just the opposite: despite the income of the worker being higher than that of the independent producer, *the latter is reluctant to give up being an independent producer.*

In India, comprehensive information on peasant producers collected under the Farm Management Surveys in the 1950s had shown that if the peasants' labour on their own farms was evaluated at the prevailing wage-rate, then a very large proportion of farms would show a deficit (Sen 1966; U. Patnaik 1987), which suggests that the independent producer would be better off if he or she abandoned being an independent producer and became a labourer. Why does this not happen?

One common answer to this question has been that independence is valued *per se.* People are unwilling to sell their birth-right for a 'mess of pottage' (Hill 1967). Hence, unless the income differential becomes substantial, they would rather linger on as independent producers in order to enjoy their freedom than be at the beck and call of someone else.

This is certainly a valid explanation. There is however an additional, more prosaic explanation for this phenomenon, and this consists in the existence of unemployment alongside wage-labour. The independent producer would compare the return per labour-time he or she gets from being an independent producer, not with the wage-income of an employed worker but with the *expected* income of joining the work-force, reckoning with the probability of remaining unemployed. If the reserve army of labour (assumed for simplicity to consist of only unemployed persons with no income) is 10 per cent of the work-force, then, if the income of the independent producer who puts in a certain amount of work on the land is x and the wage-income of a labourer who puts in the same amount of work is y, even leaving aside the question of the value of independence, the independent producer might be tempted to become a labourer only if $x < .9y$. Hence with x merely less than y if the independent producer does not become a labourer, this should not *per se* be a matter of surprise.

But that is not all. If, for instance, $x = .9y$, then a person will not be indifferent between being a labourer and remaining an independent producer, because there is a risk of being unemployed and hence earning zero income associated with being a labourer; this would deter him or her from ceasing to be an independent producer.[2] The person would require an *additional compensation* to overcome this risk before considering a move from being an independent producer to becoming a labourer working for an employer; and the magnitude of this additional compensation will depend upon his or her attitude towards risk. A person who is *totally risk-averse*, i.e. does not wish to jeopardize his or her living at all, will never move to becoming a labourer.

Since most people, especially at lower levels of income, are highly risk-averse, the temptation to avoid moving from the status of being an independent producer will be strong; when one adds to it the desire for independence, which is valuable *per se*, it becomes clear why people continue to stay on as independent producers instead of becoming labourers despite lower incomes in the former occupation.

A reflection of this fact is found in India in another set of data, namely the income difference between 'attached' (or permanently employed) labourers and 'casual' labourers. The daily wage of 'attached' labourers is *distinctly* lower than that of 'casual' workers. This is because of two reasons: first, in the latter case there is a certain probability of *not* finding employment so that the income of the attached worker has to be compared with the *expected* income of the casual worker; and second, even if the *income of the attached worker is equal to the expected income of the casual worker*, there is a risk associated in the latter case of not finding employment which is absent in the former.

It follows, therefore, that the classical liberal argument that individuals voluntarily agree to an arrangement where they work as labourers by abandoning independent production because of the higher income they get as labourers owing to technological progress, does not hold for two distinct reasons. First, there is a reluctance to abandon independence and become subservient to someone else. Second, because of the existence of unemployment, the wage-rate of an employed worker must be much higher than the return to labour-day by an independent producer to induce such a producer at all to become a labourer, to compensate both for the probability of unemployment and for the risk of unemployment; the technological change adduced by a section of classical liberalism to explain this transition must therefore be quite substantial to make such significantly higher wages possible.

The emergence of unemployment along with the shift to wage-labour, together with the absence of any notable technological progress that could have offered greatly increased incomes to labourers, shows that the narrative of voluntary transition lacks validity. Such a dual creation of wage employment together with unemployment must have occurred only through coercion used against independent producers to *dispossess* them, rather than any voluntary choice on their part.

Coercion as the Origin of Wage-Labour

The act of dispossession is simultaneously an act of appropriation by someone else. This dispossession occurs as part of the emergence of capitalism and capitalist wage-labour, where, instead of the voluntary arrangement emphasized by classical liberalism, we have an exercise of coercion. It is not that pre-existing individuals come together to cooperate as employer and employee within a capitalist arrangement, but rather that the 'individual' itself is formed by the coming into being of the capitalist arrangement that dispossesses former independent producers who lived within a community that gets destroyed.

The process of formation of this uprooted individual who then *competes* for jobs with other uprooted individuals is a carrying forward of the process of formation of *competitive individuals* which had begun through commodity production. The 'individual' as we see the person now is the 'competitive individual', a product of the emergence of capitalism, not a social individual. At the other end, the persons engaged in dispossessing independent producers are also doing so in response to market opportunities, a market where they compete against others similarly engaged. At both ends, therefore, the competitive individual emerges, and this individual is the product of the destruction of a community.

The individual about whom Marx says that Adam Smith and Ricardo 'saw this individual not as an historical result, but as the starting point of history; not as something evolving in the course of history but posited by nature, because for them this individual was in conformity with nature, in keeping with their idea of nature' (Marx 1971, p. 188), was the egotistical or competitive individual that emerges in its full form only with capitalism, except that Smith and Ricardo, as we discuss below, do not see competition for what it really is – a Darwinian struggle.[3] Neo-classical economics was to apotheosize this individual even further by making him totally and intrinsically egotistical by nature.

The contrast here between classical liberalism and Marx is thus quite sharp. Classical liberalism begins with the concept of an already existing individual engaged in pretty production, in Adam Smith a 'jack of all trades'. Capitalism, or the emergence of the employer–employee relationship, entails the coming together voluntarily of these individuals. The competition under capitalism on this view is itself, therefore, based on a voluntary agreement. It is not competition destructive of cooperation but competition cooperatively arrived at, an arrangement of competition arrived at cooperatively, which is why classical political economy (and classical liberalism) sees capitalism as the end of history. 'Henceforth there has been history; in future there will be none' (Marx and Engels 1976). If the workers do not get the best out of such cooperation then that is because of their fault, their tendency to breed too rapidly the moment they become somewhat better off. This is a matter that requires amelioration in a different way, by workers changing their habit rather than by going beyond capitalism.

In Marx, however, the pre-capitalist individual is already located within a network of social relationships; his coming into his own as an individual arises because of the dissolution of that structure and his being set free from access to any means of production. The formation of the individual is simultaneously the formation of competitive individuals and a denial of cooperation, which is possible only with a different mode of production.

Much has been written about the history of this dispossession in Britain through the enclosure movements, which had occurred in two rounds. The sixteenth-century enclosures which did not have the support of the state, as Britain had not had its bourgeois revolution until then, excluded producers from common land which was taken over for sheep farming by the more powerful landed interests. Those producers whose economies got disrupted by this measure had to migrate to swell the ranks of agricultural labourers in the villages themselves, or migrate to towns in search of employment where they faced hostility for having abandoned their traditional callings. The second and far more pervasive episode of enclosures which occurred in the eighteenth century had the support of the state and the concurrence of Parliament, since the bourgeois revolution had already occurred in England in the seventeenth century. This round of enclosures, while ostensibly creating enclosed and bounded private property *universally*, that is, by the big landowners as well as the small ones, also entailed an exclusion from common land of the smaller producers, which disrupted the economy of petty production and forced many to become labourers, failing which they frequented poor houses and wandered about as vagabonds. The immediate provocation behind this round of enclosures was not any particular factor like the enhanced profitability of sheep farming, but the general spread of capitalism and the opportunities for profit-making that it opened up.

The entire history of capitalism consists in carrying the logic of the enclosures all over the globe. The process of exclusion of numerous petty producers from the land, first by making their economies unviable through the enclosure of the 'commons' and subsequently by buying their lands cheap, initially carried out in the metropolitan countries where capitalism developed, was then extended all over the globe. It had a particularly brutal character in the 'new world' where the exclusion of the pre-capitalist producers from land was violent. They were confined to small reservations while the land from which they were excluded was used for the settlement of European immigrants, thereby alleviating to a degree, though by no means entirely, the pain of unemployment back home in the metropolis. This was the pattern in the temperate regions of European settlement such as Australia, America, New Zealand and Canada.

In the tropics, however, a very different form of exclusion from land was practised. This took the form not of dispossession in favour of European *settlers*, since there was relatively little settlement anyway. There was dispossession in favour of moneylenders and landlords, including European planters, because of the introduction of an inflexible tax on *land* as distinct from on *produce*, as for instance Mughal India had, which had automatically adjusted the tax burden to the size of the harvest (Habib 1995).

But the tax itself meant the taking away without any *quid pro quo* by the colonizing power in the metropolis, a part of the independent producer's produce, hence a reduction simultaneously in the amount of goods absorbed within the colony of conquest. It entailed, in other words, not so much exclusion from land of the independent producers (though it also did that as we noted earlier), but above all exclusion *from the products of the land*. Thus, the logic of exclusion from land that capitalism imposed on the individual producers or users of land was universal; its form, however, varied in different parts of the world. It was exclusion from land-use in the metropolis itself through the enclosures. It was a violent version of similar exclusion from land-use in the new world. And it was exclusion from the *products* of land-use in the colonies of conquest. All these, as Marx had pointed out, represented various forms of primitive accumulation of capital.

The Corroding Effect of Commodity Production

Commodity production is the progenitor of capitalism. This is usually interpreted as commodity production introducing differentiation among the petty producers, which in turn leads to some of them moving up to the status of capitalists while others sink to the ranks of labourers. As the foregoing suggests, however, this snail's pace of differentiation is greatly accelerated by a more powerful route through which the introduction of commodity production generates capitalism, and this is by causing the exclusion of petty producers from the commons and making their economy unviable to a point where many of them become labourers in search of jobs.

Long-distance trade plays an important part in this process. We have already discussed in chapter two the specificity of the Marxian notion of a commodity, and the difference between classical and Marxian notions of the commodity. The classical notion sees the commodity as possessing both use-value and exchange-value for both the producer and the consumer. The Marxian notion, however, sees the commodity as being a combination of use-value and exchange-value only for the consumer, or the buyer; for the seller, it is exclusively an exchange-value *and not a use-value* (Kautsky 1903). For the seller, in short, the commodity signifies only the command over so much money; the seller is concerned with its physical and chemical properties only to the extent that it remains saleable, i.e. only from the point of view of the buyer, but not *per se*.

It follows, therefore, that mere exchange does not constitute commodity production. Even exchange that is mediated through money does not necessarily constitute commodity production. Commodity production occurs only when, for one of the parties to the exchange, the commodity represents pure exchange-value, pure command over money, *devoid of all personal relations*.

Such exchange does not usually characterize local trade. A group of buyers and sellers who meet regularly face-to-face and engage in exchange do not constitute a system of commodity production. Such exchange can go on for millennia without having any corroding impact on the pre-capitalist mode of production within which it occurs; this is why in older countries like India and China there has been pervasive exchange, even mediated through money, for centuries without generating any tendency towards capitalism.

The exchange that can have a corroding effect and constitutes commodity production in the authentic sense is one that entails long-distance trade, where supply is for an unknown market shorn of all personal relations and ties (P. Patnaik 2015). Of course, not all long-distance trade necessarily has this corroding effect, nor can it be called commodity production. For instance, long-distance trade that merely constitutes a carry-over of local trade, a mere extension of local trade, can have little corroding effect. But when long-distance trade constitutes the predominant element, not just an extension of local trade, it can have major consequences. And this is especially true when a country gets opened up for long-distance trade, i.e. when long-distance trade occurs quite independently of, and separately from, local trade.

These consequences need not always be towards the development of capitalism. As the experience in Eastern Europe shows, the opening up of profitable long-distance trade in a feudal society can have the effect of tightening serfdom. The so-called 'second serfdom' that came about in Eastern Europe was caused by the attractions of profitable long-distance trade. But in certain circumstances, notably when the feudal structure has been somewhat loosened already, the sudden emergence of profitable long-distance trade can bring about an exclusion of independent producers from the use of common land, rendering many of them unviable and making them move out of villages in search of jobs, which only some succeed in obtaining.

The emergence of long-distance trade also has the effect of causing a differentiation among independent petty producers, with some moving up to the status of capitalists or proto-capitalists and others moving down to the status of labourers. This happens because long-distance trade exposes petty producers to greater risks than local trade and hence greater indebtedness, leading eventually to dispossession of many petty producers. Commodity production, in short, entails greater risk for the petty producers engaged in it, a fact that may not even be appreciated by them initially when they engage in it. In colonial conditions of course, commodity production is forced on the peasantry because of the inflexibility, both in terms of the amount and the timing, of the revenue demand, for the fulfilment of which the peasants have to borrow from traders in the form of advances and are forced to cultivate specific crops. This too results in a differentiation among the petty producers, with some moving up while others move down. The basic point however is this: the collapse of petty production is intimately linked with commodity production, which in turn, when not enforced by the revenue demands of a colonial state, is linked to long-distance trade.

Imperialism as an Abiding Feature of Capitalism

We have seen that the process of exclusion of petty producers from the use of the land to which they had been accustomed earlier, which marked the emergence of capitalism, was also carried out all over the globe in different forms. In the 'new world' it took the form of outright exclusion of the earlier inhabitants from land-use through violence; in the tropical colonies where there was little European settlement, it took the form of exclusion of the colonies from using the products of the land, which were appropriated *gratis* for use in the metropolis.[4] This international exclusion comes under the rubric of imperialism, and *it continues throughout the history of capitalism because a whole range of products produced in these outlying regions are both indispensable for metropolitan capitalism and also un-producible (in adequate quantities and round the year) in the metropolis.*

Such products are not just confined to oil whose centrality for imperialism even today has been widely noted and would be readily conceded. And obviously, Keynes' exclusive emphasis on the inflow of Spanish gold into Europe, no matter whether it was important in initiating capitalism as he believed, was only a part – and an episodic one at that – of an overall enduring relationship between the metropolis and the outlying regions.

While the relationship in the colonial period, though not sufficiently appreciated, is clear, the real question is: how would one characterize this relationship today, in the post-colonial phase of capitalism? With the end of colonialism, obviously, the 'drain' of surplus from the colonies to the metropolis, i.e. the appropriation *gratis* of this surplus in the form of tropical commodities required by the metropolis, has largely come to an end. A certain element of 'drain' still continues, for instance through payments for intellectual property rights, through unequal exchange and such like, but the amount involved is nowhere near the amount involved in the colonial period. Of this amount in the colonial period, Marx, echoing the Indian nationalist writer Dadabhai Naoroji, had written as follows in a letter to Danielson, the Narodnik economist, in 1881:

> What the English take from them annually in the form of rent, dividends for railways useless to the Hindus; pensions for military and civil service men, for Afghanistan and other wars, etc., etc. – what they take from them *without any equivalent* and quite apart from what they appropriate to themselves annually *within* India, speaking only of the *value of the commodities* the Indians have gratuitously and annually to *send over* to England – it amounts to *more than the total sum of income of the sixty millions of agricultural and industrial labourers of India!* This is a bleeding process, with a vengeance!

Of course, much more refined estimates are now available of the colonial 'drain' (U. Patnaik 2017); but it is significant that Marx, just before his death, had come to realize its importance for capitalism. The magnitude of this drain has of course dwindled after decolonization, which raises the question: how then can we still talk of 'imperialism'?

We have seen earlier that imperialism entails the imposition of a squeeze on the working people of the third world, so that the growing needs of the metropolis for products of the fixed amount of tropical and sub-tropical land-mass (fixed, because of capitalism's abhorrence for state activism without which land-augmenting measures are not possible) are met without giving rise to inflationary pressures. The colonial system of using the taxation system for 'draining' away the surplus (which of course was just one of the instruments, the other being the 'deindustrialization', i.e. displacement of pre-capitalist craft producers brought about by the import of capitalist products into the third world) played this role admirably. But the 'drain' implied that the exclusion of the colonial working people from the products of the land-mass they inhabited was *simultaneously an exclusion of the colony as a whole from these products.*

Contemporary imperialism still entails the exclusion of the *working people* of the third world from the products of the land-mass they inhabit, *but not the exclusion of the third world as a whole from the value of the products of this land-mass.* The absence of the 'drain', in short, entails the import of an equivalent value (let us assume this, and ignore unequal exchange and such like) from the metropolis, which means that the third world country does not hand over its produce *gratis* any longer. But the working people of the third world are still excluded from these products, which is how the metropolis gets these products. In fact, the whole neo-liberal arrangement makes this exclusion possible.

The manner in which this happens will be examined in a later chapter. The point to note here is that imperialism, in the sense of imposing a squeeze on the working people of the third world to exclude them from the products of the tropical and sub-tropical land-mass, is as much a feature of capitalism today as it was in the past; in fact, capitalism cannot do without it. This squeeze, which has been called an 'income deflation', gives new meaning to Marx's remark about capital accumulation producing wealth at one pole and poverty at another. This poverty takes the form of nutritional deprivation in the context of contemporary capitalism, which continues unabated despite remarkable technological progress that has occurred in recent years, and which has significant implications for the issue of individual freedom.

Notes

[1] See also Hill (1967).

[2] The standard deviation of the probability distribution of the expected earnings is a measure of risk, while the mean of the probability distribution is the expected (or the 'best guess') income. Even when the 'best guess' income when a person becomes a labourer is equal to what that person earns as an independent producer, the risk associated with being a labourer still has to be reckoned with.

[3] Marx on the whole was insufficiently appreciative of the difference between his own concepts and similar concepts used by classical political economy. The individual that Smith and Ricardo saw as the starting point of history and the individual that Marx saw as emerging from the historical process are not identical, just as the competition in which this individual is engaged, according to Smith and Ricardo, is not identical with competition according to Marx's conception.

[4] It follows from our foregoing discussion that primitive accumulation of capital can occur both in 'stock' and in 'flow' terms, i.e. can take the form of snatching away of assets as well as snatching away of the products of the assets.

CHAPTER NINE

Competition under Capitalism

Karl Marx certainly did not believe in the malleability of capitalism. He could not have made a case for socialism if he had thought that capitalism was malleable enough to be 'rectified' or 'improved' through state intervention. But on why he thought this was the case, the common understanding is one that is quite insufficient.

Sociological Perception of the Limits of State Intervention

The common understanding why Marx thought so is that the agency that was supposed to bring about this 'improvement', namely the state under capitalism, was not itself an independent entity that could act as an embodiment of 'reason', free of the influence of vested interests, in particular class interests, as Keynes had believed. In a capitalist society the state was controlled by capitalists, so that it would not be allowed to act in any way that went against the interests of the capitalists.

This common understanding, which is certainly rooted in Marx's own writings, represents what I call a sociological perception. Such a perception suggests that the state can enforce certain changes but not others. It certainly cannot impose changes that impinge on the fundamental exploitative character of the system. It can even allow changes, within limits and under certain circumstances, that affect the *degree* of exploitation within the system, for the sake of its survival and longevity. But it can never abrogate its exploitative character (whence it follows that even though it may have somewhat greater leeway in intervening in non-zero-sum-game situations like mass unemployment, it can never achieve full employment in the true sense, for that can cause either a reduction in the degree of exploitation or a money wage-price explosion).

Putting it differently, the state generally acts in the interests of the system, and these may sometimes demand that short-term adjustments should be forced on the capitalists for the sake of the long-term survival and health of the system.

There are several hurdles according to this view in the way of a 'reformist' state exceeding its limits. These are in the ideological sphere and in the political sphere. But in case even these hurdles are overcome and the state persists in its attempt to alter the system in a fundamental way, then the standing organs of the state, such as the bureaucracy and the armed forces, would step in to paralyse and eventually overthrow the government that sought to turn the state in this particular direction. Put starkly, if the 'ideological state apparatus' represents the first hurdle against any fundamental change in the system, then the repressive state apparatus represents the ultimate hurdle, overcoming which is the essence of a social revolution that establishes a new state based on new property relations.

I call this understanding sociological because it sees the root of the non-malleability of capitalism not in terms of its inner functioning, its own immanent tendencies, but in the incapacity of the agency that could bring about any change in the system, to do so. And this incapacity arises not because it makes the system dysfunctional in any way, but because the system *for non-economic reasons* constrains the capacity of this agency, namely the state. The non-malleability, in short, arises not from the side of the economic logic of the system but from the side of the external agency. This agency is hamstrung not because it has to confront the economic logic of the system which it would perforce have to disrupt and thereby render the system dysfunctional, but because there are social constraints upon the government manning the state, in the form of electoral pressure, political hurdles and eventually military intervention. The constraints thus are not economic but sociological; they relate to the social coherence of the overall system rather than to the economic logic that drives it.

This way of looking at the constraint upon the ability of the state to 'improve' the functioning of capitalism, what I have called the sociological way, is certainly not incorrect; in fact, it is rooted in Marx's own writings as well as those of other Marxists. But it is only a part of the truth. There is a more immediate obstacle in the way of the intervening state that arises from the economic logic of the system itself and that holds even when there is no threat of the repressive state apparatus coming into play. This has not received the attention it deserves. We discuss it now.

Competition and Agency

Capitalism is essentially characterized by competition. This is not competition as is commonly understood in neo-classical or even in classical economics. In neo-classical economics competition takes the form of *perfect* competition which *ceteris paribus* not only equalizes wage-rates across the economy but drives the special category of income called profits to zero, which therefore rules out any class division among economic agents and assumes perfect social mobility.

Classical economics also recognizes competition but of a milder kind, not 'perfect competition' but 'free competition', where the wage-rate and the profit-rate are equalized across sectors but the latter does not fall to zero. There are, in other words, class divisions (rooted in the kind of considerations we discussed in the first part of this book), and no perfect social mobility. Marx took over this classical notion of competition but recognized an additional feature of it, namely a Darwinian struggle for the survival of the 'fittest'. Among the capitalists this takes the form of incessant attempts to introduce technological progress and reduce the cost of production; likewise, the system is characterized by competition among the workers, which, as we have seen, is the main source of work motivation and work discipline.

Under capitalism, where there is no explicit coercion but formal equality in the market place and voluntary contracts between the capitalists and the workers, work discipline is maintained by the fear of unemployment, for which there has to be some actual unemployment, that is, competition between the employed and the unemployed, and hence, by extension, competition among the employed themselves. Capitalism is thus characterized by the pervasiveness of competition. Immanent in the category of the egotistical, competitive individual is this trait of being driven by a Darwinian struggle. The individual is not created as such by nature; the competition which characterizes capitalism and which is quite different from that visualized by classical economics creates such an individual.

It is because of this competition that economic agents act the way they do: they are *compelled* by competition to act as they do. Capitalism, while *formally* maintaining individual agency, effectively subverts individual agency. Individuals act as they do, not because of their own volition, not because they have the freedom to act anyway they like but choose to act the way they do; it may appear, superficially, that the latter is the case, but in reality they have no choice: if they did not act as they do then competition would drive them out of the position which they occupy within the system. And if economic agents have no choice, then there is no question of their agency.

The role that each individual is compelled to play depends, of course, upon his or her class position. The recognition of universal alienation, of the fact that each individual is compelled by the system to act in a way not necessarily of his or her own volition, does not therefore entail a negation or obliteration of class positions; on the contrary, alienation occurs and the individual is compelled to play a particular role only in the context of his or her particular class position. Competition, especially between the employed and the unemployed, makes workers play the role depicted in Charlie Chaplin's *Modern Times.* Competition among the capitalists coerces each of them to accumulate capital whether they like it or not. The specific role played, in other words, depends on the class position of the individual; but the point is that the individual cannot act on the basis of his or her own volition.

The class position of an individual within capitalist society, in turn, is fixed more or less at the very birth of that society, when the process of primitive accumulation set up the basic dichotomy between the workers and the capitalists, a dichotomy that continues to be spontaneously reproduced over time through the system's own inner logic. The class division in a capitalist society, in other words, emerges in the course of its real history, its genealogy traceable to the moment of its birth. Liberalism's downplaying of classes, therefore, is the other side of its ignoring real history and dealing only with an imagined history where 'social contracts' and 'early and rude stage of society' figure prominently despite having little or no historical authenticity.

Let us, however, get back to our argument. Capitalists accumulate not because they *choose* to do so, but because they are *compelled* by competition to do so. This does not of course mean that all capitalists act identically: while their motivations are identical, their estimations of the consequences of particular actions would differ, making them act non-identically. It also does not mean that they invest all their savings, thus vindicating Say's Law (at least as the average state of affairs through cycles, as many Marxists who rule out the possibility of perennial *ex ante* over-production believe);[1] the fact that wealth can be held in the form of money implies that not all savings are necessarily invested in the form of additions to capital stock. In fact, the compulsion to be careful about investment, about the form in which they hold their wealth, whether in the form of money or capital stock, is itself a product of competition.

With each economic agent acting under compulsion to play out a part, there is an aggregate outcome in the form of certain immanent tendencies of the system. Among these is the tendency towards the centralization of capital, that is, the formation of ever-larger and ever-fewer blocks of capital over time. This tendency underlies the capitalists' drive to accumulate; since in this Darwinian struggle larger capital survives while smaller capital goes under (as the minimum scale of investment required to introduce technological change itself increases over time), every capital is desperate to become larger through accumulation. Likewise there is a tendency towards the destruction of petty producers, especially those engaged in craft production, and of petty traders.

In Marx's discussion of immanent tendencies, there is one unwarranted inclusion and one unwarranted exclusion. The exclusion refers to what has just been mentioned, namely the destruction of petty production, which Marx, concerned with examining an isolated capitalist economy and not one ensconced within a pre-capitalist setting, did not have any occasion to discuss at length (except in passing *inter alia* in the *Manifesto*);[2] it was left to Rosa Luxemburg ([1914] 1963) to do so. The inclusion refers to the tendency mentioned by Marx of an increase over time in the *value* organic composition of capital, whence he derived his falling tendency of the rate of profit. While there is no doubt that over time, the *mass* of the means of production which one worker works with increases, there is no reason to expect that this would necessarily express itself in terms of a rise in the organic composition of capital in *value* terms, as Marx had suggested. It follows that there is no *necessary* reason for a falling tendency of the rate of profit, though it does not follow from this that the rate of profit will necessarily *not* tend to fall; it is simply that nothing can be said *a priori* on the subject.

The point however is this: the immanent tendencies are both the consequence and the cause of each economic agent's being under compulsion to act is a particular way. The individual economic agents then become merely the means through which the system's behaviour manifests itself, the means of realizing the 'spontaneity' of the system. In fact Marx even calls the capitalist, the supposed hero of the drama of capitalism, 'capital personified'. Capital, in other words, works out its immanent tendency through the behaviour of the capitalist, who has little choice in the matter.

An important conclusion that follows from this about individual *freedom* is worth repeating. Under capitalism everybody is alienated, in the sense of being unfree to act as one likes. It is not just the workers but even the capitalists who are alienated. True, the alienation of the capitalists is not identical in nature to the alienation of the workers; nonetheless, universal alienation is a characteristic of capitalism.

It follows then that individual freedom, which the liberal tradition sees as the greatest virtue of capitalism, is actually absent under this system. This is so not just because of material deprivation, that is, not because of the oft-repeated argument that it 'creates poverty at one pole and wealth at another', thereby thwarting the possibility for most people to realize their potential. That is certainly true, but the absence of individual freedom is above all because there is universal alienation, in the sense of people being coerced into acting in particular ways that are not of their choice. A necessary condition for individual freedom, then, is to have a non-'spontaneous' system transcending capitalism.

Marx on 'Combinations'

The discovery of the 'spontaneous' character of the capitalist system is, I believe, one of Marx's greatest scientific achievements, and distinguishes him from his predecessors, though this is not the common understanding of his *differentia specifica.* The common understanding emphasizes the concept of surplus value and the explanation of how a surplus value can emerge despite equivalent exchange in the market as the specific scientific contribution of Marx; and associated with this is his recognition of the significance of the reserve army of labour.

The existence of a reserve army of labour rather than the working of the Malthusian theory of population as the explanation for the fact that wages remain tied to some subsistence level, thereby allowing the capitalists to take the difference between the real wage and labour productivity as surplus value, was a great scientific advance over classical political economy. In fact, some have considered the reserve army of labour as the most important concept introduced by Marx's *Capital.*

But the idea that Marx simply took over the classical theoretical schema, and used it for his own purposes after substituting the reserve army for Malthusian theory, which has also led to writers like Paul Samuelson (1971) calling Marx a 'minor post-Ricardian', misses the real revolution in the analysis of capitalism brought about by Marx. This consisted, in my view, in his perception of capitalism as a 'spontaneous' system, which represented a complete change of theoretical *weltanschauung* (Lange 1963). True, in Ricardo too there is an impersonality about the behaviour of the system; but in Marx this impersonality arises because of the effective denial of any *agency* to the economic actors who are nonetheless engaged in action, involving a loss of individual *freedom*. All Marxian concepts are embedded within this *weltanschauung*.

Marx was not just Ricardo *plus* history. Nor was he simply Ricardo placed within a narrative of history, understood as an 'inversion' of Hegel's narrative, to produce a teleological vision of socialism that differed from the earlier versions of utopian socialism. Marx's concern was about human freedom, *including individual freedom*, and he was aware that this was impossible within a set of production relations that compelled people into acting out specific roles. Human freedom, he saw, required breaking out of the 'spontaneity' of the system, which needed a change in property relations in the direction of socialism.

Socialism was not the inevitable outcome of the working out of history but the condition for human freedom, and hence the desideratum of a quest for freedom through conscious action by people trapped within a spontaneous mode of production (capitalism), which in turn is part of a spontaneous process of history (which Marx called historical materialism).

When workers form associations to overcome competition among themselves, that is the first step towards overcoming the spontaneity of the system. These associations are not just larger supra-individual globules competing among themselves: they do not just replace competition among individual workers by competition among associations, as John Stuart Mill's 'wages fund' theory would have suggested, and which Citizen Weston argued at the International Workingmen's Association, and against which Marx wrote his pamphlet *Value Price and Profit*. They are combinations for workers' struggle against the capitalists.

At the same time, it was actually impossible within the system to abolish competition among workers and bring about a situation where there would only be a tussle between the capitalists and workers. Adam Smith had already pointed out that the capitalists were everywhere in tacit collusion; but it was impossible within the system just to present the colluding capitalists with a collusion among workers. This is because the abolition of competition among workers requires also the abolition of the reserve army of labour (for the reserve army entails competition between the employed and the unemployed), *which was impossible within the system as it would make the system dysfunctional*. The point therefore was to find a way *out of* this system, made dysfunctional anyway by workers' associations in case such associations become very successful. For such a way out, the collective spirit among workers which such associations generated was crucial. They were the first rudimentary steps for going beyond capitalism.

The significance of associations, therefore, lay not just in their capacity to launch economic struggles; it lay, above all, in the fact that they nurtured a collective spirit among workers as a preliminary step in the process of transcending capitalism. In *The Poverty of Philosophy* Marx talks about English economists being puzzled by the fact that workers who form unions for improving wages continue supporting these unions from their existing meagre earnings even when the latter are singularly unsuccessful in obtaining any wage increases; they do so because keeping the union going becomes far more important for the workers than the gain of higher wages. In other words, the associations formed for obtaining gains acquire a significance transcending such profit-and-loss calculations. The association becomes from the point of view of the workers an end in itself, a step beyond an exclusive preoccupation with individual self-interest.[3]

But the associations themselves, not very successful in obtaining higher wages and yet powerful instruments for inculcating a collective spirit among the workers, which itself is a blow against the spontaneity of capitalism, cannot see their way forward towards socialism and take the transitional steps towards it. The need for bringing theory to them, which Marx and Engels had mentioned in the *Manifesto* and which formed such an important role in Lenin's thinking (1902), becomes relevant in this context. The need for this lies precisely in the fact that in a capitalist society the workers are deliberately kept in a state of ignorance, a fact implicitly admitted by Keynes when, notwithstanding his vastly different *weltanschauung,* he too placed his faith in the 'educated bourgeoisie', within which he counted himself, as the initiators of change.

The Domains of Spontaneity and Conscious Praxis

The spontaneity of capitalism covers not just the individual economic agents within it, but the state as well. If the state does not play the role, as it normally does, of supporting and sustaining the immanent tendencies of capitalism and if on the contrary it blocks such tendencies, then the domain of conscious praxis as opposed to spontaneity gets extended thereby, exactly as in the case of associations of workers. The system then spontaneously attempts to assimilate this domain of conscious praxis back within the domain of spontaneity, as distinct from directly using the repressive organs of the state to reverse such praxis as one may think on the basis of the sociological perception.

There is a tendency among many to look at capitalism *exclusively* as being characterized by class struggle. Everything that occurs in capitalism is then seen to be the result of class struggle between organized workers and organized capitalists, each of whom is engaged in advancing its material interests. Such a pure 'class-struggle view of capitalism', however, is erroneous. It obliterates completely the domain of spontaneity and any role that spontaneity plays in the operation of the system. But if spontaneity did not matter and the functioning of the system could be seen only as the outcome of the struggle between the two classes, then we would never have economic crises under capitalism *which neither the workers nor the capitalists want.* Crises arise precisely because of the spontaneity of the system, and this spontaneity is a perennial feature of it. In fact one can say that while the organization of workers seeks to overcome the spontaneity of the system, the organization of capitalists seeks to reassert the spontaneity of the system.

The essential mechanism via which such reassertion happens is the following: as the system becomes dysfunctional because of state intervention to reform it, it brings hardships for *all* and becomes unsustainable. Two possible avenues then open up: one, to press on with further reform in the system; or two, to retreat from the reform already carried out. The pressure for following the latter course becomes all the greater now, because the system can now use repression, not gratuitously but apparently legitimately, for the benefit of *all* to restore the state to its conventional role.

True, if the system is in the midst of a depression and mass unemployment, then state intervention can serve to get the system out of such a state without causing any immediate difficulties; on the contrary, such intervention via 'socializing' investment can benefit all. Even so, usually there is opposition to state intervention even in such a situation, unless that intervention takes the form of inducing the capitalists through all kinds of incentives to invest more (which is typically, however, of little use).

Keynes had misinterpreted this opposition to state intervention as arising because of lack of knowledge on the part of the 'financial interests'. This opposition, he had thought, would disappear once they understood that the theory suggesting that a fiscal deficit 'crowds out' private investment was plain wrong. This belief, that the spread of knowledge would overcome opposition to state intervention, was an erroneous perception on the part of Keynes as subsequent events have shown. The opposition to state intervention for overcoming unemployment, especially through fiscal means,[4] arises not because of ignorance, but because it enlarges the domain of conscious praxis. The state essaying such intervention is escaping the spontaneity of the system, which the capitalists instinctively find unacceptable. Even if state intervention is persisted with despite such opposition and justifies itself by bringing relief to all, its institutionalization as a *permanent* feature of the system revives the struggle between conscious praxis and spontaneity which eventually makes the system dysfunctional.

The emergence of such dysfunctionality, as noted earlier, would present the state that is intervening in the system with a choice: either carry the intervention to an even higher level, or retreat from the level to which intervention has been carried thus far. This advance to a higher level of intervention at every juncture would eventually lead to a transcendence of the system; alternatively, a retreat from the level of intervention already achieved would eventually lead towards a restoration of the spontaneity of the system.

There is, in short, no half-way house, no intermediate stage between capitalism and socialism, no system apparently based on 'reason' and drawing on the qualities of both that society can settle at, which overcomes spontaneity but does not change the property relations underlying capitalism. Analyses such as Keynes' believe in the existence of such a half-way house, which entails a permanent institutionalization of state intervention to overcome the spontaneity of the system, and yet a preservation of the property relations which entails spontaneity. These two domains, however, cannot simply coexist. A 'socialization of investment' without a socialization of the means of production and of economic life cannot survive for long.

Exactly the same can be said about those theories which wish to bring about egalitarian redistribution of income and wealth within capitalism. Here, of course, unlike with mass unemployment in a depression, even the transitional gains for *all* will not be there. While some, no doubt numerically large, will gain by such redistribution, others, fewer in number, will lose. Hence there will be strong opposition from the very outset to such redistribution. This opposition may be overcome and egalitarian redistribution carried through in certain exceptional circumstances, such as when the system is facing an existential crisis, as in the aftermath of the Second World War. But when this happens, the conflict between spontaneity and conscious praxis once again makes itself felt, though perhaps over a longer period of time, and, in complex ways discussed below, brings those pursuing such 'reforms' to a pass where they have either to go forward or to retreat.

Let us examine the ways in which the system becomes dysfunctional through state intervention. If 'socialization of investment' permanently undertaken leads to a permanently high level of employment, then it would lower *ex ante* the degree of exploitation in the system, which would manifest itself as an unending inflationary spiral. In fact, the rate of inflation will go on accelerating over time as people learn to anticipate inflation from their past experience. Accelerating inflation would make the system dysfunctional.[5]

Likewise, if redistribution of wealth and income occurs within any country to any significant extent, then capital will counteract it by moving to some other country where such redistributive measures have not been put into effect. This will cause stagnation and unemployment in the country initiating egalitarian measures, and hence cause hardships to the working people in that country. The point in short is that any significant tinkering with the spontaneity of capitalism causes hardships, ironically, for the workers themselves.

Sometimes the subversion of conscious praxis by spontaneity may be a long drawn-out affair. But the point is that the two cannot coexist for very long. Even when they do appear to coexist, the underlying conflict continues to rage. And since some immanent tendencies of capitalism still continue to work, like the tendency towards centralization and the formation of larger and larger blocks of capital, the state of coexistence gets disrupted after some time with the now larger blocks of capital going outside national boundaries forcing an opening of national boundaries to global capital flows, and hence making the reaction against egalitarian wealth and income distribution that much more effective. This has happened of late when the egalitarian distributional shift introduced by post-war social democracy has been notably reversed in the absence of an agenda of *forward* movement, that is, an agenda of carrying state intervention even further.

Imperialism as a Means of Overcoming Dysfunctionality

The dysfunctionality engendered by the coexistence of the domains of conscious praxis and of spontaneity, can however be kept at bay because of the capitalist region's control over the 'outlying regions', which is the essence of imperialism. In fact this is a crucial role played by imperialism. But imperialism, while muting the contradiction between the domains of praxis and spontaneity, does not eliminate it; besides, as we shall see, imperialism cannot even play this role of muting the contradiction *permanently.*

The successes of the trade union movement in the metropolis in obtaining wage increases in the late nineteenth and early twentieth centuries without throwing the system into dysfunctionality was made possible by turning the terms of trade against the primary commodity producers who belonged by and large to the tropical and sub-tropical colonies and semi-colonies over which the metropolis had control (P. Patnaik 1997).

Kalecki (1954), who had estimated the share of wages in national income in the metropolitan economies to have remained more or less constant between 1880 and 1939 (though there is some scepticism about this constancy hypothesis), had attributed this constancy to the play of two different factors whose effects cancelled one another. One was the rise in the degree of monopoly which would *ceteris paribus* have lowered the share of wages, and the other was a fall in the ratio of raw material prices to unit wage costs which would otherwise have raised the share of wages. The mutual cancellation of these two forces left the wage-share constant.

The mutual cancellation of these two opposite tendencies, however, was not just accidental. The existence of the raw material producers as a class of *price-takers*, which implies that they cannot enforce any particular *ex ante* share on the produce at an expected price which fully incorporates the actually occurring inflation, also prevents the price system from exploding. Otherwise, any rise in money wages in excess of labour productivity which the workers would enforce for raising their wage-share would never succeed in raising wage-share. It would cause a wage-price spiral. And this spiral would cause accelerating inflation over time, as inflation begins to get anticipated by the workers, which would make the system dysfunctional. But it does not do so and the system does not become dysfunctional, because the share of raw material producers who are price-takers gets adjusted downwards to an appropriate extent.

The two mutually opposing influences underscored by Kalecki therefore did not cancel one another accidentally; their mutual cancellation was part of the *modus operandi* of capitalism. That is how the system avoids dysfunctionality even in the face of wage increases or of increases in the mark-up margin.

While their being price-takers is because the raw material producers are located within an ocean of labour reserves, they remain in this position and are brought to this position because of the political control of the metropolis on the territories to which they belong. Such control opens up these territories and their people for encroachment by capital, which on the one hand causes a 'drain' of surplus from the periphery to the metropolis, and on the other, a 'deindustrialization' in the periphery. These twin processes create the large labour reserves in the periphery that turn the raw material suppliers into price-takers.

The fact that control over the outlying regions, which was the essence of imperialism, played the role of keeping down the dysfunctionality within capitalism, does not mean that it can keep playing this role *ad infinitum.* Every adverse shift in the terms of trade against primary producers to prevent an episode of wage-price increase from getting out of control, reduces the share of primary commodities in the gross value of output produced in the metropolis. And such a decline in the share of primary commodity producers reduces the scope for any *further* decline in primary producers' share as a means of controlling price-rise. The role of imperialism in this respect, therefore, is historically self-limiting.

Of course, keeping the system stable by having a group of price-takers is not the only role that control on the outlying regions is called upon to play: imperialism is crucial for capitalism, as mentioned earlier, for an *additional* reason as well (U. Patnaik and P. Patnaik 2016).

Capitalism cannot do without a whole range of goods which it cannot produce within the regions that constitute its base. These are goods specific to the tropical and sub-tropical regions, and include not only minerals of various kinds but also a range of agricultural goods which cannot be produced at all or produced only for a certain period of time in the temperate region where capitalism developed and continues to reign supreme.

These goods are typically subject to increasing supply price, either because their supplies are exhaustible as in the case of minerals, or because they are produced on the tropical and sub-tropical land-mass which is fixed in supply and can be augmented only though measures and practices requiring investment by the local state which capitalism is loath to promote. It obtains its supplies by acquiring control over land-use in the tropics and the sub-tropics, while excluding the local population from the products of this land. As the demand for tropical and sub-tropical products increases in the metropolis this exclusion must correspondingly increase, which means *inter alia* declining per capita food availability in the tropical and sub-tropical regions.

In the colonial period these goods, obtained by excluding the local population from using the land for their own consumption needs, were obtained to a large extent *gratis* by the metropolis, through the so-called 'drain of surplus' effected by using the colonial taxation system. While the end of formal colonialism has put an end to this system of free appropriation of such goods, keeping local demands for the products of tropical and sub-tropical lands restrained through a squeeze on the local population continues. The goods released through such restraint, or other substitute goods producible on that land, are made available in adequate amounts to meet metropolitan demand, so that there are no undue inflationary pressures that could undermine the metropolitan currency or even the currency of the periphery.

It follows, therefore, that immiserization of the working people in the periphery occurs for two distinct reasons: one is the turning of the terms of trade against the primary producers for stabilizing the system in the metropolis; and the other is the reduction in their absorption of the products of the tropical land-mass to satisfy the metropolis' demand for such goods.[6] Such immiserization generates political opposition within the periphery which provides an additional restraint upon the system's ability to stabilize itself at the expense of the periphery.

A Summing Up

Let us now pull together the threads of the argument. Capitalism is not just an exploitative system; it is also a spontaneous system where, in its pristine state, every economic agent is part of this 'spontaneity' and acts not according to his or her own volition but in a manner dictated by that agent's position in the system. The immanent tendencies of the system arise from this spontaneity whose roots lie in the phenomenon of competition. It follows that in this system there is universal alienation and individual freedom is essentially negated. The state under capitalism is generally a part of this spontaneity.

Workers forming associations to fight for better wages is the first break in the spontaneity of the system. The state intervening to control the system in certain circumstances is also a break in this spontaneity. The system's response to any such break is essentially and invariably hostile. It tries to roll back, or weaken as far as possible, the workers' associations; it tries to reassimilate the state back into its spontaneity. Even when an apparently 'reformed' capitalism exists for some time, the underlying conflict remains, with the attempt at reassimilation always going on.

This attempt comes to fruition when the break in spontaneity makes the system dysfunctional after some time. This dysfunctionality is aided by the fact that even within the 'reformed' capitalism, the fundamental immanent tendencies do not cease to operate. Centralization of capital, which is one such immanent tendency, eventually brings to the centre-stage capital of such large size (including in the form of enormous masses of finance capital concentrated *inter alia* in the hands of banks) that it disrupts the apparent stability of the 'reformed' system and brings its dysfunctionality to the fore.

The hardships it unleashes, even on the workers, presents the elements within the state who were behind the 'reforms' with a choice: either carry reforms further forward towards a further socialization of economic life, or roll back the reforms already carried out. This is how Keynesianism was abandoned. The idea of freezing capitalism in a reformed form is a chimera.

This dysfunctionality however can be kept at bay even in a capitalist society where 'reforms' have been superimposed upon its basic spontaneity, if it has control over the outlying regions. Such control was earlier exercised through colonialism. Though colonialism is over, imperialism in a broader sense continues. But this control too cannot be exercised *ad infinitum*, which once more brings the basic dysfunctionality introduced by such 'reforms' to the fore.[7]

This entire perception of imperialism however, again, contrasts with the perception of classical liberalism derived from classical and neo-classical economics which sees such international economic relationships through the prism of mutually beneficial cooperation, a point we shall take up in the next chapter.

Let us come back to the Marxist perception. Imperialism, notwithstanding the fact that it plays a central role for capitalism, though now using means other than what colonialism had done earlier for playing a similar role, has got its limitations compared to earlier. It cannot give capitalism the kind of leeway today that colonialism had given against the dysfunctionality that would be unleashed by 'reforming' capitalism; an important reason for this, we have seen, is the extremely low level to which the share of primary commodity costs in the gross value of output has been driven down in metropolitan capitalist countries.[8]

The scope for internal 'reform' within capitalism today is thus much less than earlier. The basic point here however is that the more proximate obstacle to 'reforming' capitalism arises not so much from repression by the state against those pressing for 'reforms', but from the dysfunctionality arising from the imposition of 'reforms' on the spontaneity of the system, i.e. not from sociological but from economic factors.

Notes

[1] This belief on the part of Nikolai Bukharin was the crux of his critique of Rosa Luxemburg. See Bukharin's piece reprinted in Kenneth Tarbuck, ed. (1972).

[2] Of course, in the discussion of 'Primitive Accumulation of Capital' in *Capital*, vol. 1, Marx talks of the destruction of petty production. But this is done in the context of capitalism's birth, not as a perennial feature of the system.

[3] This, incidentally, is why looking at such associations as individuals forming *coalitions* to promote their self-interests is so completely wrong. Even though that may be the origin of such associations, they soon transcend such characterization.

[4] Intervention through monetary policy is more acceptable because it operates through the behaviour of the capitalists instead of through by-passing them; but monetary policy is quite ineffective in overcoming a situation of unemployment.

[5] The role of the primary commodity producers of the periphery in preventing accelerating inflation in the capitalist sector is discussed in the next section, whence it follows that the widely prevalent proposition in 'mainstream' theory that there is a unique Non-Accelerating Inflation Rate of Unemployment (NAIRU) under capitalism is invalid. But, as discussed below, the potency of this offset to accelerating inflation declines over time.

[6] The distinction between these two reasons can be understood as follows: suppose there was no adverse terms of trade movement for tropical or sub-tropical primary commodities; even then, local absorption of such commodities would have to be curtailed for ensuring larger supplies to meet growing metropolitan demand. That requires a reduction in the *level of activity* in the periphery, the way colonial deindustrialization had induced. In *addition,* if there is a rise, say, in the degree of monopoly in the metropolis which raises the profit-margin there, this would cause a fall in terms of trade for the tropical and sub-tropical primary commodities which would immiserize the peasants.The working people as a whole suffer in both cases.

[7] This point about the role of imperialism in keeping at bay the contradictions of capitalism is discussed further in the next chapter.

[8] The fact that the role of imperialism to keep at bay the dysfunctionality of the system arising from praxis declines over time, *does not mean that imperialism becomes unnecessary for capitalism.* There are, in short, two separate issues that we must distinguish between. One relates to the need of the metropolis to obtain tropical and sub-tropical products, the demand for which increases with capital accumulation, without creating undue inflationary pressures either in the metropolis or in the periphery itself; the other issue relates to the need of the metropolis to stabilize its economy in the event, say, of higher wage demands, by turning the terms of trade against the periphery so that metropolitan capitalism does not become dysfunctional. Imperialism's role in achieving the second objective declines over time (as does its role of providing a market for metropolitan products). But imperialism continues to be crucial for the first role.

CHAPTER TEN

Imperialism or Economic Cooperation?

The basic universe of analysis in both classical and neo-classical economics is a closed capitalist economy with only workers and capitalists, and a state whose primary function is to ensure that the rules of the game are followed. Whatever is said about international trade is really an extension of this analysis rather than in any way fundamentally altering it. Not surprisingly, international trade, like all exchange in the market, is essentially seen to be beneficial for all those who engage in it, and hence for the countries to which they belong. This claim of trade being beneficial flies in the face of historical evidence, but it has had not only remarkable durability but also remarkable success, as is evident from the fact that it provides the theoretical underpinning for the WTO agreement to this day.

Put differently, just as the domestic capitalist economy was seen by these strands of economics to be characterized by a form of implicit cooperation between individuals despite its competitive appearance, with economic agents coming together voluntarily to set up the arrangement we call capitalism and gaining from this act of coming together, likewise, international trade, though occurring within a competitive setting, was seen as a means of realizing international cooperation from which all participating countries gained. There was no such thing as oppression or exploitation of one country by another through international trade.

This had an important implication. In colonies of settlement the local inhabitants were stripped of their land, but this was a once-for-all development; by contrast, in colonies of conquest where there was not much settlement from the metropolis, the impact of domination of these colonies manifested itself through trade relations. Therefore, the view that international trade benefited all participating countries meant a denial of economic 'imperialism' vis-à-vis the colonies of conquest; and since the once-for-all snatching of land from local inhabitants in colonies of settlement did not entail any expropriation from them on a *continuing* basis, such as what an unequal relationship of the sort captured under the term imperialism would have entailed, the view of international trade benefiting all meant in reality a total denial of the phenomenon of economic imperialism altogether.

Imperialism on this view could be seen at best only as a *political* phenomenon manifest in the fact that self-rule did not exist in the colonized countries. The political control exercised over them *could* of course entail economic oppression, but only if it either caused a trade pattern different from what should otherwise have obtained in the absence of political control; or if it left the controlled countries with *negative* gains of trade, that is, simply filched commodities from them. But the first possibility was one for which there was no theoretical scope either in classical or in neo-classical economics, since it would be inoptimal from the point of view of the metropolis; and the second possibility was one for which political control rather than trade *per se* would be held responsible, and there was little evidence according to classical liberalism of its occurring in the normal course anyway (that is, outside of the period of rapacious rule by mercantile companies). As a result, the real-life phenomenon of economic imperialism as it obtained in the normal course was perceived ironically as economic cooperation between countries.

A Critique of Ricardo's Theory of Comparative Advantage

Adam Smith, we have seen, had sympathized with the plight of Bengal in the late eighteenth century which was being drained of its surplus, citing it as an instance of a land in decline; but this, according to him, was a result of the rapacity of the East India Company, a monopoly trading company of the pre-capitalist era. Rule by the British crown as in the American settler colonies, by contrast, was associated by him with growing wealth. The erroneousness of this perception of Adam Smith has already been discussed by us earlier, and we shall not dwell on it any further here.

The basic theoretical foundation for all subsequent discussion on international trade that underlay the classical liberal perception was laid by David Ricardo ([1817] 1951) with his theory of comparative advantage. Taking for simplicity a two-country case, this showed that the total output, taking both countries together, would be vector-wise larger with international trade, so that each could become better off through having access to a vector-wise larger bundle of goods. There was thus a real solid reason for international trade that conferred a benefit on both countries engaged in it. This fact explained international trade and also provided a normative justification for it.

To prove his point, however, Ricardo chose an example that was palpably fallacious and did not actually prove his point. The example involved two countries, England and Portugal, each of whom produced two goods, cloth and wine. Since England had a comparative advantage in cloth production, in the sense of having a lower cost ratio relative to wine than Portugal, its specializing in cloth and Portugal's specializing in wine, and England's trading its cloth for Portuguese wine, would make both countries (Pareto-wise) better off; each would have a vector-wise larger bundle of goods, and this would be true even when one of the countries could produce *both* goods cheaper than the other.

The problem with Ricardo's example, however, is that *England in real life can never produce any wine* (U. Patnaik 2005); and if one of the trading countries cannot produce one of the traded commodities, then comparative advantage *neither explains trade nor provides a normative justification for trade.* The fact that it does not explain trade is obvious, since if a country cannot produce one of the goods then the cost of producing that good in that country simply cannot be defined. And if trade does take place, then the bundle of goods, taking the two countries together, *can never be vector-wise larger*, which makes Ricardo's argument invalid. This is because if, say, England's pre-trade output of cloth and wine (assuming full utilization of resources) was x_1 and 0 respectively, and Portugal's y_1 and y_2, then with trade, Portugal will increase its wine production by reducing cloth production, which will *reduce* total cloth production in the two countries taken together while increasing total wine production. With one commodity's total output (taking both countries together) having declined while the other's has increased, there is no vector-wise increase in total output as Ricardo had claimed; this invalidates his normative justification for trade.

The problem here is of much wider significance. Much of the trade historically between the global North and the global South has taken the form of an exchange of primary commodities for processed goods. But most of these primary commodities are producible only within the global South, which coincides almost entirely with the tropical and sub-tropical regions of the world, and *are simply not producible in the global North* (which largely coincides with the temperate region) that is incapable of growing tropical crops, either at all, or all the year around, or in adequate quantities for its own requirement. This trade, therefore, can neither be explained by comparative advantage nor be normatively justified by it, exactly as the trade between England and Portugal could not be despite Ricardo's claim.

In fact, while the tropical and sub-tropical regions can produce *both* primary commodities *and* processed goods, and while the temperate lands can produce only the latter, there is no compelling reason for the former regions to trade with the latter regions where metropolitan countries are located. And Ricardo's claim that 'cloth' could be produced cheaper in England than elsewhere may have been momentarily true for his time, since England is where the industrial revolution had originated; but it has no validity whatsoever once other countries, including those in the tropical and sub-tropical regions, 'catch up' with the English technology of cloth production.

Thus, 'comparative advantage' neither explains nor justifies trade between these two regions. But suppose we abandon the term 'comparative advantage' and simply look at trade between the two regions, with one region specializing in primary commodities and the other in processed goods, as being merely advantageous at the moment for both. The tropical and sub-tropical region may exchange locally produced primary commodities for imported manufactured goods rather than locally produced ones, simply because imported manufactures happen to be cheaper (in terms of primary commodities). Why can't trade beneficial to both regions take place on this basis even if we eschew all talk of comparative advantage?

Here, however, we come to a second problem with Ricardo's proposition. In Ricardo's presentation labour was the sole primary input; but in real life there are other inputs, notably land, which have to be considered when we are talking about agricultural primary commodity production. If a country decides to import cloth (as it is cheaper in terms of say corn) than locally produced cloth, the displaced workers from local cloth production would not find employment in corn production *and would remain unemployed, if corn production cannot be augmented because of the absence of any unutilized land.*

Something of this kind actually happened in history. When cheap British cloth poured into India in the early nineteenth century after the industrial revolution, it displaced local handloom weavers. Since land area was limited and its augmentation required investment on a scale that only the state could undertake but was unwilling to do – because it was a colonial state, and more generally because of the opposition on the part of the (metropolitan) capitalists to state activism of this kind – the displaced weavers simply crowded into agriculture as a vast underemployed and pauperized mass. This generation of unemployment and pauperization through 'free trade' is referred to as 'deindustrialization' in Indian nationalist writings, and was mentioned earlier as a significant factor behind the emergence of modern mass poverty.

It may be thought that even though those producing local manufactured goods (crafts) get displaced, others (the peasants, for example) get cheaper cloth and hence are better off. While the country as a whole does not get a vector-wise larger amount of goods, some within the country become better off through trade even as others are pushed into poverty and unemployment.

This argument, however, is a temporary and partial argument. If some get pushed into unemployment and poverty, then they increase the pressure on available land which raises rents and lowers real wages, so that *the entire working population, including even the peasants and agricultural labourers* (those who had been earlier employed in agriculture or in corn production according to our example), becomes worse off. A sufficient condition for any particular person or group becoming better off in this situation, through cheaper imports of cloth, is that the corn income of this person or group should not go down because of the rise in poverty and unemployment that increases the pressure on land; and this condition would be satisfied primarily in the case of surplus earners (landlords, moneylenders and capitalist farmers). They, if anything, would experience a rise in their corn incomes because of the rise in rents and fall in wages as displaced craftsmen are thrown on to land. But the corn income would decline for the rest of the population, that is, for the entire working population. There is thus no normative case for importing cheaper cloth even in this situation, unlike what Ricardo had postulated.

Thus, international trade where the tropical and sub-tropical regions specialize in primary commodity production while the temperate region specializes in the production of processed goods, which is what it has been for well over two centuries, must necessarily involve coercion against the working population exercised by the metropolis supported at best by the surplus earners in the periphery. Ricardian comparative advantage, whether in the original or in some diluted form, cannot explain the trade pattern; on the contrary, it serves to camouflage the fact that coercion lies at the core of trade and of a relationship of inequality between countries that is captured by the term imperialism.

There is a further issue with the Ricardian theory which is of general importance. If one of the countries has an import surplus that generates unemployment by causing a deficiency of aggregate demand (not because of the absence of land as in the discussion above), then too it would be inadvisable on its part to follow free trade on the basis of comparative advantage. Protecting the economy, reducing imports and raising domestic production of the imported good would increase employment in the economy. Ricardo did not foresee this problem because he accepted Say's Law that rules out involuntary unemployment arising from a deficiency of aggregate demand.

In other words, underlying Ricardo's argument is the presumption that (assuming government budget to be balanced) since it must be the case that

I + X = S + M .... (A)

if M happens to be greater than X for any country, its domestic investment and savings would automatically adjust in such a manner that the equality (A) would be satisfied *at full employment*. But once we recognize the invalidity of Say's Law, *which is the same as recognizing that the money-commodity is held not only for transaction purposes but also as a form of wealth,* the normative significance of free trade disappears for *this reason as well,* in addition to the other reasons mentioned earlier. If, say, I is given in any period in a country (because expectations about the future dictate only that much investment), then an excess of M over X would simply mean a reduction in S which will come about through a reduction in output and employment. Immediately, it may be thought, there would be an outflow of the money-commodity to settle the trade imbalance, which would reduce the market prices of goods and of labour (if we abstract from oligopoly and price-fixing); and that this cheapening of domestic goods will increase their international demand restoring full employment (as Hume had argued).

This argument, however, has two obvious lacunae. First, it assumes that money plays exclusively the role of a circulating medium, not a form of wealth, which, as we have seen, is both logically and empirically untenable. If money is a form of holding wealth, then an outflow to settle the trade deficit need not lead at all to a fall in money wages and prices since there is no reason to expect a fall in the quantity of money used as the medium of circulation.[1] And secondly, since producers have inherited debt commitments in money terms, even if there is a fall in money wages and prices, it would drive many of them to insolvency; this would reduce rather than increase employment.

Thus, starting from full employment, if a country opens itself to trade, and the effect of doing so is to generate unemployment because of an import surplus, then the country would be much better off protecting itself. This means that even if Ricardian comparative advantage dictates complete specialization, the country will be better off producing some amount of the good in which it does not have comparative advantage. Comparative advantage once again loses its normative significance.

It follows from the foregoing that in a world where comparative advantage has no normative significance and does not benefit a country in the manner suggested by Ricardo, but in which trade takes place nonetheless in a manner analogous to what comparative advantage would predict, then it must be that this trade occurs under coercion. Even when such trade, while causing unemployment, does not harm the population of the country in its entirety but is beneficial for a segment of the population which gains because of access to the cheaper imported good, it must nonetheless be based on coercion since this segment typically consists of a narrow stratum of surplus earners who connive with the metropolitan country to keep the country's market forcibly open. And in a world where there *is* coercion behind trade, to justify such trade through a theory of comparative advantage whose assumptions do not fit the case is to present imperialism (that invariably underlies this coercion) as voluntary cooperation; it amounts to (not necessarily consciously) a prettification of imperialism.

A Critique of Neo-Classical Trade Theory

The neo-classical strand of economics also presents all trade as mutually beneficial, and hence camouflages the effect of deindustrialization brought about by the coercion imposed by imperialism. But while projecting all trade as mutually beneficial, it argues along lines different from Ricardo's. Ricardo had talked of different countries having different production coefficients, in his case unit labour coefficients. Neo-classical economics, by contrast, believes that all countries have the same 'production function', i.e. the same set of techniques of production, but different 'factor endowments'.

Production in the neo-classical conception is not the result of the application of labour to produced means of production as in classical economics, but the outcome of the coming together of different 'factors of production'. Factors of production can be combined in different proportions, each such combination constituting a technique of production; and there are always plenty of such techniques of production. The techniques of production available to all countries engaged in trade are identical, but since their factor endowments differ, they can profitably engage in trade.

Each country is on its production possibility frontier, with all factors fully used up even when it is in a state of autarky, but the price-ratio between goods that prevails domestically is naturally different from the price-ratio at which the country can trade. At the price-ratio prevailing internationally, if the country engages in trade by producing a different bundle of goods from what it would produce under autarky (a bundle appropriate to that price-ratio) and then trades it, it would obtain a vector-wise larger bundle of goods than under autarky. In the worst-case scenario, the bundle of goods it can obtain through trade will not be vector-wise larger compared to the state of autarky, and this would happen in the exceptional case where its price-ratio under autarky happens to be exactly the same as the international price-ratio.

The question of the country not getting a vector-wise larger bundle of goods through trade than under autarky simply does not arise according to this conception because in such a case the country would not trade at all. The basic presumption behind this theory, in other words, is that trade must be beneficial, for otherwise countries would simply not enter into it.

Much has been written on the neo-classical approach in general and the approach to trade in particular, and we need not repeat all that here, especially since some mention of it has already been made earlier. We shall make just one point: the idea of 'factor endowment' would make some sense if we were talking of 'factors' that were given by nature and were measurable in their own natural units. But when the relative 'factor endowments' can be altered because the 'factors' consist of produced goods, trading on the basis of any given 'factor endowment' is patently inoptimal, since it freezes a particular production pattern when the whole idea is to change it by changing the 'factor endowments'. A country will be deterred from producing a good if it imports that good; it will produce more of it only if it takes steps to stop the import of that good. Hence the idea of trading in accordance with relative factor endowments makes no sense; the idea instead must be to change the factor endowments, and trade would come in the way of such change.

The neo-classical approach fails even as a logically coherent approach since, in the case of produced means of production, endowment must be defined as a value-sum; and in such a case, the properties attributed to the production function by neo-classical economics simply do not hold, as we saw in chapter six earlier. There would be no monotonic relationship between, say, the capital–labour ratio and the wage–profit-rate (w–r) ratio, with the two being positively associated, as is required for the validity of the neo-classical theory.

From our point of view, however, there is a further basic problem with this theory. It presumes that unless trade is beneficial, it would not occur at all; the question of forced exchange or forced entry into international trade does not enter the picture. This approach therefore simply rules out the entire spate of unequal relationships, deindustrialization or drain of surplus by assumption. It negates imperialism simply by making the assertion that it cannot exist. This is palpably absurd for the colonial period, but it is absurd even for the contemporary world where we have independent governments. These independent governments, ironically, are *compelled into free trade* by conditionalities imposed by the Bretton Woods institutions on the strength of a theory (the neo-classical one) whose basic rationale is derived from the presumption that there is *no compulsion to trade.*

When a country is compelled to undertake free trade, whether by a colonial government or by the IMF, the denial of imperialism that trade theories advanced by classical and neo-classical economists engage in can no longer be sustained.

Free trade under colonialism, through deindustrialization, caused mass impoverishment, which could not have been possible except under duress. By pretending that there is no duress, by suggesting a trade theory that closes its eyes to such duress but underscores the role of trade as a mutually benefiting exchange, both Ricardian and neo-classical economics implicitly (not necessarily consciously) play an apologetic role.

Keynes on the Market Motive for Imperialism

With Keynes, for the first time, there is the recognition of a possible role of imperialism for metropolitan economies. This is both because Keynes was writing in the shadow of the Bolshevik revolution that had highlighted imperialism and inter-imperialist rivalry underlying the First World War and he had to reckon with the reality highlighted by the Bolsheviks; and also because at a theoretical level Keynes' rejection of Say's Law, and his consequent recognition of capitalism being not just occasionally but almost perennially demand-constrained, had created the scope for recognizing the role of imperialism.

Keynes himself makes a brief allusion to imperialism (Keynes 1949, p. 382). He suggests that the economic regime of the Gold Standard that meant fixed exchange rates and balanced budgets, which characterized much of nineteenth-century capitalism right until the First World War, ruled out any policy intervention to increase the level of activity. The only weapon available to metropolitan economies for increasing domestic employment was to capture external markets through imperial ventures which gave rise to struggles among them. But once his suggestion for socialization of investment through government intervention is accepted, metropolitan capitalism would be able to rid itself of this necessity of seeking foreign markets, and hence of struggles between capitalist powers for acquiring such markets.

As a matter of fact, Keynes was way off the mark. The entire period between the Crimean War and the First World War was remarkably free of any serious conflicts between European capitalist powers. The only major wars in this period were the wars of Italian and German Unification, which of course were quite different from imperialist wars. The reason was simple: Britain, as the leading capitalist country, kept its own markets open to rival capitalist economies while itself penetrating colonial markets to balance its trade. In fact, not only did it manage to balance its trade, it even used the 'drain' from the colonies to export capital to the very countries with which it had a trade deficit, namely the newly industrializing countries of Europe and the 'New World', to effect a massive diffusion of capitalism. It is as if these rival economies, which did not have colonies of their own to match Britain, had access to British colonies and therefore did not feel handicapped in the matter of finding markets.

But Keynes' recognition of the role of colonies for providing external markets is significant. In fact, it is the first instance of a recognition of the role of imperialism by a mainstream economic theorist (which J.A. Hobson [1902] the major English theorist of imperialism was not). Keynes, however, recognizes only the market motive for imperialism, not its role in acquiring essential primary commodities that simply would not be available otherwise. Because of this partial recognition on his part, once the state had started managing aggregate demand the need for imperialism, he could argue, would disappear. By the same token, Keynes did not recognize any coercion behind the 'normal' trade between the global South and the global North, that is, trade that would occur once the need for external markets to boost aggregate demand had disappeared, even though the former was confined to primary commodities and the latter produced processed goods. As a result, he did not detect any imperialism in the 'normal' international trade; by inference, he saw 'normal' international trade as being voluntary and hence in general to mutual benefit.

True, in his 1933 essay for *The Yale Review,* he did not endorse free trade, but not because of any recognition that free trade under normal circumstances entailed an unequal relationship between countries that was sustained by coercion. Hence, in a situation where the need for external markets has disappeared, Keynes more or less accepted the trade theory that neo-classical economics propounded, a theory that saw trade relations as being based on cooperation between countries.

Marxist Writings on Imperialism

Marx did not say much about imperialism in his analysis of capitalism in the first volume of *Capital*, the only volume he himself prepared for publication. References to the phenomenon are strewn across this volume and all the others; but it does not figure explicitly as an analytical entity. In the third volume of *Capital* there is a reference to colonial trade among the counteracting tendencies to the falling tendency of the rate of profit; and some have tried to construct theories of imperialism from the other counteracting tendencies mentioned by Marx, but these see imperialism essentially in a *functional* light.

There is, however, an underlying perception throughout Marx's writings, starting from the *Communist Manifesto*, that capitalism has a global reach; that different countries participate in trade not by calculating their gains and losses, with the choice left to them to withdraw from trade if the losses become too heavy, but rather because of the overwhelming power of capital that draws countries to the vortex of world trade. As Marx and Engels write in the *Manifesto*:

> All old established national industries have been destroyed or are daily being destroyed. They are dislodged by new industries … that no longer work up indigenous raw material, but raw material drawn from the remotest zones, industries whose products are consumed not only at home, but in every quarter of the globe. (Marx and Engels 1976, p. 188)

This perception, whether or not there is any explicit mention of it in Marx's other writings, defined Marx's entire understanding of international trade.

There are four aspects of this perception that deserve attention. First, unlike in Ricardo or the neo-classicals, engaging in trade on this perception, as already noted, is not based on any calculation of gains and losses; it is rather the spontaneous tendency of capital to draw all countries into the world market. Second, this spontaneous tendency would mean that countries reluctant to enter into world trade would be forced to do so. This means that imperialism, in the sense of the exercise of economic coercion by one country upon another, is rooted in the spontaneous tendency of capital. Third, since participation in international trade is imposed on some countries by others, it is not necessarily the case that all countries benefit from it. In fact, Marx and Engels' reference to the destruction of 'all old national industries' already incorporates the case of one country's national industry being destroyed by the products of another, or what we have called deindustrialization, with its associated economic distress. The fourth aspect, pertinent from the point of view of the argument of this book, is that the network of international trade relations is not based on cooperation between consenting participants, as classical and neo-classical economics would suggest, but on coercion and exploitation that arise not out of any malice but on account of the spontaneous tendencies of capital.

This perspective, however, mentioned in general terms in the *Manifesto,* is not developed in *Capital.* We are only left with a general perspective but not how exactly it comes to get realized, that is, how exactly the human agents through whose actions capital realizes this project of dominating the world come to act the way they do. Marx, by his own admission, had kept his discussion of trade issues for a subsequent volume, but it never got written. It is only with the later Marxist writers like Luxemburg and Lenin that there is more extended discussion of how imperialism constitutes a spontaneous tendency of capital.

Luxemburg's argument, erroneous in the original form in which it was advanced but having a core that is now (after the Keynesian–Kaleckian revolution) recognized to be valid, basically suggested that accumulation in a closed capitalist economy is impossible; that unlike in Marx who had put forward a picture of accumulation as an exchange between two departments of the capitalist economy, one producing means of production and the other producing means of consumption, accumulation under realistic assumptions could occur only through sales from the capitalist to the pre-capitalist sector. She had originally argued, incorrectly, that the entire surplus value produced in the capitalist sector had to be realized through sales to the pre-capitalist sector; but after Kalecki's work (1962) we now know the correct argument to be that without an exogenous stimulus, of which sales to the pre-capitalist sector constitute the pre-eminent example, a closed capitalist economy would settle down at a state of simple reproduction or at a stationary state. Capitalists therefore would not leave the pre-capitalist sector untouched; on the contrary, there would be pressure from them on the capitalist state to open up the surrounding pre-capitalist sector to trade, so that capital accumulation can proceed without getting halted.

As the pre-capitalist sector still left untouched by capitalism kept shrinking competition among capitalist countries for this shrinking remainder, according to Luxemburg, became more and more intense, which explained the First World War as an expression of this intense inter-imperialist rivalry. This last point, similar to Keynes' later argument, is invalid for the same reason that Keynes' argument is invalid: each capitalist country does not need a separate pre-capitalist appendage of its own; as long as the leading imperialist country, Britain at that time, which encroaches into the pre-capitalist sector, keeps its own market open for its rivals, they do not need separate empires. There was therefore no reason for an increase in the intensity of inter-imperialist rivalry unless there was an apprehension of Britain closing its markets to its rivals, of which there was no indication.

Lenin's theory ([1917] 1976) addresses this very question, of explaining inter-imperialist rivalry, by moving away from the exclusive focus on trade and the search for pre-capitalist markets to the quest for 'economic territory' in general; it locates the agency for this quest in a new category called finance capital that comes into being through the emergence of monopoly in the spheres of banking and industry, and the fusion of the oligarchies in both these spheres and their developing close relations with the state personnel. The rivalry between these rival financial oligarchies for economic territory explains, according to Lenin, the need to repartition through wars an already partitioned world, of which the First World War was a manifestation.

Lenin's theory however confined, in line with J.A. Hobson's perception, the term imperialism only to the monopoly phase of capitalism. It did not go into the question of the immanent tendency of capitalism to have a global reach *throughout its entire life*, including in its competitive – that is, pre-monopoly – phase.

Luxemburg's and Lenin's theories, notwithstanding their restricted scopes – one falling short in its explanation of the First World War, and the other exclusively focused on the conjuncture underlying the First World War and therefore not covering the earlier period – underscored the Marxist perception expressed in the *Manifesto* that capitalism's global reach is achieved by coercion, by forcibly breaking down barriers against the encroachment of capital, as the outcome of an immanent tendency of capital. This global reach is covered under the term imperialism; and the Marxist perception sees imperialism, unlike both classical and neo-classical economics, not as an expression of international cooperation from which all countries benefit, but as one of domination of one segment of the globe by another, of the countries belonging to the periphery by those at the core of capitalism.

We thus once again encounter the same contrast in the sphere of international economic relations. Classical and neo-classical economics, which underlie liberalism, see the architecture of capitalism as built upon the voluntary consent of economic agents – whether individuals or countries – who benefit from it, rather than as standing above the economic agents and driving them in accordance with the immanent tendencies of capital.

Of course, the denial of individual freedom in the two contexts, in the metropolis where the capitalist mode of production prevails and in the outlying regions which are tied to it but where the capitalist mode of production itself is not significant, takes different forms. In the metropolis, we have seen, it takes the form of denial of individual agency, since all individuals are engaged in a process of Darwinian competition against one another, whose actions therefore are not of their own volition but are in conformity with the dictates of the system. In the periphery, even though the encroachment of capitalism gives the 'individual' a legal existence which it had scarcely enjoyed earlier, it is not just the Darwinian competition typical of capitalism that gradually enmeshes the individual; the limit to individual freedom is far more direct. There is of course mass unemployment, and growing poverty; but in addition there is the indignity of being 'colonized', of being racially or ethnically victimized, all of which follow from the fact of political control exercised by the metropolis and which continue even after *formal* political control ends (a point we discuss later): no individual can be free if the country he or she belongs to is palpably unfree. The constraint on individual freedom under capitalism therefore arises in two different ways in the two contexts.[2]

When the country becomes politically free of metropolitan control, there is a brief interregnum when a *dirigiste* regime is introduced, which does not conform to classical capitalism (Kalecki 1972a). But the introduction of neo-liberal 'reforms' pushes these economies towards classical capitalism and hence necessarily towards metropolitan dominance, but this time in conjunction with domestic big capitalists and without any explicit political control by the metropolis. The question of freedom under the neo-liberal regime will be examined in chapter twelve below.

Notes

[1] Even if we do not invoke the Hume mechanism and simply assume that money wages and prices fall whenever there is unemployment, this fact too would not act in an equilibrating direction. It will simply give rise to a continuous fall in money wages and prices in both countries as each implicitly vies with the other in pushing unemployment onto the other.

[2] Marx had also made the point that no individual can be free if the country to which he or she belongs *oppresses* another, which, though rarely recognized, is of profound significance. This would make the individuals of the advanced capitalist countries unfree for *two* reasons: first, as argued in this book, they lack agency; and, second, they are also inhabitants of countries whose capitals oppress other countries, even though they themselves are not responsible for this oppression.

CHAPTER ELEVEN

Capitalism in Its Spontaneity and Appearance

Let us recapitulate the argument until now. The liberal tradition sees capitalism as emerging through a voluntary coming together of individuals. Even wage-labour is seen not as a result of dispossession of some petty producers, but as a voluntary arrangement entered into by some petty producers with other producers. International trade, likewise, arises from countries entering voluntarily into trade with one another from which all of them gain, rather than from any exploitative relationship between them as theories of imperialism would suggest. Capitalism, it would follow, is not only conducive to individual freedom but is based upon it; it is in essence a cooperativist arrangement among individual agents.

As against this, we have the Marxian notion where capitalism emerges through the exercise of coercion against some petty producers who are dispossessed from their means of production, and is sustained by the continual exercise of coercion which reproduces the social division between capital and wage-labour. This exercise of coercion, however, is not itself a voluntarist one, with some powerful persons in a neo-feudal style tyrannizing over others to cause their dispossession; if that was all there was to it, then one could say that while some lose their individual freedom, others retain their freedom. This exercise of coercion is itself a result of coercion exercised upon the coercers through competition, which means that *everybody under capitalism is unfree.* The system then acquires a spontaneous character, its overall movement being the outcome of the actions of individual economic agents who are coerced to act in particular ways, failing which they would lose their positions within it. Capitalism in its spontaneity is based, in short, on individual *unfreedom*.

Precisely for this reason however, capitalism, almost throughout its history, is characterized by a quest for individual freedom, with economic agents seeking to overcome its spontaneity by entering into combinations, for no individual agent *qua* individual can do so alone. This means however that capitalism in its spontaneity is scarcely visible; what we see is its appearance where its spontaneity is being fought by, and therefore hidden by, praxis against it. We do not see capitalism in its *ideal* form which it would assume if there were no praxis against it, but as a system in whose external appearance praxis overlies the *ideal* form underneath.

This makes capitalism a unique mode of production. It has been usual within the Marxist tradition to think of the various 'modes of production' as being, in a *formal* sense, similar to one another; and several of Marx's writings, notably the preface to *A Contribution to a Critique of Political Economy,* can be adduced to support this view. This usual view, however, has missed an important point: namely that capitalism as a mode of production is *vastly different* from others not just in the details of its content, which of course is to be expected, but even in the way it has to be cognized. In the case of feudalism, for instance, the 'normal' working of the system for long stretches of time, barring periods of sporadic peasant revolts, is visible in an un-obscured form; for capitalism however its 'spontaneity', which is an essential part of its 'normal' working, is always obscured by the simultaneous presence of its opposite, namely the tendency to overcome spontaneity by overcoming competition among workers through the formation of 'combinations'. True, even when there are no actual peasant revolts under feudalism, there is nonetheless an element of peasant solidarity directed against the depredations of the feudal lord which can be taken as an implicit peasant opposition; but there is a difference between implicit opposition which scarcely affects the functioning of the system and explicit rupture of the 'spontaneity' which a 'combination' among workers represents under capitalism.

Put simply, the existence and functioning of trade unions, though often seen as being part of the 'normal' working of capitalism, really represent the initial intrusion of an opposite tendency into the *essence* of the working of capitalism. This also explains why capitalism is invariably and spontaneously engaged in attempting to weaken or destroy trade unions, and does succeed in doing so occasionally when the conjuncture is favourable for capital.

Under capitalism, in other words, what appears as its quotidian character is not its real essence. This is so not just for the reason that Marx had discussed, namely the appropriation of surplus value by capitalists despite the existence of equivalent exchange, but for a totally different reason as well, namely the existence of 'combinations' in a universe that in its pure state is characterized by pervasive competition between atomized individuals. This quotidian existence of the system with a camouflaged real essence is what differentiates capitalism from all previous modes of production.

Centralization of Capital

Capitalism, in short, never appears in its true character. It appears as an entity mired always in struggle, admittedly trade union struggle most of the time, but trade union struggle that by its very nature overcomes competition among workers. This has significance: the 'combination' that a trade union represents must never be confused with a 'coalition' among individual workers that we had mentioned earlier, for a coalition serves individual self-interest while a 'combination' represents a transcendence of individual self-interest, as Marx had noted in *The Poverty of Philosophy*.

It is worth quoting Marx here to get some idea of the import of combinations:

> Large-scale industry concentrates in one place a crowd of people unknown to one another. Competition divides their interests. But the maintenance of wages, this common interest which they have against their boss, unites them in a common thought of resistance – combination. … If the first aim of resistance was merely the maintenance of wages, combinations, at first isolated, constitute themselves into groups as the capitalists in their turn unite for the purpose of repression, and in the face of always united capital, the maintenance of the association becomes more necessary to them than that of wages. *This is so true that English economists are amazed to see the workers sacrifice a good part of their wages in favour of associations which, in the eyes of these economists, are established solely in favour of wages.* (Marx 1976, pp. 210–11; emphasis added)

In other words, combinations, formed initially for defending workers' material interests (wages), soon become for them desirable *per se*, irrespective of whether such combinations bring them any material gains.

It follows that under capitalism, its *essential property* of being characterized by pervasive competition never fully reveals itself because of the simultaneous presence of its very opposite, namely, the negation of competition among the workers because of combinations (though competition continues to remain between the employed and the unemployed workers, or between the active and the reserve armies of labour); the shoots of the negation of capitalism appear *always* enmeshed with capitalism itself as part of its quotidian existence, which is not true of any earlier mode of production.

This simultaneous *visible* presence within the system itself of the shoots of its negation is of course more pronounced at certain times than at others. It is less pronounced under the regime of globalization than earlier, which makes the current regime closer to the undisturbed spontaneity of the system than, say, the post-war *dirigiste* regime, whether in the metropolis or in the decolonized countries of the third world. The reason behind this waxing and waning of the presence of its negation within the functioning capitalist system itself is the following.

Centralization of capital, which is an immanent tendency under capitalism, reintroduces competition among workers at a higher level even after this competition has been overcome at a lower level. When workers in a particular factory form a trade union and overcome competition among themselves, the same capitalist then sets up another factory whose workers now compete against those of the first factory; even if the latter workers get unionized, unless the two unions coordinate among themselves, there will be competition between the two sets of unionized workers which would reassert the ascendancy of capital. Thus, centralization of capital, i.e. the formation of larger and larger blocks of capital (in the present case, a larger capital spread over two factories compared to the original one confined only to one factory), is a way of reasserting the spontaneity of the system by re-establishing competition between workers when it appears to have been overcome through 'combinations' at one particular level.

Globalization of capital, likewise, which carries centralization of capital to a still higher degree re-establishes competition, this time between, say, American workers and Indonesian workers, which checkmates, from the point of view of capital, the effects of the overcoming through unionization of the competition among American workers. The reason why the spontaneity of the system appears more pronounced under the regime of globalization is that under this regime it is capital that becomes globalized, while workers' combinations are non-existent at a global level. Whenever the level at which capital operates is higher than the level at which workers' combinations operate, there is a reassertion of greater spontaneity, while this spontaneity tends to get challenged through the simultaneous presence of its opposite when the two levels are the same.

Put differently, while capitalism, unlike earlier modes of production, always manifests itself not in its *ideal form*, because of the simultaneous appearance of economic agents' continuous collective praxis against this *ideal form*, the system spontaneously also seeks to overcome this praxis to establish the *ideal form*; and one of the most important mechanisms through which it does so is the spontaneous tendency towards centralization. In those rare moments when the centralization of capital has raised the level of operation of capital while workers continue to function at their old level of operation, the underlying nature of capitalism in its *ideal form* becomes visible through the 'cloud cover' of the praxis against this *ideal form.* This does not of course mean that centralization once again *atomizes* the workers by rolling back the combinations they have formed; it only means that the competition they had overcome at one level reappears at a higher level. The period of globalization is one such moment.

This has an important implication. Isaiah Berlin (1969) had questioned the very idea of an 'objective' identity of a person, such as class identity, that is distinct from other identities that are clearly visible. Akeel Bilgrami (2022) has criticized this position on the ground that at certain times, for instance during revolutionary uprisings, people suddenly come together to *act* as a class, which therefore acquires as much visibility as a category as any other; their class identity manifests itself at such times. What our argument suggests, however, is that the partial manifestation of a class identity is a *perennial phenomenon*, as perennial as any other identity; revolutionary uprisings are not the sole manifestation of class identity, but rather the limit point at which it becomes total and overwhelming. This bursting forth of class identity in the form of sudden and overwhelming political praxis occurs because of the denial of the possibility of successful quotidian struggle for improving the material conditions of life of the working people, or the denial of democratic rights to them.

Of course, our argument may be objected to on the grounds that it obliterates the distinction Lenin had drawn between trade union consciousness and class consciousness; that we are mistaking trade union consciousness for class consciousness, which is altogether different. It would be argued that workers coming together to form 'combinations' in the shape of trade unions, even when these are admittedly distinct from 'coalitions' where individual interests still reign supreme, exhibit only trade union consciousness, but cannot be taken to be exhibiting class consciousness which they can acquire only through a comprehension of *theory* that is brought to them from 'outside'.

This criticism however treats class consciousness as the outcome as some kind of sudden 'enlightenment' and the two kinds of consciousness as totally disjoint phenomena. There is, on the contrary, a rudimentary class consciousness even in trade union consciousness (Lenin had talked of it as 'class instinct' – Krupskaya 1933); and, at the same time, there is never any state of being *fully* 'class conscious'. There are varying degrees of class consciousness among the workers at all times, and the acquisition of class consciousness gets hastened through praxis that plays a pedagogic role as well.

A Clarification

The point made above about capitalism not being visible in its pure or ideal form must be distinguished from a kindred point one often comes across in economics. The latter relates to the fact that no phenomenon is observable in its pure form, that there is always some *random* disturbance around it, because of which it is visible only in a distorted form. The point being made here, however, is altogether different; it refers not to any random disturbance or fuzziness surrounding the pure phenomenon, which is capitalism that we are studying in the present context, but rather to the fact that this pure phenomenon always, except in some fleeting historical moments that offer us the rare chance to observe it with some clarity, appears overlaid with its opposite, namely the praxis that it has called forth.

One instance where this divergence between the true character of capitalism marked by pervasive competition, and the way it appears because of the simultaneous visible presence of its opposite tendency in the form of combinations among workers, manifests itself is in the discussion of the determinants of wages under the system. In the earlier part of volume 1 of *Capital* wages are seen to equal the value of labour power, that is the amount of labour embodied directly and indirectly in the production of a unit of labour power, which means in the subsistence basket (not physical subsistence but a historically determined level of subsistence) required for producing (and reproducing) a unit of labour power. This perception of the determination of wages is in keeping with the general discussion of the determinants of value of all commodities, of which labour power is one, in volume 1 of *Capital.* But the determination of wages later in volume 1 itself, and in Marx's other writings, is seen to depend upon the bargaining strength of trade unions, and the latter in turn is seen to depend upon the relative size of the reserve army of labour, which is an entirely different conception.

One way of reconciling these two different theoretical positions would be to say that whatever wage-rate is determined by trade union-bargaining *is* the value of labour power. But there is a clear conceptual difference between the value of labour power as seen on a par with the value of other commodities, that is, the value of what is required at the historically given subsistence level for the production (and reproduction) of labour power, and value of labour power seen as simply the value of whatever wage the trade unions succeed in enforcing. The two cannot be taken as referring to the same concept.

The real difference between the two perceptions lies in the fact that they belong to different levels of discourse. It becomes clear if we distinguish between capitalism in its ideal form, and capitalism as an empirical entity where there is a simultaneous presence of the opposite of its spontaneity. The value of labour power seen as the value of the historically determined subsistence basket that is required for the production and reproduction of labour power characterizes the first perception; the value of labour power seen as the value of whatever wages that the trade union which has come up in opposition to the spontaneity of the system succeeds in enforcing, characterizes the second perception.

Such a distinction, between the system in its ideal form and the system as it actually appears empirically, holds according to us for capitalism but not for any earlier mode of production; and that is the specificity of capitalism as a mode of production. Put differently, capitalism does not appear, unlike earlier modes of production, in its purity; it appears invariably as a mode together with its opposite. This gives capitalism its *sui generis character* and has a number of important implications.

The Freneticism of Capitalism

Our argument can be put in a different way. Capitalism is the only mode of production that almost from its very inception, faces uninterrupted resistance. The capitalism we observe is not capitalism in its ideal form but capitalism that is contested, capitalism that is engaged explicitly in a struggle for its being. Unlike other modes of production where this struggle was sporadic, in capitalism this struggle in its explicit form is perennial. Of course, this struggle is not necessarily for socialism; to make this quotidian struggle into a struggle for socialism requires a *theoretical* understanding that has to be developed. But it is a theoretically uninformed, an un-self-conscious struggle against capitalism in its pure or ideal form; a struggle against a system that coerces individual economic agents into acting out specific roles under the pressure of competition.

It follows that capitalism is a frenetic mode of production, the very opposite of the relative tranquillity of feudal economic life. It is characterized not only by the freneticism arising from its own immanent tendencies – i.e. competition, centralization, accumulation and crises (which too are expressions of this freneticism) – but also by the freneticism arising from the fact of being perennially caught in the act of combating those forces that constitute the simultaneously present negation of the system's own essence.

There is no such thing as placid or peaceful or stable capitalism, such as, for instance, bourgeois economics with its equilibrium paradigm, endowed with 'stability' and 'optimality' properties, presents. It is not even a case of frenetic movements *around* a given equilibrium (such as what Schumpeter, who had said '[o]ne can have a stagnant feudalism and a stagnant socialism but never a stagnant capitalism', had visualized). There is simply no empirical equilibrium for the system, not even as a centre of gravity around which it can oscillate.

When Marx had talked of the Indian peasant continuing to cultivate his 'miserable patch of land' even as momentous conflicts raged around him to determine the fates of empires,[1] the placidity of the common people and the tranquillity of economic life he was referring to were not really confined only to Asian conditions (or the Asiatic mode of production, despite its being perhaps the specific backdrop that Marx had in mind); such placidity and tranquillity had more or less characterized all feudal societies. While all feudal societies witnessed periodic wars to determine who should appropriate the peasants' surplus, the peasants themselves continued ploughing the land placidly. The freneticism characterizing capitalism, which engulfed the society as a whole, was altogether lacking in feudalism, whether of the European or the Asiatic kind.

True, this freneticism that was a novel and *sui generis* feature of capitalism, and had been absent from all earlier modes of production, did not operate with uniform intensity. In view of what we have mentioned above, this freneticism may be less pronounced at certain times than at others. It is less pronounced when centralization has taken the operation of capital to a higher level than the level at which labour is organized, and therefore taken the system closer to its spontaneous functioning with the forces of its simultaneous negation, present within the system, being more subdued; on the other hand, it is more pronounced when the opposite happens.

This freneticism also explains why capitalism is necessarily a transitional mode of production, why the dream of its being the final mode of production that will last forever can never be fulfilled; in fact, if it survives a little longer, then it would put the future of mankind in jeopardy. The reason is that everything about capitalism, from the mindless exploitation of nature to the rapacious plunder of the earth's resources from those who may have had earlier access to it, such as for instance the snatching of tropical produce from the inhabitants of the region, has something frenetic about it. The transitoriness of capitalism follows from the fact that in its absence human survival itself may be a transitory phenomenon.

Two Distinct Arguments

The point we have been making needs to be distinguished from another point often made about the capitalist system, though both stress the transitoriness of capitalism in different ways. This latter point relates to the ideological let-down by capitalism. To clarify matters, therefore, let us spend a little time over this latter point.

The bourgeois revolution of 1789 ushering in capitalism was based on the slogan 'Liberty, Equality and Fraternity', which represented some of the noblest of sentiments upon which to base the foundation of human society.[2] The point about ideological let-down is not that these sentiments themselves are flawed, but that capitalism betrays these sentiments through the institution of private property, and of competition acting as an external coercive force on all economic agents.

This makes the transition from feudalism to capitalism fundamentally different from the transition from capitalism to socialism. The former represented a transition between two distinct sets of ideals; the latter represents not a transition between two distinct ideals but a difference over how to achieve the same given set of ideals.

The socialist case is that the institutions of capitalism subvert the achievement of the ideals of 'Liberty, Equality and Fraternity', that capitalism is based on a gigantic betrayal where what it promises and what its institutions which are legitimized through those very promises are inherently capable of achieving, are two very distinct entities. The socialist argument, in short, is that social ownership of the means of production is necessary for achieving the ideals which the bourgeoisie had set before the people and around which it had mobilized their support for acquiring state power through the bourgeois revolution, though of course, in the process of achieving these ideals, socialism goes beyond these ideals themselves.

The Keynesian prescription of 'socialization of investment', even if it could be achieved without socializing ownership of the means of production as Keynes had believed, would still not be sufficient to negate this historic betrayal, because the promise of the bourgeois revolution went much further than simply keeping the system within the limits of tolerance of the working masses. Keynes was clear that the 'world will not for long tolerate the levels of unemployment' that free market capitalism, 'except for brief periods of excitement', invariably entails; his emphasis was on making the system 'tolerable' from the point of view of the workers. The fact that even when the system is 'tolerable' it would still fall far short of the promise of 'Liberty, Equality and Fraternity', though an indubitable fact, did not worry him.

The promise of the bourgeois revolution, in short, went far beyond the paternalism of 'social engineering' within a bourgeois society. But Keynes at least was aware of the need for such 'social engineering', which other 'bourgeois' writers are not. The socialist argument is concerned, to start with, with the realization of the ideals of the bourgeois revolution; it aims to negate the betrayal of these ideals by the bourgeoisie, which even Keynesian 'social engineering' does not negate.

Precisely because the socialist argument is based not on a negation of the ideals of the bourgeois revolution but on their affirmation, and because bourgeois theorists, not surprisingly, fiercely contest this argument, the capitalist mode is characterized by intense ideological struggles, far more intense than in any earlier mode of production. The role of ideological struggle, in other words, becomes far more important under capitalism than earlier. Both capitalism and socialism are engaged in an ideological struggle that is 'post-enlightenment', that debates the implications of the 'enlightenment' but within an intellectual setting conjured up by the 'enlightenment' itself.

The argument for overcoming capitalism arises with the birth of capitalism itself. It arises at the level of theory with the socialist argument about the betrayal by the system of its own ideals. But the point we were making earlier relates not to any ideological struggle, but to the practical struggle in which workers engage in their quotidian life, which also represents a rejection of capitalism in its pure form. The formation of 'combinations' constitutes a negation of competition which is at the core of capitalism. The fact that capitalism appears to take such 'combinations' in its stride gives the impression that it does not represent a challenge for it. But this is not true; its attack on trade unions whenever the opportunity arises is proof as much of its bitterness towards unions, as of the unions' struggle against the system reaching its *denouement* in the transcendence of the system itself.

The Transitoriness of the Capitalist System

Curiously, an inkling of the transitoriness of capitalism is there in economics even among those traditions that have nothing to do with socialism. This manifests itself for instance in the perception, common to many writers, of the falling tendency of the rate of profit. Adam Smith directly linked the falling tendency of the rate of profit to competition under capitalism. He did not provide a logically valid explanation for such a tendency; to infer from the fact that rapid capital accumulation in a particular branch of production brings down the rate of profit in that branch, the proposition that the same would happen for the economy as a whole, is an untenable logical step.

The rate of profit could come down if the share of wages went up for independent reasons (such as greater trade union strength), or if there was increasing supply price for certain commodities which went directly or indirectly into the production of every commodity (as Ricardo postulated), or if there was a rising capital–output ratio over time (as Marx visualized). Since Smith visualized neither of the latter two tendencies, his theory could acquire coherence only if the share of wages went up; this certainly happened according to him when the demand for labour outstripped supply because of capital accumulation, but there was no reason why such an increase would be a permanent phenomenon. Hence, unless there was some natural limit to the supply of labour, there could be no secular tendency towards a fall in the rate of profit.

But Smith's postulating a falling tendency of the rate of profit was not a logically inescapable prognostication, nor even a reading of something that was manifesting itself in real life; it was more perhaps an expression of the apprehension that such a frenetic system as capitalism simply could not go on, that it was bound to come to a stop somehow.

Much the same can be said of Ricardo's theory of the falling tendency of the rate of profit, though it is logically much better grounded. Capital accumulation makes demands upon nature, of which the demand on land for producing food crops and raw materials is the most obvious expression. Since the supply of good-quality land cannot increase, capital accumulation would naturally push the economy into using increasingly inferior land, or using the given available land more and more intensively with growing disadvantage. In either case there would be a fall in the rate of profit both in agriculture and elsewhere in the economy, through a shift in the terms of trade in favour of agriculture.

While this is logically valid unless technological progress of a 'land-augmenting' kind prevents such a fall in the rate of profit, it has not happened historically because of the use of coercion against tropical suppliers of food and raw materials. Such coercion has squeezed out a surplus from them to suit the requirements of metropolitan capital without shifting the margin of cultivation in any way; in fact, the secular tendency for the terms of trade has been to move *against the primary commodities,* as a host of writers from Prebisch and Singer onwards have pointed out.

The significance of Ricardo's proposition, however, lies elsewhere: in his apprehension that a frenetically accumulating system makes demands upon natural resources that simply cannot be met in a sustained manner; that the capitalist system with its immanent freneticism can therefore only be a transitory phase in human history.

Lenin of course drew explicit attention to this transitoriness, from the phenomenon of imperialism and wars that also followed from the freneticism that characterizes capitalism. Imperialism, by which Lenin did not mean the entire phenomenon of capitalist domination of the 'outlying regions' but rather only the late nineteenth and early twentieth-century phenomenon of a quest for 'economic territory', was characterized according to him by rivalry among the major capitalist powers. This rivalry for acquiring 'economic territory' was itself rooted in the fact of competition, and gave rise to wars for a repartitioning of an already partitioned world.

It arose from the fact that through centralization, what had earlier been competition between capitals had now become a struggle among rival monopoly-combines, with each such combine bringing its state directly into this struggle. Competition projected on to the world stage between the rival monopoly-combines was the crux of the economic relationships characterizing imperialism; and such rivalry arose not just for known sources of raw materials, but also to keep rivals out of spaces in which *potential* sources of raw materials could be located. Lenin's idea, in short, was to underscore the phenomenon of rival capitalist powers engaged in frenetic competition on the world scale, and how this would plunge humanity into devastating wars. If mankind was to avoid such wars, then it had to go beyond capitalism to usher in socialism, or, as the Bolshevik programme put it, to 'turn the imperialist war into a civil war' for overthrowing the system.

One can also see in Keynes' prescription for stabilizing the capitalist system, an effort to reduce this freneticism. He talks about the economic motivation for imperialism disappearing if his prescriptions were put into effect. He also visualizes the 'rentier aspect of capitalism' disappearing over time (the euthanasia of the rentier). Both of these, he believes, would produce a more tranquil environment within which a cultivation of the finer tastes could be possible.

The Question of Individual Freedom

Given the spontaneity of capitalism where every individual is made to compete against another and therefore forced to act in a manner that is not of his own volition, individual freedom becomes a mirage. A condition for the realization of individual freedom is the overcoming of the spontaneity of the system through the assertion of individual agency; but this assertion of individual agency is possible only through a simultaneous dissolution of individual agency within a collective agency, that is, through 'combinations' that overcome competition between individuals. 'Combinations' amount therefore to introducing a counter to the spontaneity of capitalism. Individual freedom under capitalism, in short, can be asserted only to the extent that the individual as a member of a collective can overcome the spontaneity of the system.

It now seems, however, that the system always attempts to reassert its spontaneity against such praxis towards the realization of individual freedom, through a spontaneous reorganization of capital into an even more centralized entity, i.e. by carrying centralization of capital to a still higher level. The improvement in the state of individual freedom through collective agency within capitalism, therefore, has no permanence; it can be rolled back over time.

Even this reorganization of capital into a higher level of centralization is achieved more or less spontaneously; any actual intervention by the state to hasten centralization, which one may observe in practice, must not mislead one into thinking otherwise. Such intervention by the state is meant only to expedite a process that is already immanent within the system.

It follows that no improvement in individual freedom under capitalism has any degree of permanence within capitalism. Advances in individual freedom achieved through combinations can be followed by regressions in individual freedom brought about by greater centralization of capital.

The complete untenability of the proposition that capitalism ensures individual freedom can be gauged from this. This claim is erroneous for one obvious reason and two subtle ones. The obvious reason is the existence of imperialism whose essence lies in the subjugation of the 'outlying regions' and its inhabitants to the will of metropolitan capital; no individual freedom is clearly possible for the inhabitants of a region that is implicitly or explicitly a 'conquered territory'. The two subtle reasons relate to the metropolis itself, i.e. to the very nature of capitalism as a mode of production. The first is the argument we have been advancing all along, namely that individual freedom is simply non-existent under capitalism which is a spontaneous system where the individual lacks agency. Second, the individual can effect an improvement in his or her freedom only through collective intervention, i.e. intervention by an agency which represents a 'combination'. Such a 'combination' *does* provide agency and hence breaks the spontaneity of capitalism; but such an achievement of the collective agency itself is never final, since there can be, and invariably is, a turning of the wheel that reverses this achievement. Neither as a 'monad' nor as a member of a 'combination', in other words, can the individual *under capitalism* ever claim success in achieving individual freedom.

The whole course of capitalism represents a struggle for achieving individual freedom, a struggle that is never won because of the very logic of capitalism. This struggle can succeed only when the competition characterizing capitalism and the spontaneity it generates have been overcome by the creation of a new economic order, an order that carries to its conclusion the collective spirit that had sprung up under capitalism and, in opposition to it, an order that constitutes socialism.

Notes

[1] This remark is made in Marx, 'British Rule in India', reproduced in Husain, ed. (2006, p. 16).

[2] We are not here going into the contradictions that exist between these ideals, since our concern is with the *ab ovo* betrayal of these ideals by capitalism.

CHAPTER TWELVE

Freedom in the Era of Globalization

'Globalization' has many dimensions, but, from an economic point of view, its essence consists in more or less free flows of commodities and capital, *including finance*, across state boundaries. Globalization of capital entails a rolling back of trade union activism, and also of the kind of state intervention that underlay the so-called Golden Age of capitalism that characterized the quarter-century or so after the Second World War. It represents a movement in the direction of reasserting the 'spontaneity' of capitalism and of revealing its real nature by removing the cloud covers that usually serve to obscure it.

The fact that in the third world especially the material conditions of life of the working people have *deteriorated* during the period of globalization is clear, though, oddly, it continues to be disputed. A direct indication of it, taken from India, is that notwithstanding an increase in the rate of GDP growth in the era of globalization according to official statistics, there was an increase in the percentage of rural population not having access to 2,200 calories per person per day (the definition of poverty originally applied by the country's Planning Commission) from 58 in 1993–94 to 68 in 2011–12 (liberalization in India began properly in 1991); the corresponding percentages for urban India (where the benchmark is 2,100 calories per person per day) are 57 and 65 respectively.[1]

Such an increase in nutritional deprivation is often explained away by suggesting that a change in tastes has occurred on the part of the population, away from foodgrains to meat, fish and milk products. This explanation however is erroneous, first, since we are talking of calorie intake and not direct ingestion of foodgrains; and second, because it goes against the evidence all over the world that a rise in real income in the range we are talking about, is invariably associated with an increase in calorie intake (so that, if the real per capita income of the Indian poor was rising, they would not be posting a lower per capita calorie intake). Thirdly, even within India, years of higher real per capita income, such as years of good harvest, are associated with higher average calorie intake. The apparent nutritional deprivation, therefore, does indubitably represent real deprivation.

This is hardly surprising: the reassertion of spontaneity of the system means the resumption of the process of encroachment by capital on the domain of petty producers and the dispossession of the latter who join the ranks of job-seekers in the capitalist sector. The capitalist sector, however, does not generate sufficient jobs despite the increase in the GDP growth; *in fact employment growth comes down relative to the earlier, dirigiste, period,* despite the increase in the GDP growth. This happens owing to the much higher rates of growth of labour productivity compared to earlier, which, as we shall see, are also a consequence of the reassertion of the spontaneity of the system.[2]

Nutritional deprivation is not a new phenomenon in these countries. It had happened in India, for instance, over much of the colonial period earlier: per capita foodgrain availability had fallen by 25 per cent over the last half century of colonial rule for which we have data (Blyn 1966), suggesting an acute increase in nutritional poverty. What is striking about the period of globalization is not just the re-emergence of such a process of absolute impoverishment in the third world, but a restraint too on the absolute level of the material conditions of life of the workers in the advanced capitalist countries; and everywhere the scope for praxis by the working people to fight against this has been greatly attenuated, since the international mobility of capital-in-production enfeebles the trade unions which continue to be organized on national lines.

We mentioned earlier the contradiction between the spontaneity of the system and praxis to overcome it. Globalization entails an ascendancy of the spontaneity of the system over praxis, and hence a rolling back of agency, which also impinges in an immediate sense on the development of combinations of workers as it intensifies competition among workers of different countries.

Globalization and Democracy

If the globalization of capital-in-production enfeebles trade unions, the globalization of capital-as-finance enfeebles the nation-state. Since we live in a world of nation-states, free mobility of finance across the domains of such states implies that if any state's policy differs from what finance capital considers 'appropriate', then it leaves the shores of that state *en masse*, precipitating a financial crisis. Nation-states, in other words, always have to make sure that they 'retain the confidence of the investors', i.e. are on the right side of globally mobile finance capital, by pursuing policies that are palatable to finance.[3]

This itself amounts to an abridgement of freedom for the people. Democracy entails the freedom of the people to elect a government of their choice, one that would pursue policies that the people largely approve of, which is why different political formations vying for electoral support come before the people with different agendas. But if all political formations have the same agenda, namely the one that globally mobile finance capital approves, for fear that they would otherwise trigger a capital flight with deleterious consequences in the event of their coming to power, or, even if some of them which have a different agenda before the elections go back upon it after the elections and pursue the same policies that were being followed earlier (as Syriza did in Greece), then the people's choice becomes meaningless.

Put differently, democracy implies in principle, the sovereignty of the people; what globalization of finance does is to institute the sovereignty of finance capital which necessarily displaces the sovereignty of the people, and hence entails an abrogation of democracy and freedom. Even if the people willy-nilly accept such a displacement of their sovereignty, that makes no difference to the issue; the fact of abrogation of democracy is not thereby altered an iota.

This is not just a formal point. The demands of finance capital are by no means identical with the demands of the people. For instance, in any third world society, there is a dire need for improving the condition of the people through larger welfare expenditure on education and health care. Such expenditure, if it is to genuinely improve the condition of the people, must be financed not by taxing the beneficiaries themselves, but by either taxing the rich or by a larger fiscal deficit. Both these, however, are anathema for finance capital. It opposes fiscal deficits beyond a very small amount relative to the GDP of a country (usually 3 per cent these days); indeed, most countries have even adopted legislation to this effect. And any larger taxes upon the rich, it is feared, will drive away 'investors' to other destinations where the tax rates are comparatively lower. Because of this, a programme of welfare expenditure that should obtain overwhelming popular support, remains unimplemented.

True, many of the third world governments do not push the system to its limits; and it is not necessarily the case that they would have been eager to implement such welfare measures if globalization had not restrained them. But the restraining effect of globalization, and indeed its decisive role, is undeniable, so much so that even avowedly socialist governments, which come to power by promising change, end up by accepting the status quo as long as they remain trapped within the vortex of globalized finance.

Much the same can be said of redistributive measures relating to income and wealth. Hardly any political formation in the third world, including even those committed to social democracy, has a programme of redistribution on its agenda, for fear no doubt of damaging the so-called 'investor confidence'; and this is so despite the fact that inequalities have increased quite sharply during the years of globalization. In India, for example, according to an estimate by Chancel and Piketty (2017), the share of the top 1 per cent of the population in the national income of the country was just 6 per cent in 1982; it increased to 22 per cent by 2013–14, two decades after India had adopted a neo-liberal regime in 1991. Obviously, inequality-generating tendencies are immanent to such a regime; the point to note is that using the weapon of political intervention to counter such immanent tendencies, which used to be the case earlier, is no longer in vogue, not because such an objective has become less urgent (on the contrary, even the 'rich persons' club', the World Economic Forum, is talking about its necessity), but because the scope for doing so when globalized finance faces the nation-state is limited, and perceived to be so.

To recapitulate, the phenomenon of a nation-state facing globalized finance abridges the freedom of the people, in the sense of eliminating their capacity to improve their living conditions by exercising their political franchise, as the state itself gets assimilated into the spontaneity of the system. This happens in multiple ways. First, the people are denied any meaningful choice between alternative political formations at the time of elections, which amounts to an abrogation of democracy. The agendas which the different political formations present before the people are more or less identical in their economic content; and if perchance one of them comes with a different agenda and the people do elect that formation, then it usually ends up betraying the people perforce by discarding its own agenda.

Second, these identical agendas of the different political formations are generally in conformity with the demands of globalized finance, so that it is not just a matter of lack of choice; rather, it is a matter of privileging the demands of globalized finance capital over the interests of the people.

Third, there is an elimination of serious redistributive or welfare measures from the agendas of the political formations. This is particularly striking in view of the immanent tendency under neo-liberal globalization towards growing inequalities in income and wealth that thus are not countered.

Tendency towards Increasing Inequality and Poverty

This immanent tendency towards growing inequality, in turn, arises within a setting of neo-liberal globalization owing to three inter-related factors. First, globalization links the real wages of workers everywhere. Even though labour is not freely mobile across countries under the current globalization, since capital becomes mobile, resulting in a shift of activities from higher-wage advanced capitalist countries to some lower-wage third world countries, it ensures that advanced country wages, and hence by implication wages everywhere, become subject to the restraining effects of the vast third world labour reserves. Advanced country wages do not rise because of their capitalists' threat to move activities to lower-wage third world countries; and third world wages do not rise as the workers there are located in the midst of vast labour reserves (themselves a legacy of the colonial era), which, far from getting depleted through such relocation, actually grow because of the dispossession of petty producers and meagre employment growth in the capitalist sector owing to the accelerated growth in labour productivity, both caused by globalization and its associated neo-liberal policies. This is a point elaborated below.

The vector of real wages all across the world therefore becomes non-increasing. For the United States, for instance, Joseph Stiglitz (2013) has estimated that the average real wage of a male American worker in 2011 was no higher than in 1968; in fact it was marginally lower.

Second, even as this happens, the vector of labour productivities all across the world keeps increasing, which results in an increase in the share of surplus (the excess of labour productivity over the wage-rate, divided by labour productivity) everywhere. This is the cause of the increase in income inequality, since the surplus is the source of the income of the capitalists and of the large number of persons engaged in higher-paid activities in the service sector.

Such an increase in income and wealth inequality undermines democracy everywhere. It is also by no means a transitory occurrence that can be expected to disappear over time. Its non-transitoriness arises because of a phenomenon which constitutes our third factor, namely, even as activities shift from the advanced countries to the third world countries with their vast labour reserves and hence lower wages, *these reserves do not get exhausted*;

on the contrary, their relative size compared to the total actively employed work-force actually *increases* despite such a shift of activities.

This is so for a number of reasons. First, there is a removal of all restrictions on the introduction of labour-displacing technical and structural changes, such as existed during the *dirigiste* period of post-decolonization development in many third world countries. Second, there is an actual introduction of labour-displacing technological change because of the greater openness of economies. Freer trade forces domestic producers to introduce technological change that is typically labour-displacing in order to withstand external competition both in the export market and in the domestic market. Third, the withdrawal of state support from the petty production sector brings down its profitability, which in turn is accentuated by greater encroachment upon it by the capitalist sector; this makes a number of peasants and petty producers migrate to the cities in search of work and swell the labour reserves. And fourth, the growing income inequality that arises for all these reasons itself contributes towards the non-exhaustion of labour reserves and hence a further rise in inequality. This is because any increase in income inequality changes the pattern of demand towards less employment-intensive goods: the domestic elite, towards which income distribution shifts when there is a rise in inequality, has a lifestyle and consumption pattern that is imitative of the lifestyle and consumption pattern of the elite in the metropolis, and the goods consumed by the latter are less employment-intensive than those consumed by the working people in the third world. It follows from this last point that if the labour reserves do not get depleted to start with, then *ceteris paribus* they will never get depleted but will keep growing as a proportion of the work-force; a process of cumulative causation, in other words, is involved here.

The increase in income (and hence wealth) inequality then becomes not a transient, vanishing phenomenon but an enduring one in the era of globalization. Within the third world itself, the income squeeze on the peasantry (and other petty producers) and hence the increase in the relative size of the labour reserves that get swollen by peasant migration to cities, not to mention the natural growth in the population, can have the effect not just of increasing income (and wealth) inequalities, but even of raising the proportion of persons living in absolute poverty, defined by a nutritional norm.

We have given above the figures for India that confirm this. But one can draw a similar inference for the world as a whole. For the world as a whole, the annual average per capita cereal output (triennium average divided by mid-triennium population) was 355 kg for 1979–80 to 1981–82 (1980 to

1982, in short) and fell to 343 kg by 2000–02; even in 2016–18 it was 344 kg, while the proportion available for use as food declined owing to a sharp rise in the use of grain for ethanol production between the second and the last triennia. This strongly suggests an increase in malnutrition and hence the proportion of nutritionally deprived population in the total world population over the period since neo-liberal globalization has begun to hold sway.

Globalization, in short, has not only increased income and wealth inequalities substantially and thereby undermined the foundations of democracy everywhere, but is also likely to have increased the proportion of nutritionally deprived 'poor' in the world's population.[4] In view of the hype about growth in the third world lifting 'millions of the world's poor above the poverty line' before the pandemic, this claim may appear odd at first sight; but it is well established from food and nutrition data that are much firmer than any so-called 'poverty line' estimates. At the same time, globalization, for reasons we have seen, prevents any redistributive measures or welfare measures to alleviate the impact of growing inequality and poverty.

Globalization, therefore, puts much of the world's population in a bind: they keep becoming worse off, and yet lack any capacity to effect a change in their predicament in this globalized world. The fact that some countries in Asia, which include India, have experienced high GDP growth rates in the period of globalization should not obscure this basic reality. In India, for instance, the high growth rate has only meant an accentuation of the hiatus between the 'haves' and the 'have-nots' *within* the country.

It is this sense of being 'boxed in', of being subject to ever-worsening living conditions, and at the same time being deprived of the capacity for collective political intervention to stem this worsening situation, which constitutes a serious loss of freedom for the people. What is more, even the capacity of a country to delink from globalization, that is, to have an alternative regime where capital controls are put in place, so that the writ of globalized finance does not run and the nation-state reacquires the capacity to pursue policies of its choice, thus allowing the people to collectively intervene through politics to improve their condition, also gets limited. We now turn to the reasons for this.

The Constraints on Delinking

The most serious constraint on delinking is the transitional pain it brings, and that too precisely to those sections of the population whose long-term interest lies in delinking. The *immediate* outflow of finance consequent upon, and even in anticipation of, the decision to delink creates a financial crisis for the country attempting to delink, so that this immediate crisis forces the government to rethink about delinking and even reverse that decision. But even if there is no financial crisis, and controls over capital outflow are imposed immediately as the decision to delink is announced (which of course will necessarily have to come as a surprise), a problem still arises with regard to the balance of payments.

Many third world countries, of which India is a major example, systematically run current account deficits on their balance of payments, and these are financed by the inflow of finance on the capital account. A decision to delink, even if it does not lead to any substantial capital *outflows* (because of the immediate clamping down of controls on such outflows), will certainly lead to a cessation of capital *inflows*, which will then make the balance of payments unsustainable, requiring *import controls*. Such import controls, however, will force immediate cuts in domestic absorption, and typically in domestic consumption, which will impinge particularly on the poor, the very segment in whose interest delinking is being undertaken.

This is a transitional problem in the sense that a large economy attempting to delink will be able to increase its production capacity of most goods after a certain period; but there are some commodities, of which oil is a classic example, where a country cannot just import substitute at will. True, such a country can make specific arrangements for importing oil (or other essential imports). But there is an obvious practical constraint here, which brings us to the second constraint upon delinking in the contemporary world.

Since globalization serves the interests of metropolitan capital which now has the freedom to move across country borders, it has the backing of major advanced country governments. This is so despite the fact that the US itself has started imposing tariffs of late. Hence, any country delinking from globalization immediately incurs the wrath of the advanced country governments which promptly impose sanctions upon trade with this deviant country; and given the power of the advanced countries, above all the US, most countries of the world agree to impose sanctions, which makes it extremely difficult for this country to make the kinds of arrangements for importing oil and other essential goods that could have overcome its difficulties. The sanctions against a host of countries, including Cuba, Venezuela and Iran at present, underscore this problem. The point, however, is that any such sanctions also affect the poor adversely, which makes the delinking project lose its appeal among them.

The bourgeoisie in the third world, which is integrated with globalized finance capital and is a beneficiary of globalization, is strongly opposed to delinking anyway. The support for this project therefore can come only from the workers, peasants, agricultural labourers, craftsmen, artisans and fishermen; and the project itself can be launched only with a political formation that enjoys their support, and has the courage and honesty to stick to its agenda if elected. But such a political formation launching a delinking project which would already be facing unrelenting opposition from the domestic bourgeoisie and urban middle classes, not to mention the advanced country governments, soon loses even such support from its own base as might have helped it to face up to its opponents and detractors, because of the difficulties created by trade sanctions. Even if its loss of support is not very substantial, such loss can still make a difference to its ability to survive and proceed with its delinking agenda.

Hence, even as globalization 'boxes in' the world's poor and working population through its own immanent tendencies and deprives them of their capacity to intervene politically to improve their plight, it puts up formidable barriers to any delinking from its ambit. It places vast masses of the people of the world in a difficult situation from which apparently there is 'no exit'.

Two Concepts of Nationalism

Ironically, such a delinking project faces opposition from large sections of even progressive opinion in the west, on the purported ground that it represents an undesirable retreat into 'nationalism'. This opposition, however, is based on a flawed conception of 'nationalism' that sees it as one homogeneous category, not distinguishing between European 'nationalism' and anti-colonial third world 'nationalism', between a 'nationalism' that was espoused by Hitler and a 'nationalism' that was espoused by Gandhi or Ho Chi Minh.

The term 'nationalism' that came into vogue in Europe in the wake of the Westphalian peace treaties in the seventeenth century differed in at least three fundamental ways from the anti-colonial 'nationalism' that emerged in the third world in the twentieth century. First, it had always located 'an enemy within' so that it was never inclusive, while the anti-colonial nationalism in the third world was inclusive, incorporating within its ambit everyone irrespective of religious, linguistic, ethnic and gender differences. Indeed it *had* to be inclusive in order to take on the might of the colonial power that thrived on creating divisions among the colonized. Secondly, European nationalism had been imperialist from the very beginning, while third world anti-colonial nationalism sought to build bridges with other similar struggles around and largely eschewed such an imperialist project. And thirdly, European nationalism saw the nation as standing above the people, an entity for which the people only made sacrifices, while third world anti-colonial nationalism saw the *rationale* of the nation as consisting in an improvement in the condition of the people.

The class bases of the two kinds of nationalism were also fundamentally different. European nationalism was quintessentially bourgeois nationalism, its role and complexion changing in accordance with the phases of bourgeois development. Anti-colonial nationalism in the third world, on the other hand, though it gave expression to the anger of all classes against the colonial yoke, was above all peasant nationalism, since the peasantry was the most numerous and oppressed segment within the colonial order.

The terms European and anti-colonial nationalism are not geography-specific. The aggrandizing nationalism of Europe also had a presence within the third world, and was *opposed* to the anti-colonial struggle. It had sought not the mobilization of all against the colonial power, but of one particular segment of the population against another based on ethnic or religious differences. It not only continues but has acquired a fresh impetus of late (for reasons we shall discuss later), and is expressing itself in the form of authoritarian and fascistic movements all over the world. Its *differentia specifica* lies precisely in the fact that it does not offer to the people the prospect of any improvement in their condition, since its analysis of this condition, if at all there is one, is utterly superficial, putting the blame for it on the 'other', a different ethnic or linguistic or religious group within the country.

The problem with the western progressive opposition to delinking is that it sees *all* nationalism as being synonymous with this 'European' nationalism, as being essentially hegemonic and proto-fascist, which is far from the truth. Delinking from globalization to improve the condition of the workers, peasants and other sections of the working people in the third world (and elsewhere) is diametrically the opposite of a proto-fascist project. But the effort at delinking, in addition to all the other problems it faces, has also to contend with this ill-informed ideological prejudice.

The Onset of Crisis and the Growth of Neo-Fascism

Not only does globalization put the working people of the third world into a straitjacket which they cannot get rid of and which keeps squeezing them harder and harder, but as it enters into a crisis, it creates conditions for the explicit attenuation of democracy and the growth of fascistic tendencies. The rise of authoritarian and fascistic tendencies has got a fillip from the economic crisis into which globalization has entered for some time.

The cause of the crisis lies in what we have already mentioned earlier, namely, the rise in the share of surplus in each country's output and in that of the world as a whole. Since consumption out of a unit of surplus is on average lower than out of a unit of wage income, such a steady shift from wages to surplus has the effect of lowering the time-profile of consumption and hence the time-profile of world aggregate demand for any given time-profile of investment. But there is no reason to expect the time-profile of investment to either increase or even to stay unchanged as the time-profile of consumption falls, because investment itself responds to changes in demand; the time-profile of investment itself therefore also comes down, adding to the tendency towards stagnation.

Against this tendency towards stagnation, there are no counteracting tendencies of any significance. Since larger state spending financed by increasing tax revenue at the expense of the working people scarcely entails any net addition to aggregate demand (as the working people consume the bulk of their incomes anyway), the state can counter the stagnation only by larger expenditure that is financed either by a fiscal deficit, or by larger taxes imposed on the capitalists and the rich in general. But the ability of the state to do so gets limited for fear of offending globalized finance capital.

The only possible counter to this tendency towards stagnation, therefore, is the formation of asset-price bubbles that stimulate larger spending through their wealth effect, especially in a large economy like the US which has a powerful effect on the world economy. But even if such bubbles do get formed, their collapse once again plunges the world economy into a crisis, as has happened of late.

The inability of the system to overcome the crisis makes it vulnerable to resistance; what it attempts therefore is a discourse shift, towards blaming in each country the hapless 'other' who is held responsible for the crisis. For this it enlists the support of fascistic and semi-fascistic groups which always exist in any modern society, but are usually confined to its fringes. They move centre-stage in periods of crisis for two reasons: first, their perennial slogan of vilifying and excluding the 'other' finds more takers in such periods; and second, for reasons just discussed, big capital promotes them with large financial and media backing in such periods as part of its effort to bring about a discourse shift. The economic issues affecting the lives of the people either drop out of discussion altogether as people are made to become polarized along ethnic or religious lines; or, alternatively, the blame for the economic travails of the majority is also laid at the door of the 'other'. In either case, the focus shifts to the need for excluding the 'other' rather than for discussing the roots of the crisis and its remedies with the exercise of reason.

Unlike in the 1930s, however, the emergence of fascistic governments does not even overcome unemployment through larger military spending. That, as just mentioned, would require larger government expenditure financed either by larger borrowing (as in the 1930s) or by larger taxes on capitalists, neither of which is acceptable to globalized finance capital.[5] Nonetheless, neo-fascism comes to the aid of the system in at least two ways: first, by distracting attention from any serious discussion of economic issues to a demonization of the 'other' and the generation of hatred against the 'other'; and second, by making the state far more repressive than before, so that the scope for any democratic protests around the economic plight of the people, and even against arbitrary measures of the government against the targeted minority, is snuffed out. We in India are in the process of witnessing such a change occurring in the nature of the state, pushing it in the direction of an authoritarian and fascistic state.

Thus, if globalization even in its heyday, i.e. even before the onset of crisis, constricts the freedom of the people by putting them in a straitjacket that gets tighter over time, while taking away effectively their capacity for political intervention, let alone for political intervention for bringing about a delinking from globalization, it becomes even more constricting as it enters a period of crisis. It witnesses a snuffing out of formal democratic structures, an abridgement of democratic rights, and the spread of hatred among communities.

This argument may appear puzzling for two reasons. First, it may be asked: while fascistic forces have no doubt raised their heads in many parts of the world, what does globalization have to do with it? On the contrary, are these forces not motivated by a 'nationalist' desire to retreat into their local shells rather than being open to global scrutiny that being linked to globalization entails? Second, it would be argued that globalization has been accompanied by greater concern not only about human rights in general, but also about their violation in any part of the world, since every part now becomes visible to the whole world. Globalization, in short, acts as a force in favour of democracy and human rights, rather than of fascistic movements and the snuffing out of human rights. Let us look at this objection to our argument.

The Contrast with the 1930s

Globalization certainly seeks to justify itself in terms of its concern for human rights and democratic values globally; but it is also true that no fascistic formation comes to power anywhere without the financial backing of a segment of the big bourgeoisie (and over time of the big bourgeoisie as a whole) which also happens to be a votary of globalization. The fascistic formation therefore, even as it abridges human rights domestically and faces global criticism for it, has no intentions of delinking the country from globalization.

Its assault on democratic institutions is carried out within a context where the country's domestic corporate-financial oligarchy remains integrated with globalized finance capital, which is why the criticism of such regimes for their human rights record never reaches a point where they become seriously inconvenienced by it.

This situation is in sharp contrast to that prevailing in the 1930s, the earlier occasion when fascistic elements had been in the ascendancy. That had been a period of intense inter-imperialist rivalry. Fascism then had not just been an internal phenomenon promoted by a segment of the big bourgeoisie (with its acceptance willy-nilly by other segments of the big bourgeoisie); it had also additionally been a means of upsetting the prevailing imperialist arrangement, the existing global power relations of the time.

Put differently, fascism in the 1930s had arisen in a context where each of the different finance capitals had a national character, was aided by its particular nation-state, and was engaged in a conflict with other similar finance capitals belonging to other major countries and aided by their nation-states. The fascism of the 1930s, in short, had arisen in the context of inter-imperialist rivalry. In contrast, fascist tendencies today arise in the context of a globalized finance capital, of which the finance capitals originating in particular countries and presided over by their respective corporate-financial oligarchies constitute different components; that is, today's fascism is arising when inter-imperialist rivalry is extremely muted.

As long as the governments of individual nation-states backed by these corporate-financial oligarchies remain a part of this global arrangement, any human rights violations by them, though arousing global criticism, would continue to be tolerated without bringing them much discomfort. In other words, the human rights rhetoric of contemporary globalization is perfectly compatible with the coming into power of fascistic elements in particular countries, precisely because such coming into power does not threaten any repartitioning of the world through wars as it had done in the 1930s, or even any withdrawal from globalization today.

A Summing Up

Let us now recapitulate the argument of this chapter. We had talked earlier of the spontaneity of the system being challenged by praxis; in special circumstances, as in the post-war period when capitalism faced an existential threat, it had to make significant concessions to the working people. Globalization is a means of rolling back this post-war regime, of reasserting the spontaneity of the system.

For large masses of the workers, peasants, agricultural labourers and petty producers, especially in the third world, for whom freedom consists in their ability to struggle to improve their living condition, globalization entails a loss of freedom compared even to what they had enjoyed under earlier *dirigiste* regimes that had functioned within a democratic set-up. They become victims of growing inequality, and even growing absolute nutritional poverty, through the spontaneous working of the neo-liberal arrangement that characterizes contemporary globalization. At the same time, their capacity to bring about changes in this spontaneous *denouement* through collective political intervention is also taken away from them because of this very phenomenon of globalization, under which finance is *globalized* while the state remains a *nation*-state. And getting out of this globalization altogether is also extremely difficult, since any delinking brings in its wake transitional difficulties which are not just immense in themselves but become even more formidable because of trade sanctions imposed at the behest of the advanced capitalist countries. The working people of the third world are thus kept in a bind within the regime of globalization.

As globalization gets engulfed in an economic crisis, this bind is further tightened through the institution of authoritarian and fascistic political regimes that launch an assault on individual rights and democratic institutions: the abridgement of freedom is then carried to an even higher level. The immanent tendencies of capitalism that bring it to the stage of neo-liberal globalization bring mankind, therefore, to a pass where the conflict between individual freedom and the economic system becomes palpable.

Notes

[1] For the 1993–94 figure, see U. Patnaik (2013). She has kindly made available to me the figure for 2011–12. These figures are based on the findings of the large-scale sample surveys carried out every quinquennium by the official National Sample Survey. The figures for 2017–18 were never published by the government because they were reportedly quite startling. Leaked figures published in newspapers report that in rural India, per capita real expenditure of the *entire population* declined between 2011–12 and 2017–18 by as much as 9 per cent, which certainly suggests a considerable worsening of the level of poverty.

[2] If, despite higher overall GDP growth under neo-liberalism, the rate of growth of output in the petty production sector is lower than under the earlier *dirigiste* regime, and if employment growth in the capitalist sector is lower than before, then the rate of fall in poverty ratio must be lower. But if the poverty ratio did not show much of a fall earlier under *dirigisme* (i.e. if the rate of fall was close to zero earlier) then the ratio must be *rising* under neo-liberalism.

[3] This is the reason why Keynes, who had wanted intervention by the nation-state to maintain near-full employment, had opposed internationalization of finance. He had said, 'let finance above all be national' (Keynes 1933).

[4] This is stated only as a likelihood because one cannot *strictly* draw an inference about the proportion of the nutritionally deprived in total population from macro-level data about food availability.

[5] For an analysis of business upswing in Nazi Germany, see Kalecki (1972b).

CHAPTER THIRTEEN

The Struggle for Individual Freedom

We have seen that liberalism as a political doctrine sees capitalism as an economic system that promotes individual freedom. It is underpinned by an economic analysis that runs through both classical and neo-classical writings, notwithstanding their other important differences. This analysis sees capitalism essentially as a voluntary arrangement where individuals come together to set up the system, including even the employer–wage-labour relationship. Capitalism, in short, is based on cooperation between self-interest-promoting individuals where each is better off than if he or she worked independently. Even economic relations between nations, including trade relations, are such as would ensure that each nation gains from them. With this perception of the system it is hardly surprising that this system is supposed to represent the flowering of individual freedom.

As against this there is a diametrically opposite view that comes out of Marxist economic analysis, which sees capitalism as emerging on the basis of coercion; it is also continuously sustained by coercion, though not necessarily in the form of brute force. This coercion that engenders the system and sustains it is not just exercised by one group of persons, or one class, *on its own volition* against another; on the contrary, even those exercising coercion are under compulsion to do so. The entire system therefore is one of universal alienation, where every economic agent, even while appearing to have agency, actually lacks agency. Each is driven by competition to act in specific ways that do not necessarily conform to his or her own volition. True, the capitalists' alienation is different from the workers', but both are alienated in the sense of having to act in ways demanded by the system rather than by their own volitions. Capitalism is therefore a system of pervasive *unfreedom* of individuals, which is why it is characterized from almost its very beginning by attempts to limit competition that, for workers, takes the form of entering into 'combinations'. These combinations acquire an irreducible character, *quite different from coalitions*. What we see as quotidian capitalism therefore is not its pure form (of atomized agents belonging to any particular class engaged in competition with one another), but one where this pure form is covered by individual agents' attempts at attaining freedom through combinations – in the workers' case, through trade union action. Trade union actions receive a setback through the spontaneous tendency towards centralization of capital that tends to revive competition among workers at a higher level; such actions can therefore never succeed in providing economic agency to the individual until the system itself is transcended for an alternative non-alienating one, socialism.

The period of globalization marked by the hegemony of international finance capital provides confirmation of this. Not only are workers' combinations weakened, but competition between workers of different countries becomes sharper owing to the global mobility of capital-in-production; it is now willing to relocate activities from the metropolitan economies to any corner of the globe where it finds lower wages and a disciplined work-force. In addition, globalization of finance means that the ability of individual workers to acquire *political* agency to change their economic conditions, which had emerged as a historical possibility owing to the spread of democracy in the post-Second World War period, also disappears. The fact that finance becomes global while the state remains a nation-state means that the state willy-nilly has to obey the dictates of finance; otherwise it faces an exodus of finance that threatens a debilitating financial crisis. And getting out of the web of globalization is fraught with serious transitional difficulties even in large economies that can survive on their own by instituting self-sufficiency through the domestic production of most goods. A neo-liberal economy created by globalization thus 'boxes' in the individual economic agents, with the box becoming tighter over time; and as neo-liberal capitalism enters a period of crisis, it forms an alliance with neo-fascism which constitutes a further, palpable negation of individual freedom (P. Patnaik 2021b).

A Revival of New Liberalism?

But the question arises: can't globalized finance be confronted through a coordination among nation-states that produces a surrogate global state that can institute Keynesian policies to breathe meaning into democracy and individual *political* agency?

Keynesian analysis, it would be recalled, had a *sui generis* character: the 'new liberalism' it had propounded had argued that socialism was unnecessary for overcoming the flaws of the capitalist system (mass unemployment), flaws which old liberalism was not even willing to concede (and 'mainstream' economics does not do so even today), and that such flaws could be overcome through state intervention within capitalism itself. It would hold that this proposition, which had been originally advanced in the context of the 1930s, would be as true today as it had been in the 1930s.

In fact, contemporary 'new liberalism'[1] believes that the *impasse* that capitalism faces today can be compared to what it had faced in the inter-war period; it constitutes a reappearance of the 'Keynes–Roosevelt moment' of the 1930s, which can also be resolved by reviving in some form the regime of post-war *dirigisme.* An editorial in *The Financial Times* puts this similarity between the current conjuncture and that of the 1930s quite clearly:

> Today's situation resembles that of the 1930s. Back then, centrist liberals from US president Franklin Delano Roosevelt to British economist John Maynard Keynes saw that liberal democratic capitalism, in order to survive, had to be shown to work for everyone. The victory of their ideas set the stage for the success of western capitalism in the decades after the second world war. Now, like then, capitalism does not need replacement even if it may need repair. (8 May 2020)

What such 'repair' may entail today was suggested in an earlier editorial of the same paper:

> Radical reforms in reversing the prevailing policy direction of the last four decades will need to be put on the table. Governments will have to accept a more active role in the economy. They must see public services as investment rather than as liabilities and look for ways to make the labour market less insecure. Redistribution will again be on the agenda. ... Policies until recently considered eccentric such as basic income and wealth taxes will have to be in the mix. (3 April 2020)

This is clearly an agenda for reversing neo-liberalism and reviving the *dirigisme* of the post-war years. But this agenda is untenable. The replacement of post-war *dirigisme* by neo-liberal globalization, we have seen in earlier chapters, was not an accidental phenomenon; it arose from the fact that post-war *dirigisme* had run into severe dysfunctionality, at the root of which was the conflict between what the system needs in its spontaneity (such as a reserve army of labour and control over the resources of the 'outlying regions') and what pervasive state intervention had secured both at home and abroad (such as high rates of employment in the metropolis, and third world states' increasing control over their own national resources, including land-use, after decolonization). The inflationary upsurge that engulfed post-war *dirigisme* was an outcome of this conflict, and controlling such an upsurge became both necessary and also possible because of the emergence of an international finance capital through the process of centralization of capital that continued unabated even under post-war *dirigisme*.[2]

It became utterly necessary because of the enormous weight of financial assets in asset-holders' portfolios whose loss of real value in the event of inflation had to be avoided; and it became possible because the neo-liberal regime imposed on the world by globalized finance capital meant that income compression could be exercised globally, and especially in 'sensitive' third world economies witnessing increases in primary commodity prices, at the first sign of the emergence of inflation.

Problems with a Coordinated Fiscal Stimulus

A simple return to the post-war *dirigiste regime* under which individual nation-states intervened to stimulate their respective economies is not possible today. This is so both because globalized finance, whose local pillars are the corporate-financial oligarchies of particular countries, will resist any such return as it would abrogate its hegemony; and also because any single country attempting such a return will experience an exodus of finance precipitating a crisis for it. This opens up two possibilities: one is the institution of a new and different, supra-national, *dirigiste regime.*

As regards such a different, more updated *dirigisme*, a *dirigisme* that is supra-national, involving coordinated action by several nation-states including fiscal action, which would prevent globalized finance from coercing *individual* nation-states to accede to its demands as it has been doing under globalization, there is not even any serious proposal for it in the contemporary liberal discourse;[3] and the then US president Joseph Biden's plans for reviving the US economy through state expenditure financed by an increase in corporate taxes and in fiscal deficit had not found any response in the European Union, which makes it rather still-born.[4] Besides, in the US itself, the revival of inflation because of specific factors (despite the existence of substantial unemployment and unutilized capacity) has led to a clamour for rolling back whatever stimulus the Biden administration was planning to provide. Even at a conceptual level, the need for such coordinated action among nation-states, which in effect amounts to setting up a surrogate 'world state' to confront globalized capital for 'reversing the prevailing policy direction of the last four decades', has scarcely figured in the liberal discussion.

There is a remarkable difference in this respect between the situation in the inter-war years and the situation today. At that time, ideas of overcoming the *impasse* of capitalism within a 'new liberal' framework were already current from the end of the 1920s;[5] in the present context, however, no such ideas are making the rounds, other than simply a call for a return to post-war *dirigisme*. In fact this call for a return to post-war *dirigisme* is sustained by the argument, prevalent in enlightened 'new liberal' circles, that the end of the post-war *dirigiste regime* was not a necessary, but only an accidental, development.

Even this call for a return to post-war *dirigisme*, however, is confined only to a small segment of the liberal intelligentsia; for a much larger segment, there is not even an awareness of the current *impasse* of capitalism. The role of the 'educated bourgeoisie', which Keynes had set so much store by, has itself been undermined by the spontaneity of capitalism, especially in its late stage when the system has even directly invaded the intellectual sphere to create an apologetic discourse in its favour. The absence of a conception of any new stage that capitalism may make a transition to, while overcoming its current *impasse*, is symptomatic of the poverty of the intellectual discourse that late capitalism has brought about.

There is a further problem with such a return to a *dirigiste* regime even if we assume that the advanced countries agree to have a coordinated policy of encouraging state expenditure. If any such agreement is confined only to the advanced countries while the third world economies are chained to a neo-liberal regime complete with 'fiscal rectitude', then they would remain submerged in crisis even if there is revival in the metropolis. For instance, when the metropolitan economies recover through Keynesian measures introduced in all of them simultaneously, if the consequent rise in primary commodity prices is sought to be controlled by income compression in the third world, enforced through a fiscal squeeze, then the loss of freedom for the bulk of the world's working people will remain as real as before. The working people in the third world will then continue to face mass unemployment and loss of political agency to effect a shift away from a neo-liberal regime (because of the fear of exodus of finance), exactly as before. The metropolis will in such a case experience a coordinated revival, buttressed by inflation control achieved by fiscal compression in the third world. This would be different from the post-war *dirigiste regime* in two ways: greater coordination, including fiscal coordination among advanced countries; and the loss of freedom with regard to their fiscal and monetary policies compared to the post-war years, in third world countries. Such a 'new liberal' solution to the economic crisis will scarcely vindicate the claim of capitalism to ensure individual freedom *everywhere*. But even this *denouement* can scarcely be said to be on the agenda at present.

Thus, while a simple return to a post-war *dirigiste regime* is untenable and a move to a higher form of *dirigisme is* not even on the agenda, the question remains: how do we see the future unfolding? We argued in the previous chapter that the working people in the third world, and not just in the third world, are boxed in to a 'no exit' situation by the phenomenon of globalization, which makes any praxis by them impossible even as their condition worsens over time;[6] and, in a period of crisis for the global economy, the corporate-financial oligarchies in individual countries even promote fascistic political *regimes* which let loose repression and snuff out constitutionally guaranteed individual freedom. What, then, is the 'exit' one can see from this seemingly 'no exit' situation? We argue here that any 'exit', if it is to be durable, must take the country beyond the hegemony of global finance and hence, by inference, beyond capitalism, of which the hegemony of global finance is the highest development to date.

The Way Ahead

If an internationally coordinated effort to reintroduce *dirigiste* policies is not on the agenda, which it is not, then the transcendence of the currently given situation must occur in *particular* countries, notwithstanding all the difficulties of transition we have discussed earlier; *but it has to be accompanied by capital controls, especially restrictions on the cross-border movements of finance.*

This is a plausible course of action for at least three reasons. First, the organization of workers till today is only at the national level. Hence, the only location where there can be any effective working class intervention, whether in the realm of the economy or of the polity, is the national economy. Second, the peasantry will have to be part of any resistance to neo-liberalism, and, in the absence of any international organization of the peasantry, the only location where a worker–peasant alliance can be built is at the level of the nation. Third, since neo-liberalism, having reached a deadend, has aligned itself with neo-fascism, any anti-fascist struggle that occurs in a world characterized by nation-states will naturally have to be at the level of the nation.

The struggle against the alliance between neo-liberalism and neo-fascism that has been forged of late must, therefore, be at the national level, by the workers and peasants belonging to a particular nation coming together on an agenda that seeks to improve the conditions of life and the democratic rights of the people.

The real hallmark of a seemingly 'no exit' situation is not that there is never any 'exit' from it, but that the 'exit' from it tends to be sudden, unexpected and momentous. In other words, the very snuffing out of resistance *in the normal course* implies not the perennial triumph of 'no exit', but that the struggles of the workers and peasants no longer characterize the *quotidian* existence of the system; and when this happens, the breaking out of this situation occurs in a sudden unexpected and unforeseen rush. Indeed, Marx had suggested in *Value, Price and Profit* that as workers fail to make any headway in their economic struggles, they engage increasingly in direct political struggle; and this means the possibility of sudden and momentous advance on their part. This is also the effect that the growth of fascism has, of engendering resistance in a sudden burst, precisely because more long drawn-out and normal resistance is precluded by it. Such a sudden burst of resistance however requires a programme.

Fascism in fact unites the opposition; it unites the adherents of liberalism and Marxism despite their different *weltanschauungs.* It unites them for ensuring that the usual array of democratic freedoms, whether at the individual level or at the level of organizations of the working people, gets restored. Uniting the opposition would require the adoption of a programme that must promise some relief to the working people against the immiserizing tendency of globalization, and hence putting some restrictions on the global mobility of finance which underlies its hegemony. And restrictions on the global mobility of finance would necessarily bring in their train trade restrictions, so that the balance of payments becomes viable even in the absence of large financial inflows.

Such restrictions, in turn, would require the promotion of greater self-sufficiency, an orientation of production towards the domestic market, and an emphasis on the development of peasant agriculture as well as on greater income and wealth equality as the means for expanding the domestic market. All these would involve a development trajectory very different from what prevailed under neo-liberal globalization.

The matter can be looked at a little differently. Contemporary fascism, we have seen, is *not* nationalist in the sense of being opposed to the hegemony of globalized finance; not even Donald Trump, despite his imposition of trade restrictions, had expressed any opposition to the free movements of finance. Besides, fascism is itself supported by the domestic corporate-financial oligarchy that is fully integrated with globalized finance. Contemporary fascism, therefore, far from representing a retreat from globalization, constitutes its ultimate limit, its real end-point. A political struggle against fascism must simultaneously therefore encompass, to start with, an economic struggle against at least some of the aspects of neo-liberal globalization. It must bring relief to the people, revive peasant agriculture, and reduce income and wealth inequalities. In short, it must set out by adopting a path different from that of neo-liberal globalization.

This would not mean indifference or hostility towards the rest of the world. Embracing neo-liberal globalization is not synonymous with global solidarity; on the contrary, the opposition by the anti-fascist resistance to racial, communal or ethnic chauvinism, all of which are promoted by fascism, would make a political regime that comes to power after the defeat of fascism more internationalist in its outlook, even while rolling back neo-liberal globalization.

This alternative path, apposite in the context of a third world country, with which we shall be exclusively concerned here, will of course, to start with, be a path of capitalist development, though a capitalist path of a different kind from what neo-liberal globalization had entailed. But the very resistance put up by the domestic corporate-financial oligarchy and by the advanced capitalist countries against such an alternative path, which we discussed in the last chapter, will force a shift in trajectory in the direction of socialism. If private capital, both domestic and foreign, makes a change back to a neo-liberal trajectory a condition for undertaking investment, then public investment will necessarily have to make up for such an 'investment strike' on their part, and so on. At every stage, when hurdles come up which present such a political regime with a choice, either to retreat back to a situation of hegemony by globalized finance or to move forward in the direction of greater economic empowerment of the working people, the regime will have to choose the latter option; and if it keeps choosing the latter option, then the sequence of such choices will engender a move towards socialism.

A primary difference between post-war *dirigisme* in the third world and the new *dirigiste* regimes that would emerge after the defeat of the current wave of fascism would be the latter's promotion of peasant agriculture, and the metamorphosis of peasant agriculture over time to more cooperativist or collectivist forms on a voluntary basis. This would keep enlarging the home market while providing the political base, through the maintenance of a strong worker–peasant alliance, for fighting domestic and foreign capitalist pressure.

There is no gainsaying, however, that this path of delinking from current globalization and proceeding towards socialism will be extremely difficult for any third world country, at least until a similar political change against the hegemony of finance capital occurs within some of the advanced capitalist countries themselves. But until that happens, the period of transition will be extremely difficult.

To tide over this difficult period of transition, the need for political education among the working people is of paramount importance. The sooner the 'educated bourgeoisie' – which Keynes had talked about and which the Marxist tradition also emphasizes, though within a different *weltanschuung* – is caught up by the 'educated working people', the greater are the chances of success of such a transition towards socialism, and hence also towards individual freedom for which socialism constitutes a necessary condition.

This is so because, unlike under capitalism – where there is a spontaneity to the behaviour of the system, so that economics shapes politics, for otherwise the system becomes dysfunctional because of political interference that runs counter to its spontaneity – under socialism, there is no such spontaneity. Because of this politics shapes economics, and the people can collectively shape their economic destiny by taking appropriate political decisions through their elected representative government.

The immediate question that will be raised against this is that actually existing socialism has not seen elected representative governments, and has generally ridden roughshod over individual freedom. Then how can one put much faith in socialism as the means for achieving individual freedom (though admittedly it constitutes only a necessary condition)? Let us turn to this question in the next chapter.

Notes

[1] When I say contemporary 'new liberalism', I do not mean the various academic strands located in the USA that claim a Keynesian lineage. Joan Robinson had even expressed strong opposition to post-war American 'Keynesian' interpretations of Keynes, which she called 'bastard Keynesianism' (see Robinson 1962). I mean by 'new liberalism', those who would follow the Keynesian 'reform' agenda as a feasible agenda under capitalism.

[2] While centralization of capital, entailing the accumulation of huge amounts of finance in metropolitan banks, was the general factor underlying the emergence of international finance capital, a specific factor in the background was the post-war

scenario where the leading capitalist country, the US, did not have access to any 'drain of wealth' from the colonies, as the pre-war leader, Britain, had. The US had to run current account deficits on its balance of payments (as the leader of the capitalist world is generally required to do) without the support of such unrequited transfers from colonies. These deficits, therefore, had to be financed by printing dollars, which was officially declared under the Bretton Woods system to be 'as good as gold' with a fixed price of $35 per ounce of gold (and played the same role unofficially even after the collapse of the Bretton woods system); this outpouring of American IOUs in the form of dollars *inter alia* provided the base for the enormous financial superstructure that has got built up in post-war capitalism.

[3] During the Great Depression of the 1930s, both Keynes and a group of German trade unions had suggested a coordinated fiscal stimulus by several advanced capitalist countries as a way out of the crisis, but there were no takers for the idea. See Kindleberger (1974). Today, there are no such serious proposals.

[4] Even the global minimum corporate tax rate proposed by the Biden administration has turned out to be a disappointment. Against the 25 per cent suggested by the US government, agreement was ultimately reached at 15 per cent, which does not mean much.

[5] Lloyd George, the leader of the Liberal Party in Britain, had already suggested in 1929, under Keynes' prompting, a system of public works financed by a fiscal deficit to overcome unemployment. Against this the British Treasury had famously argued, in a manner reminiscent of the contemporary argument, that a fiscal deficit 'crowds out' private investment and hence does not reduce unemployment, since the employment generated in the public works is offset by the employment lost through the reduction in private investment that gets 'crowded out'. This argument was based on the fallacy, exposed by Kahn (1931), that there is a 'fixed pool' of savings: that the increase in output caused by public works will leave savings unchanged. In fact, Kahn argued, at any given interest rate in a closed economy, a fiscal deficit generates additional private savings whose excess over private investment is exactly equal to itself.

[6] The 'no exit' situation we have been talking about has nothing to do with the pandemic. In fact our entire discussion so far has excluded the pandemic, which has only made matters worse for the working people of the world.

CHAPTER FOURTEEN

Socialism and Individual Freedom

At the risk of repetition, let us once again recapitulate the argument so far. We have defined individual freedom in this book in terms of the individual's agency in the economic and the political terrain.

The Argument So Far

Classical political economy and its precursors, among whom we looked at John Locke, contended that 'capitalism' itself (not a term used by them) constituted an improvement in the position of the erstwhile petty producers who became hired workers and therefore it was constituted through the voluntary participation of the individual, which made it essentially a cooperativist arrangement. Classical political economy also contended that any further improvement in the position of the labourers was restrained neither by the state nor by the system nor by any organized group of oppressors, but by the labourers' own habits of multiplying too rapidly whenever their economic position improved. There was no question, therefore, of any denial of freedom under capitalism; on the contrary, this was a system that arose out of the exercise of individual freedom.

Neo-classical economics, though it explicitly says little about the origin of capitalism, can also be interpreted as seeing the emergence of capitalism as a result of individuals joining together voluntarily to improve their lives. As long as the state maintains law and order and the rules of the game of competitive capitalism, and does not go beyond the appropriate levels of intervention in cases of 'externalities', individual freedom is ensured. Many neo-classical economists would support state intervention even beyond this limit for bringing about an improvement in the distribution of endowments, but the transfer of endowments from some individuals to others in such a case has to be a 'lump-sum' transfer that does not affect the 'efficiency' of the system, and the extent of transfer has to be decided by a 'democratic' state where the government is elected through individuals exercising their political agency (as is the case in western democracies). Capitalism with such a 'democratic' state with an elected government represents, therefore, the full flowering of individual freedom.

The New Liberalism of Keynes argued that *laissez faire* capitalism *did* indeed entail a denial of freedom, since it was generally characterized by 'involuntary unemployment'. An improvement from a state of 'involuntary unemployment' entails a non-zero-sum game, and it can be effected with state intervention which requires nothing more than a correct *theoretical* understanding of the problem. Since state intervention can overcome the denial of freedom that 'involuntary unemployment' entails, capitalism modified by such intervention by a 'democratic' state with an elected government can achieve the full realization of individual freedom.

All these strands of political economy which see individual freedom as being achieved under capitalism within a western 'democratic' framework constitute a liberal position. Or, looking at it from the other end, the liberal position sees capitalism within a western 'democratic' framework as the end of history (rather like the Prussian state in Hegel's analysis), though it arrives at this conclusion via diverse political economy routes. The basic difference between this position and that of Marx is the latter's recognition of capitalism as a 'spontaneous system' where individual economic agents are obliged to play specific roles as a result of the unavoidable competition that the system foists on them, and the state too is not free to act in any manner it wishes. Capitalism entails, therefore, a *denial* of freedom in the sense of a denial of agency to the individual even when that individual is apparently taking all decisions entirely on his or her own.

It is to escape from this state that the workers form combinations to limit competition among themselves, and thereby to assert their aspiration for freedom. The struggle between these two opposing tendencies – on the one hand, the immanent tendency of the system to reduce individual economic agents to the status of mere cogs, and on the other hand, the attempt by individual economic agents to overcome this tendency by entering into combinations – is everywhere visible on the surface in capitalism. But given the very nature of capitalism, that is, given the spontaneous forces it puts into play, the struggle I have just outlined is necessarily unequal: the *political* agency of the individual is limited because all efforts by state intervention (of the sort that Keynesian New Liberalism outlines) to give it support can only do so by going against the immanent tendencies of the capitalist system, and that renders the system dysfunctional, inducing ultimately, *within its confines*, a retreat from such intervention.

Individual freedom in any genuine and substantial sense in this perception therefore is an impossibility under capitalism, a conclusion that acquires special force when we reckon with the fact that the domain of capitalism covers not just the workers and capitalists in the metropolis, but also the working people in the periphery who are ruthlessly subjugated to the will of metropolitan capital. This is particularly evident in its latest phase, the phase of neo-liberal capitalism.

It follows from this analysis, which links the loss of individual freedom with the spontaneous tendencies of capitalism, that freedom is only achievable when capitalism is transcended. Since socialism alone is conceived as a non-spontaneous system – that is to say, a system where the workers can collectively control their destiny – it offers a systematic political economy that is compatible with individual freedom. Workers control their work environment through factory councils; and they control the working of the economy through political intervention via the state which is no longer constrained by the immanent tendencies of a spontaneous system. Both these become possible because of the social ownership of the means of production that overcomes private property, and hence can overcome competition. Individuals, in short, can be free as *individuals* only by being part of a *collective* that constitutes the foundation of socialism.

And yet, paradoxically, 'actually existing' socialist societies have also been characterized by a denial of individual freedom in a different sense from that occurring under capitalism. The restraint upon human agency exercised by the 'spontaneity' of capitalism has been replaced in actually existing socialist practice by the restraint exercised by political control. This is a failure on its part because nothing in the idea of workers' control and social ownership is tantamount to the idea of freedom-undermining political control. It is a distortion of the promise of socialism. This failure has been sought to be explained, with justification no doubt, by the specific historical circumstances of its birth; and whenever any transition to socialism occurs even in the future, such distortions arising from the specific circumstances of its being surrounded by hostile capitalist powers will inevitably occur.

Even if we diagnose these failures of actually existing socialism in these ways, any effort at rectification of such distorting failures becomes impossible if there are *misconceptions about the nature of socialism*. Some of these misconceptions gain currency merely as *ex post* justifications for what has actually occurred; but others are genuine theoretical misconceptions about socialism. All these misconceptions have to be removed if the appropriate praxis towards socialism is to avoid the failures of the past. The present chapter is addressed to this issue: it discusses some prevalent misconceptions about socialism which have been conducive to an abrogation of individual freedom under it.

Misconceptions about Socialism

The basic misconception lies in seeing socialism as yet another mode of production on par with earlier modes of production, which then, on a certain reading of historical materialism, treats the socialist project as one of enhancing *production* rather than enhancing *freedom.* Historical materialism, it is argued, holds that a mode of production becomes historically obsolete, and hence ripe for transcendence, when the relations of production which characterize it become a fetter on the further development of productive forces. It follows that the succeeding mode of production must unleash once again the development of the productive forces which had reached a state of stagnation under the earlier mode, which means that this development must occur at a faster rate than under the mode of production being transcended, prior to its transcendence. The common inference from this is that the transition to socialism must involve much higher rates of GDP growth than during the period immediately preceding it. This emphasis on production has typically characterized all socialist countries including the Soviet Union, as much in the 1920s and 1930s as after the Second World War, and China to this day.

There is nothing wrong, of course, with emphasizing production. In fact, when countries transitioning to socialism are surrounded by hostile capitalist powers keen to thwart this transition, acquiring a strong production base is an essential condition for the success of the transition; the point, however, is that when this emphasis is erected into a rationale for the socialist project, the project inevitably comes in the way of enhancing *freedom,* which was always the rationale in Marx underlying the socialist project.

The contradiction between these two considerations manifests itself in several ways, of which we shall mention only two. The first is quite obvious: it relates to the fact that the development of the productive forces in an economy making a transition to socialism typically takes the form of rapid *industrialization*, at least if the transition occurs in a relatively underdeveloped economy, where a surplus is squeezed out of the peasantry;

the Soviet Union was indeed a relatively underdeveloped economy at the time of the October revolution and so, despite all the care taken to draw distinctions within the peasantry and to ensure that only the rich peasants are squeezed and not the other segments, there was an inevitable rupture of the worker–peasant alliance upon which the revolution was founded, which in turn led to the strengthening of the authoritarianism of the ruling party in order to 'save the revolution'. In the Soviet Union, this was manifested in the forced collectivization of agriculture in the 1920s, both a symptom and a consolidation of the authoritarian tendency in the realm of the polity.

The second, a less discussed problem, relates to the adoption of central planning as the means of rapid development. Central planning necessarily entails an abridgement of individual freedom. This is because, looking upon labour as a 'resource', which central planning necessarily does, amounts to an objectification of it, which is a denial of individual agency, a denial of the worker, *as part of the collective*, being the historical subject under socialism.[1]

The essence of socialism must lie in an alternative work motivation and work discipline. Work motivation and work discipline are ensured under slavery by the fact that the slave is the property of the master who can use physical coercion upon the slave. Under feudalism, likewise, work motivation and work discipline are ensured by the *monsignor*'s whip. Under capitalism, where there is no explicit coercion, the implicit coercion of the 'threat of the sack', that is, the threat of being thrown out of employment and being consigned to the ranks of the reserve army of labour, plays the same role. Under socialism, however, there must be neither explicit nor implicit coercion: work motivation and work discipline must come from the *volition* of the workers, that is, the conscious commitment of the individual worker to the overall collective to which he or she belongs. The realization of a centrally worked-out plan, however, requires workers being *directed.* Volition, in other words, is necessarily replaced by centrally exercised political coercion as the source of work motivation and work discipline,[2] which is a negation of socialism.

Central planning which is characteristic of a 'command economy', that is, an extremely centralized economy, is bound to be accompanied by a highly centralized polity, typically represented by a one-party dictatorship; and this political form too abridges individual freedom. Seeing central planning as a necessary accompaniment of socialism, which follows from the perception of socialism as enhancing the development of productive forces, leads to a situation where individual freedom remains ever-elusive.

An early manifestation of this tendency to use coercion for work discipline and work motivation was the call, which Lenin had very strongly opposed, for the 'militarization' of trade unions that had surfaced in the Soviet Union in the 1920s. But prioritizing production for a strengthening of the workers' state, slipping into the use of state coercion to impose work discipline and work motivation on the argument that the state using this coercion is after all a *workers'* state, is corrosive of the 'community', and the 'subjecthood' of the class alliance underlying it, that brought about the revolution in the first place. The dictatorship *of* the proletariat then gets transformed over time to a dictatorship *on behalf of* the proletariat.

Decentralized Non-Commodity Production

The spontaneity of capitalism arises from the fact of competition in which every economic agent is caught, which is a hallmark of commodity production and is carried to its zenith under capitalism. So the question arises: if both commodity production and central planning are to be avoided under socialism, since both lead to a denial of freedom, how should one then envisage the functioning of a socialist economy?

Here we come up against a second misconception, which is to pose central planning and commodity production as the only two alternatives. This happens because central planning is seen as the *only* possible alternative to commodity production, a perception based on an erroneous understanding of commodity production. which we have discussed already in chapter two. Commodity production is not synonymous with *any* production for the market, or *any* production for exchange even when it is mediated by money. In Mughal India, for instance, the surplus appropriated by the emperor was sold on the market for money, but that did not make Mughal India a commodity-producing economy. Commodity production entails that the produce is *not a use-value for the producer* but *pure* exchange-value, simply a sum of money; it is necessarily associated with impersonality. Commodity production therefore can be suppressed under socialism without necessarily introducing central planning.

Socialism must mean the direct involvement of workers in the taking of decisions that affect their economic and political lives. For this, the socialist society must be characterized by a set of sub-national or regional units (communes) which are largely self-sufficient in economic terms and largely self-governing politically, where workers take decisions collectively. (Where the commune itself is too large, direct decision-making by workers may occur at a sub-commune level.)[3]

These collective units may exchange outputs among themselves, which would not constitute commodity production. Some production would also occur in centrally managed units and be distributed by the central government, constituted from elected representatives of the entire working people of the country, to these dispersed communes. Likewise, a central authority (which could be an independent constitutional body and not necessarily the central government itself) would tax away a part of each commune's income, and distribute it between the central government for its expenditure and the communes for meeting their investment needs.

Such fiscal intervention would serve two distinct purposes: the promotion of equality (defined in a specific manner as we discuss below) among the communes, and an adjustment of the overall rate of investment in the economy. The latter can be brought about in the following manner. If the resources appropriated from the communes by a central authority and distributed among them are statutorily required to be used exclusively for investment purposes (and not for consumption) while the tax levied impinges (partly at least) on collective consumption, then an alteration in the ratio of resources mobilized to the GDP becomes simultaneously a means for altering the balance between consumption and investment. For instance, if the communes as a whole have been investing at a rate that is too high relative to the growth in the number of workers (even taking into account the growth in labour productivity brought about by technological progress, and even after considering the possibility of internal voluntary migration), then the appropriation (and distribution) of fiscal resources relative to the gross domestic product can be reduced; similarly, in the opposite case it can be increased. And in this manner total investment can be socialized despite a decentralized economic arrangement. We discuss this in greater detail below.

There would also be other bodies, like factory councils, to oversee the conditions of work in each factory. *The self-managed commune however is the locus where decisions affecting individual workers are taken by a collective that includes the individual workers themselves.* An important decision, apart from the specific projects on which the commune's investment resources are to be spent, would be the degree to which the benefits of technological progress should be enjoyed through greater output for a given labour-force, or through greater leisure for a given output.

All this, however, would still not prevent individual freedom being encroached upon by the collective even at the level of the commune, let alone in the aggregate. Against such encroachment, therefore, the individual must enjoy a set of constitutionally guaranteed, justiciable, fundamental rights, which would include both economic rights (such as the right to employment, free food, free housing, free education and health care, and old age pension and disability benefits), and political rights like the right to freedom of expression, to religion and so on. These rights would constitute the *differentia specifica* of a socialist society compared to capitalism, for capitalism can never guarantee fundamental economic rights, in particular the right to employment.

Such a socialist universe would be characterized by a multiplicity of political parties, each bound by the constitution and by elections to government and other bodies, though these elected representatives would respect as far as possible the decisions taken at the direct assemblies of the commune.

If we keep in mind this vision of a socialist society and economy, we will have to conclude that these misconceptions I have pointed out about socialism are what thwart its realization. Even leaving aside the historical circumstances in which actually existing socialism had been born, it was also imbued with a theoretical misconception of socialism that made the freedom of the individual a matter of secondary importance, secondary to what was considered the primary objective of a socialist economy and polity, namely, a rapid development of the productive forces. For this, a command arrangement was considered necessary; *but this conception was itself erroneous.* It must be abandoned and the conception of socialism must be seen essentially as a freedom-enhancing rather than a production-enhancing project.

The Exaggerated Fear of Capitalist Restoration

I have said that 'productionism' (for more on this notion, see U. Patnaik and P. Patnaik 2021) amounts to a misconception about socialism, and de-emphasized the centrality given to production in the understanding of socialism. But it is important to stress that de-emphasizing production must be done with the right purpose and motivation, which has not always been done in historically existing socialist societies. A proper understanding of the socialist ideal would de-emphasize production because, as I argued above, it thwarts the socialist goal of enhancing human freedom. But in socialist China in earlier decades, de-emphasizing production was motivated quite differently – by a cry for 'class struggle' instead. During the Cultural Revolution one of the two warring sides was supposed to be upholding 'production' while the other was upholding the primacy of 'class struggle', not just struggle against the defenders of the old order, but also against elements *within the class alliance itself that made the revolution.* Thus 'production' and 'class struggle' were seen to be opposite points of view, the former representing a rightist and the latter a leftist tendency. Both tendencies, however, have this attitude in common: they destroy the 'subjecthood' of the class alliance that brought about the revolution.

The transformation that allows a society to transcend capitalism will necessarily be based on an alliance between workers and petty producers, especially peasants. If this transformation is to move forward towards socialism, then the peasants must be induced to move towards collective forms of property *voluntarily*, without being subjected to any coercion. Here, ever since the days of Lenin's *Two Tactics of Social Democracy*, the understanding has been that while the rich peasants will oppose such a move, the poor peasants will approve of it. On this conception, in the course of the onward progress of the revolution, the class alliance must keep changing, first making itself broad-based to incorporate the entire peasantry, and later turning against the rich peasants when a transition is made from the *democratic* stage of the revolution to the *socialist* stage of the revolution.

This, however, is an altogether unrealistic perspective. If the rich peasants know that the revolution they are supporting in its democratic stage will eventually turn against them, they will not support it to begin with; or they will not support it sufficiently wholeheartedly to ensure its victory. The revolution, therefore, cannot turn against *any* of its supporting classes during *its entire course*. It has to change its character by inducing *all* classes who make the revolution to *voluntarily* support such change from the outset. Collectivization therefore must be voluntarily effected, through inducement rather than the use of force against any section.

This, to be sure, may not be easy to accomplish, but it is essential. The reason why it is considered so necessary to carry on class struggle against some segments of the original class alliance, notably the rich peasants, is that they are supposed to constitute a proto-capitalist class, so that if they are not opposed, the revolution will get engulfed by a capitalist restoration. The entire emphasis on *class struggle* in the transition to socialism, as opposed to voluntary metamorphosis of the rich peasants through inducements, arises from the fear of capitalist restoration; and this fear is rooted in the phenomenon of commodity production which prevails in such a transitional society and which, it is argued by this conception, constitutes a fertile breeding ground for capitalism.

This whole conception is questionable. As we have already seen, commodity production itself does not simply mean any production for the market; genuine commodity production arises only when the product that is produced is no longer a use-value for the person producing it, but represents a pure exchange-value, that is, a pure sum of money. Commodity production therefore must entail the cessation of all personal relationships, which typically arises in the case of long-distance trade, rather than in producing for a known local market. Countries like India have had millennia of production for the market, typified by the C–M–C circuit, without the capitalist mode of production emerging out of it. Thus, this conception which de-emphasizes production for the sake of class struggle misconstrues the nature of commodity production, including in an aspiring socialist society.

The emphasis on *class struggle* after the revolution, as I said, serves to dismantle the class alliance that brought the revolution into being in the first place, to take 'subjecthood' away from this class alliance, and this has the freedom-threatening outcome of vesting all subjecthood in the hands of a small group, typically the 'Party'. Thus, as it turns out, the emphasis on class struggle plays the same role as the emphasis on production; both are different ways of destroying the 'subjecthood' of the class alliance that brought about the revolution. Both ignore the necessity of preserving the 'community' in the form of the class alliance, which is a necessity because it is essential for the success of the transition to socialism.[4] That class alliance has to be forged and preserved throughout the entire period of transition, and though, of course, its character will change through this period, that change must be brought about through inducement and not the use of force. So, to sum up, if emphasizing production leads to a suppression of individual freedom, so does what is apparently its opposite, namely class struggle within the alliance that effected the revolution.[5]

Such a de-emphasizing of class struggle *within* the alliance during the transition to socialism which the alliance is seeking has an important further implication. *It makes the transition from capitalism to socialism altogether different from all earlier transitions from one mode of production to another.* The earlier transitions had all been spontaneous transitions, in sync with the spontaneous character of history recognized by historical materialism. Though a bourgeoisie, for instance, may have been in the forefront of the transition from feudalism to capitalism and may have effected the bourgeois revolution, it did not have a planned or conscious objective in terms of the nature of the economy or society towards which it was working; and that is even more true of the earlier transitions to slavery or to feudalism. But the transition from capitalism to socialism is altogether different, because the class at the forefront of this transition is clearly aware of where it wants to go.

It may have to make tactical adjustments along the way; it may not proceed towards its objective in a direct linear manner, but it does not lose sight of its objective.

Once we recognize this fact, a number of very important conclusions follow which are at variance with the standard perceptions of the transition to socialism; and I have been arguing in this chapter that it is this variance which diagnoses why 'actually existing socialism' did not live up to the promise of being the harbinger of individual freedom.

Recognizing this fact means that the preservation of the 'subjecthood' of the *class* (or the class alliance) that leads the process of going beyond capitalism (and within whose corpus the individuals freely dissolve their agency, in so far as that agency is individualistically understood) becomes essential for sustaining the entire process of transition to socialism. In fact everything else becomes secondary to this key objective of preserving its 'subjecthood'. An example will make the point.

The Pitfalls of Stage Dependence

While demarcating the transition to socialism into distinct stages, as I have done, is *analytically* important, making the achievement of the goals of the revolution *stage-dependent* is untenable. Here, one has even got to take issue with Marx's own vision in *A Critique of the Gotha Programme,* where he says that in the earlier stage of the transition payment to a worker should depend upon the work done, while in the later stage it will be determined by need, with the transition from the earlier to the later stage being determined by the further development of the productive forces. This is quite untenable for a number of reasons.

First, if, as we have seen, the development of the productive forces has to cede primacy to the need to maintain the class alliance that essayed the revolution and its 'subjecthood', then this later stage may either never come or will take so long in coming that income inequalities would have got ossified by then. Put differently, unless the so-called first stage itself is also permeated by the characteristics of the so-called second stage, the latter will never materialize. In the case under discussion, unless distribution according to needs is to a considerable extent already introduced *from the very beginning,* within the first stage itself, it will never appear at a later stage.[6] If the primacy of production has to be subordinated to the need for maintaining the class alliance, then all conclusions that follow from the primacy of production, such as a second stage succeeding the first, have got to be abandoned.

Secondly, this entire discussion downplays the importance of consumerism, of self-centredness, of a rivalrous attitude towards fellowmen and, in the present context, of the crisis induced by climate change. The transition to socialism must be accompanied by a change in all these respects. In fact the revolution itself marks the arrival of this change, and unless the transition to socialism builds on this change, starting from the morrow of the revolution, it will never succeed in bringing it about at some later date. An anti-consumerist, anti-possessive 'cultural revolution' must be an essential feature of the transition to socialism, and this must also partly compensate for the lack of development of the productive forces. In a third world society, what is required for the transition to socialism is a conscious rejection of capitalist consumerism, not an imitation of it, and not the development of the productive forces to some level where everyone can enjoy it.

In short, the need to have greater egalitarianism in income distribution, the need to introduce the criterion of 'need' into income distribution, must find expression from the very beginning of the transition to socialism rather than waiting for an adequate development of the productive forces.[7]

What has just been said of 'stages' holds also for the so-called 'laws' under socialism. If the transition to socialism is led by a voluntarily self-mutating class alliance that presides over it from the revolution (or even before the revolution) onwards, then the course of this transition depends upon the concrete problems and possibilities. To talk of 'laws' according to which this transition must be effected is, once again, to downplay the 'subjecthood' of this class alliance. True, it can be said that the 'subjecthood' of this class alliance lies precisely in recognizing these 'laws' and acting in accordance with them. But, while the constraints faced during the transition to socialism have to be recognized and overcome (which is obvious), to elevate this entire process into some 'laws' that presumably operate independently of human will and consciousness, is to negate 'subjecthood'. One can talk of 'laws' (though it would be more accurate to talk of 'tendencies') in a *spontaneous* system, but not in a system whose *differentia specifica* lies in human intervention to overcome the system's 'spontaneity'.

The Great Discussion

An even more fundamental misconception relates to the role of 'theory'. Here two different conceptions get mixed up. From the *Communist Manifesto* to Lenin's *What is to be Done?* there is a line of argumentation which states that workers on their own can develop at best a trade union consciousness, but not a socialist consciousness which requires a certain degree of theoretical awareness and which therefore has to be brought to them from outside by bourgeois or petty-bourgeois intellectuals who have declassed themselves. Alongside this, however, there is a quite different, second view that is taken to be identical with it, namely that a 'vanguard' party which is theoretically informed must always lead the proletariat.

These two, however, are by no means identical. The second view suggests a perennial division, and hence an arbitrary one, between those who 'have theory' and those who lack theory and have to be led, which the first statement that deals with a particular situation does not necessarily suggest.[8] And it is the second view that officially underlies the supposed role of the Party under 'actually existing' socialism. It is untenable because it arbitrarily separates the 'theorists' from the 'non-theorists', the Party from the Class, the 'givers' from the 'receivers' of theory, which is but a short step to the dictatorship of the Party replacing the dictatorship of the proletariat.

Even on its own assumptions, namely that theory is developed by the 'vanguard', the validity of that theory needs to be tested with reference to the experience of the proletariat, for which the proletariat must be free to express itself. The validity of the theory, in other words, cannot be tested by obliterating the 'subjecthood' of the proletariat or of the class alliance that was leading the transition to socialism. Even if the vanguard makes the theory, as long as the theory so made has got to be tested in practice, it cannot provide an argument for destroying the 'subject-hood' of the leading class alliance. But it does destroy this 'subjecthood' when the primacy of theory is taken to mean that if the claim of its validity is contested by significant sections of the class alliance, then that act of contestation constitutes a hostile act, an act of counter-revolution. From that moment onwards, the dictatorship of the vanguard replaces the dictatorship of the class alliance, and the transition to socialism where individual freedom would come into its own gets subverted.

The arrival of this moment however is not just a sociological phenomenon, in the sense of being an outcome of conflicts that characterize transitional societies; it is immanent in the very conception of theory that underlies this picture. This suggests that those who make theory and those for whom theory is made are two distinct entities; it does not visualize the process of theory-making as encompassing both. If theory-making encompasses both, that is, if it breaks down the binary between a distinct class of theory-makers and a separate one of theory-users, then the proletariat does not get dissociated even in principle from its 'subjecthood'. This dissociation, in short, arises from the very conception of theory-making as a separate activity from which some are excluded at any point of time.

If this conception is abandoned, if the distinction between theory and praxis – the latter presumed to be constituting the activities of numerous footsoldiers who put into practice the conclusions drawn from theory – is abandoned, then that amounts, in effect, to abandoning the distinction between some who direct and some who are directed. Immanent in this distinction is a subversion of the transition to socialism, a substitution of the Party for the class alliance, the replacement of the dictatorship of the class alliance by that of the Party. Once we abandon it and recognize that theorizing itself is a collective act, that even if theory is *originally* brought from outside to the workers who have till then been deliberately kept ignorant under capitalism and have not yet gone beyond trade union consciousness, this original dichotomy gets overcome subsequently, then the transition to socialism becomes a process of 'great discussion'. Bertolt Brecht had described socialism as the 'great production'; it is in fact a process of 'great intellectual production', or of 'great discussion'.[9]

This discussion cannot be confined to a universe consisting of a single Party. Even the outcome of the discussion may not be accurately summarized or implemented by a single Party. The richness and diversity of proletarian political life cannot be captured by a single Party. To be sure, if that Party was characterized by the tolerance of diversity within it, then matters could be different; but in a Party following strict discipline where divergence of opinions is suppressed within the Party, the guarantee for intellectual diversity that is so essential for the 'great discussion' can only be provided by a multiplicity of Parties.

To say that the post-revolutionary transition to socialism must be accompanied by a voluntarily induced mutation within the class alliance leading this transition rather than by 'class struggle' within it involving the violent suppression of one class by another, to say that there must be a multiplicity of Parties associated with it for a meaningful 'great discussion', to say that the binary between a set of 'theory-givers' and a set of 'theory-receivers' must be abandoned as it is the harbinger of a one-Party dictatorship, and to say that the emphasis on the development of the productive forces must be replaced by the emphasis on the enhancement of freedom, does not entail a weakening of the struggle for this transition. On the contrary, the *collapse* of actually existing socialism has been effected by the institution of a single-Party dictatorship, which, on the one hand, gets eventually alienated from the class alliance that brought about the initial revolution, rendering the latter quiescent in the face of the slide-back to capitalism, and on the other hand, spawns a class of proto-bourgeoisie within the leadership of the Party itself that leads this slide-back. The post-revolutionary state can have laws that put limits to dissent, that define constraints on the political praxis of the multiplicity of Parties, and so on. But these must be laws that come out of the 'great discussion' and hence enjoy a general consensus.

Misconceptions about the Role of the Market

The economics of the transition to socialism has been debated at great length, but, unfortunately, this debate has been marred from the beginning by misconceptions. Preobrazhensky's (1926) 'primitive socialist accumulation' was the starting point of such misconceptions, since practising it would break the class alliance underlying the revolution, institutionalizing a one-Party dictatorship that ultimately fails the revolution. In the early years after the October revolution (and in countries with a similar class profile), enlisting the support of the peasantry for the introduction of 'land-augmenting' technological progress (which increases annual output per acre through multiple-cropping and yield increases on land of a given size) must constitute the specifically socialist way of bringing about development, as opposed to an imitation of what capitalism had ruthlessly enforced in its time, namely a process of primitive accumulation. Likewise, as we have already seen, the proposition that commodity production engenders capitalism has been used, on the basis of an erroneous understanding of commodity production, to advocate the violent suppression of petty production, for which again there is little justification and which turns out to be ultimately counter-productive for the transition.

Similarly, the significance of the 1930s debate about the possibility of 'rational calculations' in a socialist economy which is characterized by central planning rather than the pervasive use of markets has been wholly misinterpreted.[10] This is a misinterpretation, and a fundamental sorting out of the confusions that surround the use of the notion of 'markets' is needed to expose it.

The misinterpretation arises because of a lack of distinction between the market as a 'computer analogue' and the market as a social institution, and taking the two as synonymous. When Ludwig von Mises argued that the absence of markets makes socialist countries incapable of allocating resources efficiently as markets under capitalism do, he expressed the belief that the actually existing markets under capitalism behaved like a computer analogue, *which is just not true.* If the market under capitalism behaved like a computer analogue allocating resources efficiently to bring about a Pareto-optimum, *then there would be no unemployment under capitalism.*

Capitalism, however, is characterized perennially by unemployment – not just technological unemployment, but also what Keynes called 'involuntary unemployment'. A situation cannot be an optimum if one of the inputs remains perennially unutilized under it. It followed, therefore, that von Mises' claim was wrong to start with. The actual role of the market is that of a social institution in a capitalist economy, an institution through which discipline is imposed to force work motivation and work discipline among workers, to force capitalists to accumulate and thereby have the wherewithal to introduce technological progress (which typically requires a minimum and growing size of the capital stock). Von Mises was thus criticizing socialism for not having a feature that capitalism, which he held as being superior in this respect, *never had anyway.*

The analysis provided by Oskar Lange is illuminating here but Lange has to be properly understood to see where the illumination really lies. When Lange (1938) criticized Mises by saying that actual markets and actual prices were unnecessary for rational calculations and that 'accounting prices' could do equally well, he was essentially talking not about what obtains under capitalism, but about the fact that an actual optimizing exercise could be carried out without the existence of markets; or, as Joan Robinson put it, he was talking about pseudo-markets. He was not even making the claim that socialism *should* have these pseudo-markets; so the interpretation placed on Lange that he was providing an actual model of how a socialist economy should run, is incorrect. His argument was a logical refutation of von Mises' point and in the process, an elaboration of what markets could *ideally* achieve. If computers existed to solve the problem and if all information could be accurately relayed to the central planning authority from the enterprises, then that authority could simply announce the optimal solution.

Lange's model, in short, took the market as a computer analogue and argued that such an analogue could be created even in the absence of actual markets. The question of whether a socialist economy *should* have markets as an actual social institution is an altogether separate issue on which it is misleading to invoke Lange.

The market as an actual social institution functioned in erstwhile Yugoslavia above all, which has been called a model of 'market socialism'. But 'market socialism' in this sense must be distinguished again from the mere use of the market in a socialist economy. In almost every socialist economy, the market existed to play the role of distributing consumer goods among the working people. The sheer existence of a market under socialism and even its pervasive use does not constitute market socialism. The latter is characterized by the determination of all major decisions in the economy on the basis of market signals. And even if means of production are socially owned, if the market has this *determining* role, as distinct from fulfilling certain specific secondary functions such as distributing a set of consumer goods, then it begins to display many features similar to capitalism – from unemployment, to growing personal and regional inequality, to inflation. Above all, it also acquires the spontaneity of the system that we noted in the case of capitalism which arose from the fact of competition; the same competition comes to characterize 'market socialism' as well.

It follows, therefore, that the term 'market socialism' is a contradiction in terms, since it mimics capitalism without necessarily achieving the minimum goals of the socialist project, such as full employment; but of course, the room for introducing a market in a socialist economy to fulfil *certain specific functions* without determining its overall dynamics certainly exists.

The Question of Wage and Unemployment

On the basis of the foregoing discussion we can say that socialism, and hence by implication even the transition to socialism, does not need the market either as a computer analogue or as a social institution for imposing discipline, especially on the working people. The market can be there for playing other roles, but not these roles.

It cannot be a computer analogue working out the optimal solution to a planning problem because, as just argued, primacy has to be given in the transition to the preservation of a self-mutating class alliance rather than to production *per se*. The obsession with the optimality of the market outcome derives both from a misreading of the role of markets under capitalism and hence of capitalism itself, and also from a 'productionist' perception of socialism which sees enhancing production and hence making optimal use of the available 'resources' as the primary aim of socialism; such a perspective is particularly inapposite in the present context when sensitivity to the issue of human demands on nature is so pervasive.

Nor can the market be a social institution imposing discipline all around, including above all on the workers, because the whole point of socialism is precisely to break from that kind of discipline.

So, the role of the market in the period of transition, and even under socialism, must be thought of as providing for exchange between enterprises, exchange between communes, and exchange between enterprises and consumers. But this would not be a market with any *determining role*; and investment decision-making will be socialized anyway even if there is no central planning (in a manner we discuss below).

There will be no unemployment in a socialist economy. Work will be shared among the available number of workers in a commune, so that any tendency for the labour-force to rise at a faster rate than labour demand (both measured in terms of man-hours) will show itself as a reduction in the number of hours worked per person rather than a rise in the number of unemployed persons. Such a reduction in the number of hours worked per person does not constitute a swelling of the reserve army of labour, *because the distinction between an 'active army' and a 'reserve army' disappears when every working person gets a fixed remuneration, a fact enshrined as a fundamental economic right of an individual.*[11]

The absence of unemployment would also increase the rate of technological progress in a socialist economy, for the desire not to create unemployment has been an important factor holding back innovations in 'actually existing socialism'.

With a substantial part of the workers' remuneration being given in the form of a 'social wage' as free health care, free education and such like, the principle of 'to each according to need' is already incorporated into a society in transition to socialism from the very beginning (unlike what *A Critique of the Gotha Programme* might have suggested). Over time, this component increases further. But even with regard to what is the 'private wage' component, there is no reason for such a society to have serious wage differences among workers. At the most two wage slabs, one for unskilled labour and one for skilled labour, defined as embodying a longer period of training, would be quite enough. (More hazardous work can be paid the wages earmarked for skilled labour.) The unemployed would also draw wages according to the appropriate slab.

This equalization of the wage-rate, however, must refer to the *wage-rate per man-hour, not per person*. Every man-hour of work must get the same remuneration, the only distinction being between skilled and unskilled work. If workers in a commune decide to have greater leisure, that is, work a lesser number of hours, then they would be foregoing some income that would have otherwise accrued to them; they would have preferred leisure over income.

We argued earlier that a socialist economy must eschew central planning. But our critique of central planning is different from the usual critique of central planning: the usual critique focuses on the near-impossibility of finding optimal solutions in a situation where massive amounts of data and massive numbers of equations are involved, which is why the exercise of optimization is often visualized as being decentralized through multi-level planning (Kornai and Liptak 1965). Our criticism of central planning however has nothing to do with the *formal* problems of arriving at optimal solutions; it has to do with our objections to the preoccupation with optimality itself.

Optimization of any kind, which *ipso facto* also includes central planning, treats workers as a *resource* on a par with the means of production. This is antithetical to socialism under which the workers are supposed to be *creative* producers. The vision of socialism as involving the planning of the entire economy, as opposed to a capitalist economy where only corporations plan the deployment of resources, even as the economy as a whole is enmeshed in anarchy, is an inappropriate one: it ignores the creative subject-role of workers in the process of production that socialism must effect.

Socialism, to recapitulate, must neither become a system of commodity production, as under market socialism, nor become centrally planned, for both these arrangements entail a denial of individual freedom. Some activities, we have seen, will have to be centrally planned, with the workers engaged in these activities being involved in the planning process; but a substantial segment of activities, if they are not to be brought under the ambit of commodity production and yet not centrally planned, will have to be carried out *locally*, at the level of communes, where enterprises will feed one another and also the worker-consumers, and be outside of the ambit of commodity production. The precise areas to be brought under the ambit of central planning will be determined through discussion, as a part of the process of the 'great discussion' mentioned above.

Decentralization of decision-making must, therefore, be an essential feature of a socialist economy. The Chinese communes in the early years were an example of this, and they also demonstrated the benefits of decentralization through the creation of additional means for development outside of the plan budgets drawn up at the centre.[12] The creation of such largely self-sufficient local economies may be thought to deprive the country of the benefits of division of labour that Adam Smith had focused on. But as the discussion in chapter four has shown, the main benefit of division of labour consists in making the production process amenable to the introduction of machinery. The social need for continuous all-round mechanization, however, is itself questionable. Let us now turn to the question of how investment can be socialized in such an economy with decentralized production.

The Socialization of Investment

The question will obviously arise: if each commune is largely autonomous and self-sufficient, then how can inequality across communes, with some being prosperous and others being distressed, be avoided? Conversely, if there is significant interference from a central authority with the objective of bringing about equality across communes, then in what sense do the communes have autonomy so that expression is given to individual participation and praxis?

The question of the absolute autonomy of the communes, of course, does not arise; this autonomy has to be tempered to achieve a degree of equality across communes and also to ensure that any undesired decline in the number of man-hours of work per person is quickly reversed. The entity entrusted with tempering the autonomy of the communes, to reiterate, need not be the central *government*; it could be a constitutional body that determines, on the basis of widespread social discussion, the pace of investment for the economy as a whole through the use of the fiscal instrument, even as it removes disparities across communes. An illustration will clarify the idea.

The index on the basis of which these decisions will be taken will have to be the commune GDP per man-hour of labour employed in producing it. A commune where the GDP per man-hour is high compared to another is likely to be more prosperous (even when this prosperity takes the form of greater *leisure* among its workers), and since the wage per man-hour will be same across all communes, it will have a larger surplus per man-hour. Now, let each commune be taxed at a common rate per unit of surplus per man-hour (there could also be progressive taxation) multiplied by the *number of workers* (not by the number of man-hours), so that leisure is not exempted from the tax-orbit.[13]

The total tax proceeds so obtained can be distributed among communes according to a diametrically opposite rule, that is, communes with lower surplus per man-hour get *proportionately more compared to communes with higher surplus per man-hour.* Since these transfers can be used only for investment, this would tend to have an equalizing effect on the investment–GDP ratio across communes. The less prosperous ones can then invest more, introduce newer technologies and thereby raise their GDP per man-hour over time.

Now, for the country as a whole, GDP per man-hour should be rising at some socially agreed rate. If it is rising at less than this rate (so that the hours of employment per person are falling at a rate greater than socially desired), then investment should be stepped up, while if it is rising at a rate higher than this social rate, then investment should be reined in. Since all transfers to the communes are used for investment purposes alone while a part of surplus is used for collective consumption, by raising or lowering the average tax rate as proportion of surplus (assuming that surplus is rising at the same rate as GDP) and hence the share of transfers in GDP, the distribution of resources between consumption and investment can be influenced.

For instance, if the ratio of net investment to capital stock (or I/K) is denoted by i, if the socially agreed rate of growth of GDP per man-hour is given by r^* and if the actual rate of growth of GDP per man-hour is given by r, then we should have

$$di/dt = a.(r^* - r) \ \ldots\ldots\ (A)$$

where a is a constant. Since the rate of growth of GDP per man-hour will be generally positively linked to the rate of growth of GDP itself, and since the average capital–output ratio can be taken to be constant over time if the composition of investment is scale-neutral, $r = f(i)$ with $f' > 0$. Equation (A) then becomes $di/dt = a.(r^* - f(i))$. With this rule of raising or lowering t being followed, the economy, it follows, will experience a stable average rate of growth of GDP per man-hour at r^*.

All this is just to illustrate how socialization of investment might work in a universe of autonomous communes. This is not the place for any detailed discussion of how a socialist economy or one in transition should actually look like or function; that will depend largely upon the specific circumstances. There will, in real life, be multiple forms of ownership, from social ownership to peasant ownership to collective ownership. These different ownerships have to evolve over time towards a common social ownership, but this evolution will take time. Likewise, there will be workers' collectives managing enterprises that belong to the communes and to the central government. These enterprises will relate to one another in multiple ways, including through the market, where prices will be fixed according to certain rules. But this would not mean 'market socialism' or commodity production, since socialization of investment and the absence of a reserve army of labour would make these markets very different from those under capitalism.[14] There being a more or less common wage-rate per man-hour with just two scales, and fiscal transfers from the rich to the poor communes, there will be no reason for inequalities to increase. In such an economy, the spontaneity of the system that stands in the way of individual freedom under capitalism would have been overcome; and individual agency would have been restored through direct involvement in decision-making at the commune level, not to mention the 'great discussion' that such a society would be conspicuously characterized by.

Notes

1 Akeel Bilgrami (2014) has argued that treating workers as a 'resource' was a feature of capitalism that emerged along with the European Enlightenment.

2 It may be thought that the workers' volition would lie in being directed, that is, in surrendering themselves to being directed by the collective. But such *passive* surrendering where the workers themselves do not actively participate in decision-making amounts to the negation of their historical role as subjects.

3 Many may carry the impression, drawn from instances belonging to early post-revolutionary Chinese experience, that communes necessarily entail collective *consumption* (common kitchen). That however is *not* how communes are visualized here.

4 This is especially pertinent for a third world society making a transition to socialism. The mass of the peasantry constitutes an extremely resolute force against imperialism in such a society, and since imperialism will be attempting to subvert any transition to socialism in such a society, retaining the allegiance of the mass of peasantry to the revolution becomes particularly crucial for its success.

5 Nothing that is said above relates to class struggle against the opponents of the revolution that started the transition to socialism.

6 In fact, the introduction of fundamental economic rights as I have suggested above, already implies a break from the principle of 'to each according to work'.

7 Emphasizing the criterion of 'need' from the very beginning, since it goes against the liberal principle of 'just desserts', that is, persons being rewarded for greater effort, may be objected to on *moral* grounds, even if not on the grounds of being conducive to greater *production*. But the moral defence of 'just desserts' is itself based on a bourgeois outlook. It presumes that each individual's effort can be independently measured and compared across individuals, that rewards can consist only of material goods and services, that the individual is necessarily mindful of these rewards, and so on. The morality of 'just desserts', in other words, is located within the context of a society consisting of 'monads'. The whole purpose of socialism is to transcend such a society and what appears 'moral' in such a society.

8 Lenin, who had strongly advanced the view that theory had to be brought to the proletariat from 'outside', certainly did not believe that there were two separate and permanent groups of 'theory-givers' and 'theory-receivers'. For an examination of Lenin's views on this, see P. Patnaik (2020).

9 Walter Bagehot had described democracy as 'government by discussion' (Sen 2018). The argument of the present book has been that, given the spontaneity of

capitalism, socialism constitutes a condition for such a government and hence for democracy. The transition to socialism must therefore be marked by an expansion of the role of public discussion in shaping the affairs of the government.

10 For an account of this debate, see Dobb (1969).

11 Even if it so happens that some workers do remain unemployed for a while, they would be getting their full remuneration. This follows from the acceptance of the principle that it is the duty of society to find employment for everyone; if it cannot find employment at any point of time for a certain number of working persons, then it must nonetheless pay them full remuneration, which would include not just the standard money income but all the facilities of free education, housing, health care and food.

12 See U. Patnaik (1998).

13 If the number of workers in a commune is N, if the number of man-hours employed is L (so that each worker puts in $L/N = l$ man-hours), then the total tax payment of the commune will be $T = t.[(O–w.L)/L].N$, where t is the tax-rate. This can be expressed as $T = t.S/l$. In a commune where workers enjoy greater leisure, that is, l is lower, the tax payment will be correspondingly larger.

14 The fact that producers cut back investment when there is inadequate demand and hence generate *greater* involuntary unemployment via the multiplier, which ensures that involuntary unemployment has no tendency to disappear on its own, arises because they see the output they produce quintessentially as exchange-value, a mere sum of money, rather than as use-value – that is, because they are *commodity producers*. The perpetual existence of involuntary unemployment therefore is a feature of an economy where production is of *commodities*. The sketch of a socialist economy given above precludes this possibility.

Bibliography

Berlin, Isaiah (1969), 'Two Concepts of Liberty', in I. Berlin, *Four Essays on Liberty*, Oxford: Oxford University Press, pp. 118–72.

Bharadwaj, K. (1989), *Themes in Value and Distribution: Classical Theory Reappraised*, London: Routledge.

Bilgrami, A. (2014), *Secularism, Identity and Enchantment*, Cambridge, Mass.: Harvard University Press.

——— (2022a), *Capital, Culture and the Commons*, Ranikhet: Permanent Black.

——— (2022b), 'Interview on "Identity, Inner Life and Stereotyping"', *Frontline*, Chennai, 11 February.

Blyn, G. (1966), *Agricultural Trends in India 1891–1947*, Philadelphia: University of Pennsylvania Press.

Bukharin, N.I. (1972), *Imperialism and the Accumulation of Capital*, reprinted in Tarbuck Kenneth, ed., *Imperialism and the Accumulation of Capital*, London: Allen Lane.

Chambers, J.D. and G.E. Mingay (1966), *The Agricultural Revolution 1757–1880*, London: B.T. Batsford.

Chancel, L. and T. Piketty (2017), *Indian Income Inequality 1922–2015: From British Raj to Billionaire Raj*, World Inequality Database.

Clower, R. (1967), 'A Reconsideration of the Microfoundation of Monetary Theory', *Western Economic Journal*, vol. 6, no. 1, pp. 1–8.

Cole, W.A. (1981), 'Factors in Demand 1700–80', in R. Floud and D. McCloskey, eds, *The Economic History of Britain Since 1700*, Cambridge: Cambridge University Press, pp. 36–65.

Dobb, M.H. (1946), *Studies in the Development of Capitalism*, London: George Routledge and Sons.

——— (1969), *Welfare Economics and the Economics of Socialism*, Cambridge: Cambridge University Press.

——— (1973), *Theories of Value and Distribution Since Adam Smith: Ideology and Economic Theory*, Cambridge: Cambridge University Press.

Dutt, R.C. ([1900] 1970), *The Economic History of India,* 2 volumes, London: Routledge and Keegan Paul.

Fleming, J.M. (1962), 'Domestic Financial Policy Under Fixed and Flexible Exchange Rates, *IMF Staff Papers*, 9.

Goodwin, R.M. (1951), 'The Non-linear Accelerator and the Persistence of Business Cycles', *Econometrica*, vol. 19, no. 1, January, pp. 1–17.

Habib, I. (1995), *Essays in Indian History: Towards a Marxist Perception*, Delhi: Tulika Books.

——— (2013), *The Agrarian System of Mughal India*, Delhi: Oxford University Press.

Harrod, R.F. (1939), 'An Essay in Dynamic Theory', *The Economic Journal*, vol. 49, no. 193, March, pp. 14–33.

Hill, C. (1967), 'Pottage for Freeborn Englishmen: Attitudes to Wage-labour in the Sixteenth and Seventeenth Centuries', in C.H. Feinstein, ed., *Socialism, Capitalism and Economic Growth: Essays Presented to Maurice Dobb*, Cambridge: Cambridge University Press, pp. 338–50.

Husain, Iqbal, ed. (2006), *Karl Marx on India*, New Delhi: Tulika Books.

Jevons, W.S. (1871), *The Theory of Political Economy*, London: Macmillan.

Kahn, R.F. (1931), 'The Relation of Home Investment to Unemployment', *The Economic Journal*, vol. 41, no. 162, June, pp. 173–98.

Kaldor, N. (1978), *Further Essays on Economic Theory*, London: Duckworth.

Kalecki, M. (1954), *The Theory of Economic Dynamics*, London: Allen and Unwin.

——— (1962), 'Observations on the Theory of Economic Growth', *The Economic Journal*, vol. 72, no. 285, March, pp. 134–53.

——— (1971), *Selected Essays on the Dynamics of the Capitalist Economy*, Cambridge: Cambridge University Press.

——— (1972a), *Selected Essays on the Economic Growth of Socialist and Mixed Economies*, Cambridge: Cambridge University Press.

——— (1972b), 'Stimulating Business Upswing in Nazi Germany', in *The Last Phase in the Transformation of Capitalism*, New York: Monthly Review Press, pp. 65–73.

Kautsky, Karl (1903), *The Economic Doctrines of Karl Marx*, Internet Archive.

Keynes, J.M. (1931), 'Why am I a Liberal?', in *Essays in Persuasion*, London: Macmillan & Co.; reprint, New York: W.W. Norton & Co., 1963.

——— (1933), 'National Self-Sufficiency', *The Yale Review*, vol. 22, no. 4, June, pp. 755–69.

——— ([1936] 1949), *The General Theory of Employment, Interest and Money*, London: Macmillan.

——— (1963), *Essays in Persuasion*, New York: W.W. Norton & Co.

——— (1979), *A Treatise on Money: The Applied Theory of Money*, in *Collected Writings of J.M. Keynes*, vol. 4, London: Macmillan.

Kindleberger, C.P. (1974), *The World in Depression,* Berkeley: University of California Press.

Kornai, J. and T. Liptak (1965), 'Two-Level Planning', *Econometrica,* vol. 33, no. 1, pp. 141–69.

Krupskaya, N. (1970), *Memories of Lenin*, London: Panther History.

Lange, Oskar (1938), *On the Economic Theory of Socialism*, Minneapolis: University of Minnesota Press.

——— (1963), *Political Economy*, vol. 1, Oxford: Pergamon Press.

Lee, R.D. and R.S. Schofield (1981), 'British Population in the Eighteenth Century', in R. Floud and D. MacCloskey, eds, *The Economic History of Britain Since 1770, Volume 1, 1700–1860,* Cambridge: Cambridge University Press, pp. 17–35.

Lenin, V.I. ([1902] 1976), *What is to be Done?*, in *Selected Works* (3 volumes), vol. 1, Moscow: Progress Publishers, pp. 119–271.

——— ([1917] 1976), *Imperialism the Highest Stage of Capitalism,* in *Selected Works* (3 volumes), vol. 1, Moscow: Progress Publishers.

Locke, J. ([1689] 2014), *Two Treatises of Government*, Online Library of Liberty, oll.libertyfund.org.

Luxemburg, R. ([1914] 1963), *The Accumulation of Capital*, London: Routledge and Keegan Paul.

Macpherson, C.B. (1962), *The Political Theory of Possessive Individualism*, Oxford: Clarendon Press.

Marshall, A. (1890), *The Principle of Economics*, London: Macmillan.

Marx, K. (1969), *Theories of Surplus Value, Part 1*, Moscow: Progress Publishers.

——— (1971), 'Introduction', in *A Contribution to a Critique of Political Economy*, London: Lawrence and Wishart.

——— (1976), *The Poverty of Philosophy*, in K. Marx and F. Engels, *Collected Works*, vol. 6, London: Lawrence and Wishart.

Menger, C. ([1871] 2007), *Principles of Economics*, Vienna: Ludwig von Mises Institute.

Mukherji, A. (1990), *Walrasian and Non-Walrasian Equilibria*, Oxford: Oxford University Press.

Mundell, R. (1963), 'Capital Mobility and Stabilization Policy under Fixed and Flexible Exchange Rates', *Canadian Journal of Economics and Political Science*, vol. 29, no. 4, pp. 475–85.

Pasinetti, L.L. (1977), *Lectures on the Theory of Production*, New York: Columbia University Press.

Patnaik, P. (1997), *Accumulation and Stability under Capitalism*, Oxford: Clarendon Press.

——— (2009), *The Value of Money*, New York: Columbia University Press.

——— (2011), 'A Simple Model of an Imaginary Socialist Economy', in K.N. Panikkar, T.J. Byres and U. Patnaik, eds, *The Making of History: Essays Presented to Irfan Habib*, Delhi: Tulika Books, pp. 640–57.

——— (2015), 'Defining the Concept of Commodity Production', *Studies in People's History*, 24 May, pp. 117–25.

——— (2020), 'Lenin on Democracy and Class Struggle', *Social Scientist*, vol. 48, no. 11–12, November–December, pp. 3–10.

——— (2021a), 'Commons, Commodities and Capitalism', *Social Research*, Special Number on the Commons, pp. 31–47.

——— (2021b), 'Why Neo-liberalism Needs Neo-fascists', *The Boston Review*, 19 July, available at https://www.bostonreview.net/articles/why-neoliberalism-needs-neofascists/.

Patnaik, U. (1987), *Peasant Class Differentiation*, New Delhi: Oxford University Press.

——— (1998), 'Alternative Strategies of Agrarian Change in Relation to Resources for Development in India and China', in D. Nayyar, ed., *Economics as Ideology and Experience: Essays in Honour of Ashok Mitra*, London: Frank Cass, pp. 253–59.

——— (2005), 'Ricardo's Fallacy', in K.S. Jomo, ed., *Pioneers of Development Economics*, Delhi: Tulika Books, pp. 31–41.

——— (2013), 'Poverty Trends in India 2004–05 to 2009–2010', *Economic and Political Weekly*, vol. 48, no. 40, pp. 43–58.

——— (2017), 'Revisiting the "Drain" or Transfer from India to Britain in the Context of Global Diffusion of Capitalism', in S. Chakrabarti and U. Patnaik, eds, *Agrarian and Other Histories: Essays for Binay Bhushan Chaudhuri*, Delhi: Tulika Books, pp. 277–317.

——— (2018), 'Profit Inflation, Keynes and the Holocaust in Bengal 1943–44', *Economic and Political Weekly*, vol. 53, no. 42, 20 October, pp. 33–43.

Patnaik, U. and P. Patnaik (2016), *A Theory of Imperialism*, New York: Columbia University Press and Delhi: Tulika Books.

——— (2021), *Capital and Imperialism: Theory, History and the Present*, New York: Monthly Review Press and Delhi: Tulika Books.

Phelps-Browne, E.H. and S.V. Hopkins (1957), 'Wage-rates and Prices: Evidence for Population Pressure in the Sixteenth Century', *Economica*, vol. 24, no. 96, pp. 289–306.

Pigou, A.C. ([1920] 2013), *The Economics of Welfare*, London: Macmillan.

Piketty, Thomas (2014), *Capital in the Twenty-First Century*, Cambridge, Mass.: Harvard University Press.

Preobrazhensky, E. ([1926] 1965), *New Economics*, Oxford: Oxford University Press, 1965.

Rawls, John (1971), *A Theory of Justice*, Cambridge, Mass.: Harvard University Press.

Ricardo, David ([1817] 1951), *Principles of Political Economy and Taxation*, in P. Sraffa, ed. (with the editorial assistance of M.H. Dobb), *Works and Correspondence of David Ricardo*, Cambridge: Cambridge University Press.

Robinson, J. (1962), 'Review of H.G. Johnson's *Money Trade and Economic Growth*', *The Economic Journal*, vol. 72, pp. 690–92; reprinted in J. Robinson, *Collected Economic Papers*, vol. 3, Oxford: Basil Blackwell, 1965.

Samuelson, P.A. (1971), 'Understanding the Marxian Notion of Exploitation: A Summary of the So-called Transformation Problem between Marxian Values and Competitive Prices', *Journal of Economic Literature*, vol. 9, no. 2, June, pp. 399–431.

Schumpeter, J.A. (1952), 'Karl Marx', in *Ten Great Economists*, New York: Oxford University Press, pp. 3–73.

Sen, A. (1966), 'Peasants and Dualism With or Without Surplus Labour', *Journal of Political Economy*, vol. 74, no. 5, October, pp. 425–50.

——— (1981), *Poverty and Famines*, Oxford: Oxford University Press.

——— (2018), *Collective Choice and Social Welfare*, Cambridge, Mass.: Harvard University Press.

Smith, A. (1981), *An Inquiry into the Nature and Causes of the Wealth of Nations*, 2 volumes, Indianapolis: Liberty Fund.

Sraffa, P. (1960), *Production of Commodities by Means of Commodities*, Cambridge: Cambridge University Press.

Stiglitz, J. (2013), 'Inequality is Holding Back the Recovery', *The New York Times*, 13 January.

Tarbuck, K., ed. (1972), *Imperialism and the Accumulation of Capital*, London: Allen Lane.

Turner, M.E., J.V. Beckett and B. Afton (2001), *Farm Production in England 1700–1914*, New York: Oxford University Press.

van Bath, S. (1963), *The Agrarian History of Western Europe*, London: Edward Arnold.

Vaughn, K. (1980), 'John Locke's Theory of Property: Problems of Interpretation', *Literature of Liberty: A Review of Contemporary Liberal Thought*, vol. 3, no. 1, Spring, pp. 5–37.

von Mises, L. ([1922] 1981), *Socialism: An Economic and Sociological Analysis*, Indianapolis: Liberty.

Walras, L. ([1874] 1969), *Elements of Pure Economics; or, The Theory of Social Wealth*, translated by William Jaffe, New York: A.M. Kelly.

Index